An Introduction to Object-Oriented Programming

Timothy Budd

Oregon State University

Addison-Wesley Publishing Company

Reading, Massachusetts · Menlo Park, California · New York
Don Mills, Ontario · Wokingham, England · Amsterdam · Bonn
Sydney · Singapore · Tokyo · Madrid · San Juan · Milan · Paris

For Beth,
who never let me work on weekends

Trademarks

Eiffel is a trademark of Interactive Software Engineering, Inc.
Macintosh is a trademark licensed to Apple Computer, Inc.
Smalltalk-80 is a trademark of ParcPlace Systems, Inc.
Smalltalk/V is a registered trademark of Digitalk, Inc.
Turbo Pascal is a registered trademark of Borland International, Inc.
Software-IC, ICpak, and Objective-C are registered trademarks of
    The Stepstone Corporation.
Unix is a trademark of AT&T Bell Laboratories.

The cover illustration shows a duck-billed platypus. This egg-laying mammal
represents an excellent example of inheritance with overriding—a key idea
in object-oriented programming.

Library of Congress Cataloging-in-Publication Data
Budd, Timothy
    An introduction to object oriented programming / Timothy A. Budd.
        p.   cm.
    Includes bibliographical references and index.
    ISBN 0-201-54709-0
    1. Object-oriented programming (Computer science) I. Title.
    QA76.64.B83 1991
    005.1–dc20   90-45504
                                                                              CIP
Reprinted with corrections April, 1991

6 7 8 9 10-MA-959493

C O N T E N T S

E
Glossary   *371*

Bibliography   *381*

Index   *391*

P R E F A C E

The inspiration to write this book arose, as did that for my earlier book on Smalltalk [Budd 87], when I was faced with teaching a course and was not able to find a suitable existing text. I had been for some years teaching a seminar on Smalltalk and object-oriented programming, using my own book as the text. Starting in the late 1980s, I received an increasing number of requests for a course structured around C++. About the same time, the popularity of the Macintosh computer brought with it a slightly smaller call for instruction in Object Pascal. Finally, the announcement of the NeXT computer resulted in inquiries about how best to learn Objective-C.

Since I did not wish to teach four different courses, each dealing with a specific object-oriented language, I resolved to teach a single course in which I would lay out the principles of object-oriented programming, illustrating these principles with examples from each of the four languages. Participants would learn a little about each language, and would complete a project in a language of their choice.

I then set out to find a textbook for such a course. What I discovered, to my surprise, was that existing texts, although in many ways quite admirable, were all oriented around a single language. Books I considered included Cox [Cox 86], Goldberg and Robson [Goldberg 83], Kaehler and Patterson [Kaehler 86], Keene [Keene 89], Meyer [Meyer 88a], Pinson and Wiener [Pinson 88] and its companion, Wiener and Pinson [Wiener 88], Pohl [Pohl 89], and Stroustrup [Stroustrup 86]. Although in the end, I selected a few of these as optional texts, I rejected all of them for use as a primary text for the simple reason that each one, to a greater or lesser extent, gives the impression that "object-oriented programming" is synonymous with "object-oriented programming in X", where X is whatever programming language happens to be the author's favorite. Instead, I started writing my own lecture notes to use as a primary text. Over the course of the next year I revised and extended these notes; this book is the result.

Various participants in my course (which turned out to be much more popular, and hence much larger, than I had anticipated), in addition to projects in the four languages that I have mentioned, successfully completed projects in Actor [Actor 87], Turbo Pascal [Turbo 88], and CLOS [Keene 89]. Since my objective was to convey the principles of object-oriented programming in a language-independent manner, I inquired specifically of these individuals whether the material discussed in my lecture notes was applicable and useful in their individual work. Based on their positive response, I believe I have at least partially succeeded in achieving a measure of language independence.

ORGANIZATION OF THE BOOK

Most introductions to object-oriented programming make the mistake, in my opinion, of introducing syntax before they introduce the object-oriented "philosophy". Indeed, that there is an object-oriented approach to thinking about computation and problem solving, and that this is quite independent of the syntax used to support the technique, is often a surprise to more than a few individuals. For this reason, the first two chapters of this book are devoted to setting the groundwork for encouraging an object-oriented way of thinking. These should not be given short shrift. In particular, I strongly encourage at least one, if not several, group exercises in which CRC cards, introduced in Chapter 2, are used as a vehicle in problem solving. The manipulation of physical index cards in a group setting is one of the best techniques I have encountered for developing the notions of behavior, responsibility, and encapsulation.

Chapters 3 and 4 discuss computer programs, and the mechanics used to implement the ideas of encapsulation and abstraction described in the first two chapters. There is a "chicken and egg" problem at the heart of these chapters. Which should be introduced first – the ideas of instances and message passing, or the concepts of classes and methods? In part, the "natural" order depends on which language the readers have access to in conjunction with the course material. The Smalltalk programming environment, for example, provides an exceedingly large collection of ready-made classes. Thus, in Smalltalk, it makes sense to explore first the creation of instances of existing classes, the sending of messages to objects, and so on. In C++ or Object Pascal, on the other hand, a programmer cannot do anything, in the object-oriented sense, until he or she has defined one or two classes. So just the opposite order of presentation seems appropriate in that setting. In practice, the introductions of the two concepts go hand in hand. So that the exposition will not be overly bulky, however, the material is divided into two separate chapters.

Chapter 5 presents the first of several case studies in object-oriented programming. These are small, but complete, applications that illustrate important points. I believe many people learn best by emulating prototypical models – "paradigms" in the original sense of the word. The eight queens puzzle, although simple, is nevertheless sufficient to illustrate the important ideas of classes, instances, behaviors, responsibility, and so on. In addition, by viewing four different solutions to the puzzle, the reader is provided a chance to compare and contrast the various features of the languages being used for illustration.

Chapter 6 introduces the notion of inheritance. Readers already familiar with object-oriented ideas may be surprised that this concept is not discussed earlier in the book. In fact, the abstract idea of inheritance is introduced in Chapter 1, however, my own view is that inheritance is not central to object-oriented *problem solving.* The concept of responsibility-driven design is important in the early stages of problem solution. Although the benefits resulting from the use of inheritance are significant, they occur only after a framework has been mapped out in which the responsibility of every component is determined.

Chapter 7 describes the important philosophical issues involved in binding times for languages. The distinction between early and late binding is sometimes subtle, and, if not grasped early, it can complicate understanding of later issues.

Chapter 8 illustrates the use of inheritance by examining the problem of mixed-type arithmetic in Smalltalk.

Chapter 9 is once again concerned more with mechanics than with philosophy. The important notions of addition, refinement, and replacement are introduced, as are a few other small elements in the object-oriented programmer's repertoire of tools.

Chapter 10 presents the first of two relatively sizable programs (the second is the billiards program in Chapter 16). This program allows the user to play the card game solitaire on a computer screen. In addition to the use of inheritance and overriding, the use of object-oriented techniques in the construction of a graphical user interface is explored.

Chapter 11 represents a slight diversion. The introduction of object-oriented concepts necessarily has an effect on the other, more "conventional," aspects of a language, resulting in features that are sometimes surprising to the unwary programmer. In this chapter we explore the reasons behind some of these changes, in particular examining memory allocation, the meaning of assignment, and the notion of equality.

Although multiple inheritance is implemented in only a few object-oriented languages, the concept is an important one to understand. Chapter 12 describes multiple inheritance in general, and explains how this idea is expressed in the language C++.

Chapter 13 discusses the important concept of polymorphism. The application of polymorphism is central to the development of true reusable code. The mechanisms used in object-oriented programming can be combined to achieve a variety of different forms of polymorphism. The Smalltalk collection hierarchy described in Chapter 14 illustrates many of these polymorphic techniques.

Along with a knowledge of inheritance and polymorphism, an understanding of information hiding, coupling and cohesion, and subclass versus user clients is imperative for anyone who wishes to complete a significant object-oriented project. These ideas are explored in Chapter 15, and are applied in a subsequent case study developed in Chapter 16.

Chapter 17 develops a number of useful data-structure classes in C++. These classes are used to illustrate concepts such as public and private inheritance, pointers versus references, and overloading versus overriding.

The concept of classes is, on second examination, not as simple as the development in Chapter 3 would lead us to believe. In Chapter 18, we examine such advanced topics as metaclasses, class methods, delegation, and parameterized classes.

Chapter 19 explores the implementation of object-oriented languages. This subject is actually not at all important for programmers who simply wish to use object-oriented techniques within the constraints of a particular programming language. Nevertheless, an individual who has had an exposure to the inner workings of a conventional programming language, such as might be acquired in a traditional course on compiler construction, will undoubtedly be curious about how object-oriented features are actually implemented "behind the scenes." This chapter is designed to satisfy that curiosity.

Finally, Chapter 20 mentions briefly many of the countless topics that could not be addressed in this book, and provides the interested reader with pointers to the literature.

This book should *not* be considered a substitute for either a language tutorial or a language reference manual for any of the four languages discussed. In each of the languages, there are numerous subtle but language-specific or implementation-specific features that I did not believe were relevant to the discussion in this text, but that are certainly important as practical matters to the programmer. In the final chapter, I provide references for each language.

NECESSARY BACKGROUND

I have presented the material in this book assuming only that the reader is knowledgeable in some conventional programming language, such as Pascal or C. In my courses, the material has been used successfully at the upper-division (junior or senior) undergraduate level and at the first-year graduate-student level. In some cases (particularly in the last quarter of the book), further knowledge may be helpful, but is not assumed. For example, a student who has taken a course in software engineering may find some of the material in Chapter 15 more relevant, and one who has a course in compiler construction will find Chapter 19 more intelligible. On the other hand, both chapters can be simplified in presentation if necessary.

ACKNOWLEDGMENTS

I am certainly grateful to the 65 students in CS589 at Oregon State University who, in the fall of 1989, suffered through the development of the first draft of this text. They received one chapter at a time, often only a day or two before I would lecture on the material. Their patience in this regard is appreciated. Their specific comments, corrections, critiques, and criticisms were most helpful. In particular, I wish to acknowledge the detailed comments provided by Thomas Amoth, Kim Drongesen, Frank Griswold, Rajeev Pandey, and Phil Ruder.

The solitaire game developed in Chapter 10 was inspired by the project completed by Kim Drongesen, and the billiards game in Chapter 16 was based on the project completed by Guenter Mamier and Dietrich Wettschereck. In both cases, however, the code itself has been entirely rewritten and is my own. In fact, in both cases, my code is considerably stripped down, for the purposes of exposition, and is in no way comparable to the greatly superior projects completed by those students.

I am also grateful to those people who provided comments, corrections, critiques, and criticisms on subsequent drafts of the manuscript. These individuals include Michel Adar, Jerrie Andreas, Brad Cox, Graham Dumpleton, Peter Grogono, Nola Hague, Marcia Horton, Ralph Johnson, Doug Lea, Ted Lewis, Stanley Lippman, Darcy McCallum, Lindsay Marshall, Markku Sakkinen, Michael Share, Dave Taenzer, Nabil Zamel, several reviewers, including Ed Gehringer, James Heliotis, Karl Lieberherr, Jeff Parker, Justin Smith, and Daniel Stearns and Keith Wollman, my editor at Addison-Wesley.

The source listings were printed using Latex macros based on C program formatting macros originally written by Éamonn McManus, of Trinity College, Dublin.

OBTAINING THE SOURCE CODE

The source code for the case studies appearing in this book, as well as an errata sheet and other information, can be obtained by electronic mail. Send a message to oopintro@cs.orst.edu for further information.

For questions or comments contact the author at the Computer Science Department, Oregon State University, Corvallis, Oregon, 97331. Electronic-mail messages should be addressed to budd@cs.orst.edu.

C H A P T E R

1
Thinking Object-Oriented

Human beings do not live in the objective world alone, nor alone in the world of social activity as ordinarily understood, but are very much at the mercy of the particular language which has become the medium of expression for their society. It is quite an illusion to imagine that one adjusts to reality essentially without the use of language and that language is merely an incidental means of solving specific problems of communication or reflection. The fact of the matter is that the 'real world' is to a large extent unconsciously built up on the language habits of the group.... We see and hear and otherwise experience very largely as we do because the language habits of our community predispose certain choices of interpretation.

Edward Sapir[1]

Object-oriented programming has become exceedingly popular in the past few years. Compiler writers and other software producers are rushing to release object-oriented versions of their products. Countless books and special issues of both academic and trade journals have appeared on the subject. Students strive to be able somehow to list "experience in object-oriented programming" on their résumés. To judge from the frantic activity, object-oriented programming is being greeted with the popularity once reserved for ideas such as "structured programming" or "expert systems."

What is object-oriented programming? Why is it so popular?

Let us answer the second question first. It is likely that the popularity of object-oriented programming stems in part from the hope, as was the hope for many previous innovations in computer software development, that this new technique will be the key to increased productivity, improved reliability, fewer cavities, and a reduction in the national debt. Although it is true that there are many benefits to using object-oriented programming techniques (and we will

---

[1]Quoted in the article "The Relation of Habitual Thought and Behavior to Language" by Benjamin Lee Whorf; reprinted in [Whorf 56].

1

outline some of these shortly), it is also true that programming a computer is still one of the most difficult tasks ever undertaken by humankind; becoming proficient in programming requires talent, creativity, intelligence, logic, the ability to build and use abstractions, and experience — even when the best of tools are available.

I suspect another reason for the particular popularity of languages such as C++ and Object Pascal (as opposed to languages such as Smalltalk) is that managers and programmers alike hope that a C or Pascal programmer can be changed into a C++ or Object Pascal programmer with no more effort than the addition of two characters to the programmer's job title. Unfortunately, this hope is a long way from being realized. Object-oriented programming is more than simply a collection of new programming languages. Object-oriented programming is a new way of thinking about what it means to compute, about how we can structure information inside a computer.

The quote at the beginning of this chapter emphasized the fact that the languages we speak influence directly the way in which we view the world. To cite one example, Inuktitut, the language of the Inuits of the northernmost regions of North America, has several dozen different words that denote various types of snow — wet, fluffy, heavy, icy, and so on. Thus, an Inuit is required by their language to be much more perceptive of snow than I am, since to discuss anything concerning snow, they must choose among myriad terms for the concept. Even though, physiologically, my eye is presumably no different from an Inuit eye, my language does not force me to make the same sort of discrimination, since all varieties of snow are to me lumped under a single term.

What is true of natural languages is even more true of artificial, computer languages. For a compiler, the difference between an imperative language such as Pascal and an object-oriented language such as Object Pascal may be only the addition of a few new keywords and statement types. Making effective use of the new facilities, however, requires a shift in perception, an entirely new way of thinking about problem solving.

1.1   A NEW PARADIGM

Object-oriented programming is often referred to as a new programming *paradigm*. Other programming paradigms sometimes mentioned include the imperative-programming paradigm (languages such as Pascal or C), the logic-programming paradigm (Prolog), and the functional-programming paradigm (FP or ML) [Hailpern 86]. It is interesting to examine the definition of the word *paradigm*. Paradigm (Latin *paradīgma*, Greek *paradeigma*) originally meant an illustrative example, particularly an example sentence showing all the inflectional forms of a word. But in his influential book *The Structure of Scientific Revolutions* [Kuhn 70], the historian Thomas Kuhn expanded the definition of the word to mean a set of theories, standards, and methods that together represent a way of organizing knowledge; that is, a way of viewing the world.

It is in this sense that object-oriented programming is a new paradigm. The object-oriented view forces us to reconsider our thinking about computation, about what it means to perform computation, about how information should be structured within a computer.

Although new to computation, this organizing technique can be traced back through the history of science in general at least as far as Linnæus (1707–1778), if not even further back to the Greek philosopher Plato (see [Wegner 86]). Paradoxically, the style of problem solving embodied in the object-oriented technique is frequently the method used to address problems in everyday life. Thus, computer novices are often able to grasp the basic ideas of object-oriented programming easily, whereas those people who are more computer literate are often blocked by their own preconceptions. Alan Kay, for example, found that it was usually easier to teach Smalltalk to children than to computer professionals [Kay 77].

In trying to understand exactly what is meant by the term *object-oriented programming*, it is perhaps useful to examine the idea from several alternative perspectives. The next few sections outline three different aspects of object-oriented programming; each illustrates a particular reason why this technique should be considered an important new tool.

1.2 A WAY OF VIEWING THE WORLD

To illustrate some of the major ideas in object-oriented programming, let us consider first how we might go about handling a real-world situation, and then ask how we could make the computer more closely model the techniques employed.

Suppose I wish to send some flowers to my grandmother (who is named *Elsie*) for her birthday. She lives in a city many miles away, so the possibility of my picking the flowers and carrying them myself to her door is out of the question. Nevertheless, sending her the flowers is a task easy enough to do; I merely go down to my local florist (who happens to be named *Flo*), describe the kinds and number of flowers I want sent, and I can be assured the flowers will be delivered automatically.

At the risk of belaboring a point, let me emphasize that the mechanism I used to solve my problem was to find an appropriate agent (namely Flo), and to pass to her a *message* containing my request. It is the *responsibility* of Flo to satisfy my request. There is some *method* — that is, some algorithm or set of operations — used by Flo to do this. I do not need to know the particular method Flo will use to satisfy my request; indeed, often I do not want to know the details. If I investigated, however, I might discover that Flo delivers a slightly different message to another florist in my grandmother's city. That florist, in turn, makes the arrangement and passes it, along with yet another message, to a delivery person, and so on. So our first principle of object-oriented problem solving is the vehicle by which activities are initiated:

Messages and methods.   Action is initiated in object-oriented programming by the transmission of a *message* to an agent (an *object*) responsible for the action. The message encodes the request for an action, and is accompanied by any additional information (arguments) needed to carry out the request. The *receiver* is the agent to whom the message is sent. If the receiver accepts the message, it accepts the responsibility to carry out the indicated action. In response to a message, the receiver will perform some *method* to satisfy the request.

We have noted the important principle of *information hiding* in regard to message passing — that is, the client sending a request need not know the actual means by which the request will be honored. (There is another principle, all too human, that we can also observe is implicit in message passing. That principle is, if there is a task to perform, the first thought of the client is to find somebody else whom it can ask to perform the work.) Information hiding is also an important aspect of programming in conventional languages. In what sense is a message different from, say, a procedure call? In both cases, there is an implicit request for action; in both cases, there is a set of well-defined steps that will be initiated following the request.

There are two important distinctions. The first is that in a message there is a designated *receiver* for that message; the receiver is some agent to whom the message is sent. In a procedure call, there is no designated receiver, although we could adopt a convention of, for example, always calling the first argument to a procedure the receiver. The second is that the interpretation of the message (that is, the method used to respond to the message) is dependent on the receiver, and can vary with different receivers. I can give exactly the same message to my wife *Beth,* for example, and she will understand the message and a satisfactory outcome will be produced. However, the method Beth uses to satisfy the request (in all likelihood, simply passing the request on to Flo), will be different from that performed by Flo in response to the same request. If I ask *Ken,* my dentist, to send flowers to my grandmother, I probably would be making an error, since Ken may not have a method for solving that problem. If he understood the request at all, he would probably issue an appropriate error diagnostic.

Let us move our discussion back to the level of computers and programs. There, the distinction between message passing and procedure calling is that, in message passing, there is a designated receiver, and the *interpretation* — that is, the selection of a method to execute in response to the message — may differ with different receivers. Usually, the specific receiver for any given message will not be known until run time, so the determination of which *method* to invoke cannot be made until then. Thus, we say there is *late binding* between the message (function or procedure name) and the code fragment (method) used to respond to the message. This situation is in contrast to the very early (compile-time or link-time) binding of name to code fragment in conventional procedure calls.

More important, behavior is structured in terms of *responsibilities.* My request for action indicates only the desired outcome (flowers for my grandmother). The florist is free to pursue any technique that achieves the desired objective, and is not hampered by interference on my part.

Although I have only dealt with Flo a few times in the past, I have a rough idea of the behavior I can expect when I go into her shop and present her with my request. I am able to make certain assumptions because I have some information about florists in general, and I expect that Flo, being an *instance* of this category, will fit the general pattern. We can use the term Florist to represent the category (or *class*) of all florists. Let us incorporate these notions into our second principle of object-oriented programming.

> **Classes and instances.** All objects are *instances* of a *class*. The method invoked by an object in response to a message is determined by the class of the receiver. All objects of a given class use the same method in response to similar messages.

As we will note in the next chapter, one current problem in the object-oriented community is the proliferation of different terms for similar ideas. Thus, a *class* is known in Object Pascal as an *object type*, and a *superclass* (which we will describe shortly), is known as an *ancestor*, and so on. The glossary given in Appendix E should be of some help with unusual terms. We will use the convention, common in object-oriented languages, of always designating classes by a name beginning with an uppercase letter, and in a different typeface. This convention is not enforced by most language systems.

There is more information that I have about Flo — not necessarily because she is a florist, but because she is a shopkeeper. I know, for example, that I probably will be asked for money as part of the transaction, and in return for payment I will be given a receipt. These actions are true of grocers, of stationers, and of other shopkeepers. Since the category Florist is a more specialized from of the category Shopkeeper, any knowledge I have of Shopkeepers is also true of Florists, and hence of Flo.

One way to think about how I have organized my knowledge of Flo is in terms of a hierarchy of categories (Figure 1.1). Flo is a Florist, but Florist is a specialized form of Shopkeeper. Furthermore a Shopkeeper is also a Human; so I know, for example, that Flo is probably bipedal. A Human is a Mammal (therefore they nurse their young), and a Mammal is an Animal (therefore it breathes oxygen), and an Animal is a Material Object (therefore it has mass and weight). Thus, there is quite a lot of knowledge I have that is applicable to Flo that is not directly associated with her, or even with her category Florist. The principle that knowledge of a more general category is applicable also to the more specific category is called *inheritance*. We say that the class Florist will *inherit* attributes of the category Shopkeeper.

There is an alternative graphical technique that is often used to illustrate this relationship, particularly when there are many individuals with differing lineages. This technique shows classes listed in a hierarchical tree-like structure, with more abstract classes (Material Object, Animal) listed near the top of the tree, and more specific classes, and finally individuals, listed near the bottom.

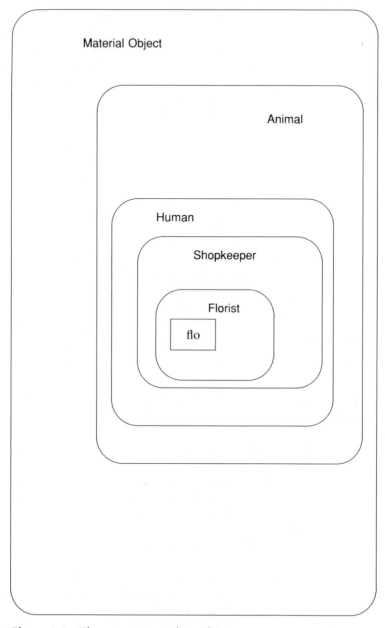

Figure 1.1   The sets surrounding Flo.

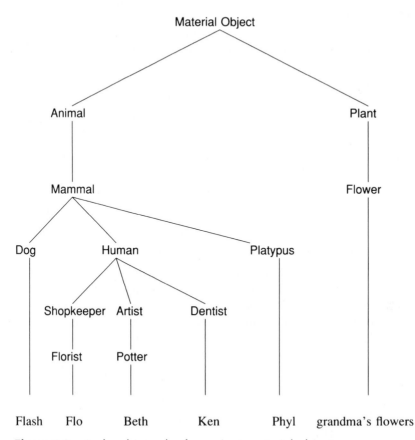

Figure 1.2   A class hierarchy for various material objects.

Figure 1.2 illustrates one class hierarchy for Flo, which also includes Beth, my dog Flash, Phyl the platypus who lives at the zoo, and for the flowers themselves that I am sending to my grandmother. Information that I possess about Flo because she is an instance of Human is also applicable to my wife Beth, for example. Information that I have about her because she is a Mammal is applicable to Flash as well. Information about all members of Material Object is equally applicable to Flo and to her flowers.

> **Inheritance.**   Classes can be organized into a hierarchical inheritance structure. A *subclass* will *inherit* attributes from a *superclass* higher in the tree. An *abstract superclass* is a class (such as Mammal) that is used only to create subclasses, for which there are no direct instances.

We will discuss inheritance, and how it is reflected in each of the object-oriented languages, in Chapter 6.

Phyl the platypus presents a problem for our simple organizing structure. I know that mammals give birth to live children, for example, and Phyl is certainly a Mammal, and yet Phyl (or rather his mate, Phyllis) continues to lay eggs. Thus we need to find a method to encode *exceptions* to a general rule. We do this by decreeing that information contained in a subclass can *override* information in a superclass. Most often, implementation of this approach takes the form of a method in a subclass having the same name as a method in the superclass, combined with a rule for how the search for a method to match a specific message is conducted.

Method binding.   The search to find a method to invoke in response to a given message begins with the class of the receiver. If no appropriate method is found, the search is conducted in the superclass of this class. The search continues up the superclass chain until either a method is found, or the superclass chain is exhausted. In the former case, the method is executed; in the latter case, an error message is issued.

Even if the compiler cannot determine which method will be invoked at run time, in many object-oriented languages it can determine whether there will be an appropriate method and issue the error message as a compile-time error diagnostic, rather than as a run time message. We will discuss the mechanisms for overriding in various computer languages in Chapter 9.

That my wife Beth and my florist Flo will respond to my message by performing different methods is an example of one form of *polymorphism*. We will discuss this important part of object-oriented programming in Chapter 13. As we explained, that I do not, and need not, know exactly what method Flo will use to honor my message is an example of *information hiding*, which we will discuss in Chapter 15.

Computation as Simulation

The view of programming that is represented by the example of sending flowers is very different from the conventional conception of a computer. The traditional model describing the behavior of a computer executing a program is the *process-state* or *pigeon-hole* model. In this view, the computer is a data manager, following some pattern of instructions, wandering through memory, pulling values out of various slots (memory addresses), transforming them in some manner, and pushing the results back into other slots. By examining the values in the slots, we can determine the state of the machine or the results produced by a computation. Although this model may be a more or less accurate picture of what takes place inside a computer, it does little to help us understand how to solve problems using the computer, and it is certainly not the way most people (pigeons and postal workers excepted) go about solving problems.

In contrast, in the object-oriented framework, we never mentioned memory addresses or variables or assignments or any of the conventional programming terms. Instead, we spoke of objects, messages, and responsibility for some

action. In Dan Ingalls' memorable phrase, "Instead of a bit-grinding processor...plundering data structures, we have a universe of well-behaved objects that
courteously ask each other to carry out their various desires" [Ingalls 81, page
290]. Another author has described object-oriented programming as "animistic;"
a process of creating a host of helpers that forms a community and assists the
programmer in the solution of a problem [Actor 87].

This view of programming as creating a "universe" is in many ways similar
to a style of computer simulation called "discrete event-driven simulation." In
brief, in a discrete event-driven simulation, the user creates computer models
of the various elements of the simulation, describes how they will interact with
one another, and sets them moving. This is almost identical to the average
object-oriented program, in which the user describes what the various entities in
the universe for the program are, and how they will interact with one another,
and finally sets them in motion. Thus in object-oriented programming, we have
the view that *computation is simulation*.

An easily overlooked benefit to the use of object-oriented techniques is
the power of *metaphor*. When programmers think about problems in terms of
the behaviors and responsibilities of objects, they bring with them a wealth
of intuition, ideas, and understanding from their everyday experience. When
computing is thought of in terms of pigeonholes, mailboxes, or slots containing
values, there is little in the average programmer's background to provide an
intuitive insight into how problems should be structured. Thus, although anthropomorphic descriptions such as the quote by Ingalls given previously may
strike some people as odd, in fact they are a reflection of the great exposi-
tive power of metaphor. It is possibly this feature, more than any other, that
is responsible for the frequently observed phenomenon that it is often easier
to teach object-oriented programming concepts to computer novices than to
computer professionals. To quote Alan Kay concerning Smalltalk once more,
"After observing this project we came to realize that many of the problems involved in the design of the personal computer, particularly those having to
do with expressive communication, were brought strongly into focus when
children down to the age of six were seriously considered as users" [Kay 77,
page 232].

Of course, objects cannot always respond to a message by politely asking
another object to perform some action. The result would be an infinite circle
of requests, like two gentlemen each politely waiting for the other to go first
before entering a doorway, or like a bureaucracy of paper pushers, each passing
on all papers to some other member of the organization. At some point, at least
a few objects need to perform some work other than passing on requests to
other agents. This work is accomplished differently in various object-oriented
languages. In blended object-oriented/imperative languages, such as C++, Object Pascal and Objective-C, it is accomplished by methods written in the base
(non–object-oriented) language. In pure object-oriented languages, such as
Smalltalk, it is accomplished by the introduction of "primitive operations" that
are provided by the underlying system.

1.3 COPING WITH COMPLEXITY

When computing was in its infancy, most programs were written in assembly language, by a single individual, and would not be considered large by our standards of today. Even so, as programs became more complex, programmers found that they had a difficult time remembering all the information they needed to know to develop or debug their software. Which values were contained in what registers? Did a new identifier name conflict with any other previously defined names? What variables needed to be initialized before control could be transferred to another section of code?

The introduction of higher-level languages, such as FORTRAN, COBOL and ALGOL, solved some difficulties (such as the automatic management of local variables, and implicit matching of arguments to parameters), while simultaneously raising people's expectations of what a computer could do in a manner that only introduced yet new problems. As programmers attempted to solve ever more complex problems using a computer, tasks exceeding in size the grasp of even the best programmers became the norm. Thus, teams of programmers working together to undertake major programming efforts became commonplace.

When this happened, an interesting phenomenon was observed. A task that would take one programmer 2 months to perform could not be accomplished by two programmers working for 1 month. In Fred Brooks's memorable phrase, "The bearing of a child takes nine months, no matter how many women are assigned"[Brooks 75, page 17].

The reason for this nonlinear behavior was complexity — in particular, the interconnections between software components were complicated, and large amounts of information had to be communicated among various members of the programming team. Brooks further said:

> Since software construction is inherently a systems effort — an exercise in complex interrelationships — communication effort is great, and it quickly dominates the decrease in individual task time brought about by partitioning. Adding more men then lengthens, not shortens, the schedule. [Brooks 75, page 19]

What brings about this complexity? It is not simply the sheer size of the tasks undertaken, because size by itself would not be a hindrance to partitioning each into several pieces. The unique feature of software systems developed using conventional techniques that makes them among the most complex systems developed by people is their high degree of interconnectedness. *Interconnectedness* means the dependence of one portion of code on another section of code.

Consider that any portion of a software system must be performing an essential task, or it would not be there. Now, if this task is useful to the other parts of the program, there must be some communication of information either into or out of the component under consideration. Thus, a complete understanding of what is going on requires a knowledge both of the portion of code we are considering and of the code that uses it. In short, an individual section of code cannot be understood in isolation.

Or consider identifier names. In most languages of the sixties and seventies (such as FORTRAN, Pascal, and C), names that represented information that was maintained for any length of time, or that could be shared with others (that is, not local identifiers) were all maintained in a common pool. Thus, all programmers had to check their names against names used by all other programmers. Pointer values that refer to elements defined elsewhere are yet another source of interdependency.

Abstraction Mechanisms

Programmers have had to deal with the problem of complexity for a long time in the history of computer science. To understand more fully the importance of object-oriented techniques, we should review the variety of mechanisms programmers have used to control complexity. Chief among these is *abstraction*, the ability to encapsulate and isolate design and execution information. In one sense, object-oriented techniques can be seen to be a natural outcome of a long historical progression from procedures, to modules, to abstract data types and objects.

Procedures.   Procedures and functions were one of the first abstraction mechanisms to be widely used in programming languages. Procedures allowed tasks that were executed repeatly, or were executed with only slight variations, to be collected in one place and reused, rather than the code being duplicated several times. In addition, the procedure gave the first possibility for *information hiding*. One programmer could write a procedure, or a set of procedures, that were used by many others. The other programmers did not need to know the exact details of the implementation — they needed only the necessary interface. But procedures were not an answer to all problems. In particular, they were not an effective mechanism for information hiding, and they only partially solved the problem of multiple programmers making use of the same names.

To illustrate these problems, we can consider a programmer who must write a set of routines to implement a simple stack. Following good software engineering principles, our programmer first establishes the visible interface to her work — say, a set of four routines: init, push, pop, and top. She then selects some suitable implementation technique. Here there are many choices, such as an array with a top-of-stack pointer, a linked list, and so on. Our intrepid programmer selects from among these choices, then proceeds to code the utilities.

It is easy to see that the data contained in the stack itself cannot be made local to any of the four routines, since they must be shared by all. But if the only choices are local variables or global variables (as they are in FORTRAN, or C prior to the introduction of the static modifier), then the stack data must be maintained in global variables. But if the variables are global, then there is no way to limit the accessibility or visibility of these names. For example, if the stack is represented in an array named datastack, this fact must be made known to all the other programmers, since they may want to create variables using the same name and should be discouraged from doing so. This is true even though these data are important to only the stack routines, and should not have any use outside of these four procedures. Similarly the names init, pop, push, and top are now reserved, and cannot be used in other portions of the program for other purposes, even if those sections of code have nothing to do with the stack routines.

The block scoping mechanism of ALGOL and its successors, such as Pascal, offers slightly more control over name visibility than does a simple distinction between local and global names. At first, we might be tempted to hope that this ability would solve the information-hiding problem. Unfortunately, it does not [Hanson 81]. Any scope that permits access to the four named procedures must also permit access to their common data. To solve this problem, a different structuring mechanism had to be developed.

Modules.   In one sense, modules can be viewed simply as an improved technique for creating and managing name spaces. Our stack example is typical, in that there is some information (the interface routines) that we want to be widely and publicly available, whereas there are other data (the stack data themselves) that we want restricted. Stripped to its barest form, a *module* provides the ability to divide a name space into two parts. The *public* part is accessible outside the module, whereas the *private* part is accessible only within the module. Types, data (variables), and procedures can all be defined in either portion.

David Parnas, who popularized the notion of modules, described the following two principles for their proper use [Parnas 72]:

1. One must provide the intended user with all the information needed to use the module correctly, and with *nothing more*.

2. One must provide the implementor with all the information needed to complete the module, and *nothing more*.

The philosophy is much like the military doctrine of "need to know;" if you do not need to know some information, you should not have access to it. This explicit and intentional concealment of information is *information hiding*.

Modules solve some, but not all, of the problems of software development. For example, modules will permit our programmer to hide the implementation details of her stack, but what if the other users want to have two (or more) stacks? As a more extreme example, suppose a programmer announces she has developed a new type of number, called Complex. She has defined the arithmetic operations for complex numbers — addition, subtraction, multiplication, and so on. She has defined routines to convert from conventional numbers to complex. There is just one small problem: You can manipulate only one complex number.

The complex-number system would not be useful with this restriction, but this is just the situation in which we find ourselves with simple modules. Modules by themselves provide an effective method of information hiding, but do not allow us to perform *instantiation*, which is the ability to make multiple copies of the data areas.

Abstract Data Types. An *abstract data type* is a programmer-defined data type that can be manipulated in a manner similar to the system-defined data types. As with system-defined types, an abstract data type corresponds to a set (perhaps infinite in size) of legal data values and of a number of primitive operations that can be performed on those values. Users can create variables with values that range over the set of legal values, and can operate on those values using the defined operations. For example, our intrepid programmer could define her stack as an abstract data type, and the stack operations as the only legal operations that are allowed to be performed on instances of the stack.

Modules are frequently used as an implementation technique for abstract data types, although we emphasize that modules are an implementation technique, and the abstract data type is a more theoretical concept. The two are related, but not identical. To build an abstract data type, we must be able

1. To export a type definition

2. To make available a set of operations that can be used to manipulate instances of the type

3. To protect the data associated with the type so that they can be operated on only by the provided routines

4. To make multiple instances of the type

Modules, as we have defined them, serve only as an information-hiding mechanism, and thus directly address only abilities 2 and 3, although the others can be accommodated using appropriate programming techniques. *Packages*, found in languages such as CLU or Ada, are an attempt to address more directly the issues involved in defining abstract data types.

In a certain sense, an object is simply an abstract data type. People have said, for example, that Smalltalk programmers write the most "structured" of all programs, because they cannot write anything but definitions of abstract data types. Although it is true that an object definition is an abstract data type, the notions of object-oriented programming build on the ideas of abstract data types, and add to them important innovations in code sharing and reusability.

Objects — Messages, Inheritance, and Polymorphism. The techniques of object-oriented programming add several important new ideas to the concept of the abstract data type. Foremost among these is the idea of *message passing*. Activity is initiated by a *request* being made to a specific object, not by a function using specific data being invoked. In large part, this is merely a change of emphasis; the conventional view places primary importance on the operation, whereas the object-oriented view places primary importance on the value itself. (Do you call the push routine with a stack and a data value, or do you ask a stack to push a value on to itself?) If this were all there is to object-oriented programming, the technique would not be considered a major innovation. But added to message passing are powerful mechanisms for overloading names and reusing software.

Implicit in message passing is the idea that the interpretation of a message can vary with different objects. That is, the behavior and response that the message elicits will depend on the object receiving the message. Thus, push can mean one thing to a stack, and a very different thing to a mechanical-arm controller. Since names for operations need not be unique, simple and direct forms can be used, leading to more readable and understandable code.

Finally, object-oriented programming adds the mechanisms of *inheritance* and *polymorphism*. Inheritance allows different data types to share the same code, leading to a reduction in code size and an increase in functionality. Polymorphism allows this shared code to be tailored to fit the specific circumstances of each individual data type. The emphasis on the independence of individual components permits an incremental development process, in which individual software units are designed, programmed and tested before being combined into a large system.

We will describe all of these new ideas in more detail in subsequent chapters.

1.4   REUSABLE SOFTWARE

People have asked for decades why the construction of software could not mirror more closely the construction of other material objects. When we construct a building, a car, or an electronic device, for example, we typically piece together a number of off-the-shelf components, rather than fabricating each new element from scratch. Could not software be constructed in the same fashion?

In the past, software reusability has been a much sought-after and seldom-achieved goal. A major reason for this is the tight interconnectedness of most software that has been constructed in a conventional manner. As we discussed in the last section, it is difficult to extract elements of software from one project that can be easily used in an unrelated project, because each portion of code typically has interdependencies with all other portions of code. These interdependences may be a result of data definitions, or may be functional dependencies.

For example, organizing records into a table and performing indexed lookup operations on this table are perhaps some of the most common operations in programming. Yet table-lookup routines are almost always written over again for each new application. Why? Because, in conventional languages, the record format for the elements is tightly bound with the more general code for insertion and lookup. It is difficult to write code that can work for arbitrary data, for any record type.

Object-oriented techniques provide a mechanism for cleanly separating the essential information (insertion and retrieval) from the inconsequential information (the format for particular records). Thus, using object-oriented techniques, we can construct large reusable software components.

We are not saying that the construction of reusable components is easy, or that it has already been done; we say merely that the tools to make such components are available. Examples of packages of reusable components that are now commercially available include the Smalltalk class hierarchy [Goldberg 89], the MacApp classes for graphical user-interface development in Object Pascal available from Apple [Wilson 90], the InterViews collection of C++ classes for user interface design [Linton 89], the ICpak 201 collection of Objective-C classes from Stepstone [Knolle 89], and the National Institutes of Health C++ collection [Gorlen 90].

1.5 SUMMARY

- Object-oriented programming is not simply a few new features added to programming languages. Rather, it is a new way of *thinking* about the process of decomposing problems and developing programming solutions.

- Object-oriented programming views a program as a collection of largely autonomous agents, called *objects*. Each object is responsible for specific tasks. It is by the interaction of objects that computation proceeds. In a certain sense, therefore, programming is nothing more or less than the simulation of a model universe.

- An object is an encapsulation of *state* (data values) and *behavior* (operations). Thus, an object is in many ways similar to a module, or an abstract data type.

- The behavior of objects is dictated by the object's *class*. Every object is an instance of some class. All instances of the same class will behave in a similar fashion (that is, invoke the same method) in response to a similar request.

- An object will exhibit its behavior by invoking a method (similar to executing a procedure) in response to a message. The interpretation of the message (that is, the specific method performed) is decided by the object, and may differ from one class of objects to another.

- Objects and classes extend the concept of abstract data types by adding the notion of *inheritance*. Classes can be organized into a hierarchical inheritance tree. Data and behavior associated with classes higher in the tree can also be accessed and used by classes lower in the tree. Such classes are said to inherit their behavior from the parent classes.

- By reducing the interdependency among software components, object-oriented programming permits the development of reusable software systems. Such components can be created and tested as independent units, in isolation from other portions of a software application.

- Reusable software components permit the programmer to deal with problems on a higher level of abstraction. We can define and manipulate objects simply in terms of the messages they understand and a description of the tasks they perform, ignoring implementation details.

FURTHER READING

The Whorf book from which the quote at the beginning of the chapter was taken [Whorf 56] contains several interesting papers discussing the relationships between language and our habitual thinking processes. I urge any serious student of computer languages to read several of these essays, since some of them have surprising relevance to artificial languages.

Another interesting book along similar lines is *The Alphabet Effect*, by Robert Logan [Logan 86], which explains in terms of language why logic and science developed in the West, while for centuries China in the East had superior technology. In a more contemporary investigation of the effect of natural language on computer science, J. Marshall Unger [Unger 87] describes the influence of the Japanese language on the much-heralded Fifth Generation project.

The quote from Fred Brooks on page 10 is from the title chapter of the book, *The Mythical Man-Month* [Brooks 75]. Although published over a decade ago, Brooks small volume is still one of the essential works every knowledgeable computer scientist should read.

In Section 1.3, we criticized procedures as an abstraction technique, because they failed to provide an adequate mechanism for information hiding. These arguments were first developed by William Wulf and Mary Shaw [Wulf 73] in an analysis of many of the problems surrounding the use of global variables, and they were later expanded upon by David Hanson [Hanson 81].

Like most terms that have found their way into the popular jargon, *object-oriented* is used with greater regularity than it is defined. Thus, the question, "What is object-oriented programming?" is surprisingly difficult to answer. Bjarne Stroustrup has quipped [Stroustrup 88] that many arguments appear to boil down to the following syllogism:

X is Good
Object-Oriented is Good
Ergo, *X* is Object-Oriented

Roger King has argued, in [Kim 89], that his cat is object-oriented. After all, a cat exhibits characteristic behavior, responds to messages, is heir to a long tradition of inherited responses, and manages its own quite independent internal state.

Many authors have tried to provide a precise description of what properties a programming language must possess to be called *object-oriented* [Micallef 88, Wegner 86]. Wegner, for example, distinguishes *object-based* languages, which support only abstraction (such as Ada), from *object-oriented* languages, which must also support inheritance.

Other authors — notably Brad Cox [Cox 90] — define the term much more broadly. To Cox, *object-oriented programming* represents the *objective* of programming by assembling solutions from collections of off-the-shelf subcomponents, rather than any particular *technology* we may use to achieve this objective. Rather than drawing lines that are divisively narrow, we should embrace any and all means that show promise of leading to a new software "Industrial Revolution." The book by Cox [Cox 86], although written early in the development of object-oriented programming and thus now somewhat dated in details, is nevertheless one of the most readable manifestos of the object-oriented movement.

Exercises

1. In an object-oriented inheritance hierarchy, such as that shown in Figure 1.2, each level is a more specialized form of the preceding level. Give one more example of a hierarchy found in everyday life that has this property. There are other types of hierarchy found in everyday life that are not inheritance hierarchies. Give an example of a non-inheritance hierarchy.

2. Look up the definition of the word *paradigm* in at least three different dictionaries. Relate these definitions to computer programming languages.

3. Take a real-world problem, such as the task of sending flowers described in Section 1.2, and describe the solution to the problem in terms of objects and responsibilities.

4. If you are familiar with two or more distinct computer programming languages, give an example of a problem showing how one computer language would direct the programmer to one type of solution, whereas a different language would encourage an alternative type of solution.

5. If you are familiar with two or more distinct natural languages, give an example of a situation that illustrates how one language would direct the speaker in a certain direction, whereas the other language would encourage a different manner of thought.

6. Argue either for or against the position that computing is basically simulation. (You might want to examine the article by Alan Kay [Kay 77].)

C H A P T E R

2
Responsibility-
Driven Design

When programmers ask other programmers, "What exactly is this object-oriented programming all about anyway?", the response tends to emphasize the language features that are introduced in languages, such as C++ or Object Pascal, as opposed to their older, non–object-oriented versions, C or Pascal. Thus, discussion usually turns rather quickly to issues such as classes and inheritance, message passing, virtual and static methods, and so on. But such conversations miss the most important point of object-oriented programming, which has nothing to do with syntax. As we emphasized in the first chapter, the most important aspect of object-oriented programming is a design technique that is driven by delegation of responsibilities. We call this technique *responsibility-driven design* [Wirfs-Brock 89b].

As anyone who can remember being a child, or who has raised children, can vouch, responsibility is a sword that can cut both ways. When you make an object (be it a child or a software system) responsible for specific actions, you expect a certain behavior, at least when the rules are observed, and you usually expect some reasonable behavior even when rules are not observed. But just as important, responsibility implies a degree of independence or noninterference. If you tell a child that she is responsible for cleaning her room, you do not normally proceed to stand over her and watch her all the time she is performing the activity — that is not the nature of responsibility.

Similarly, conventional programming proceeds largely by doing something *to* something else; modifying a record or updating an array, for example. Thus, one portion of code in a software system is frequently intimately tied, by control and data connections, to many other sections of the system. Such dependencies can come about through the use of global variables, through use of pointer values, or simply through inappropriate use of and dependence on implementation details of other portions of code. A responsibility-driven design attempts to cut these links, or at least to reduce them to as unobtrusive a level as possible.

This notion might at first seem no more subtle than the lessons of information hiding and modularity, which are important to programming even in conventional languages. But the philosophy of responsibility-driven design elevates information hiding from a technique to an art. One of the major benefits of object-oriented programming occurs when software subsystems are reused from one project to the next. For example, a simulation manager (such as the one we will develop in Chapter 16) might work both for a simulation of balls on a billiards table and for a simulation of fish in a fish tank. This ability to reuse code implies that the software can have almost no domain-specific code; it must delegate responsibility for domain-specific behavior totally to application-specific portions of the system. The ability to create such resuable code is not one that is easily learned — it requires experience, careful examination of case studies,[1] and use of a programming language in which such delegation is natural and easy to express. In subsequent chapters, we will present several such examples.

2.1 CRC CARDS

It is often useful, when you are designing an object-oriented application, to think about the process as being similar to organizing a group of individuals, such as a club or association. There is a currently popular bumper sticker which asserts, in slightly more picturesque terms, that phenomena can occur spontaneously. Of course, anybody who has tried to run an organization based on that belief knows that, in reality, it is not true. If any particular action is to happen, somebody must be responsible for doing it. That is, no action can take place without an agent performing the action. Thus, the secret to good object-oriented design is first to establish who is responsible for each action that is to be performed.

One technique that is extremely useful in driving home in a physical way both the need for the separation of responsibilities and the necessity of assigning a responsibility for every action is the use of index cards to represent individual classes. Such cards are known as CRC cards, since they are divided into three components: class, responsibility, and collaboration [Beck 89]. A CRC card is simply a 4-inch by 6-inch index card that has been divided into three distinct areas (Figure 2.1).

Each class in our design will be described by a separate CRC card. During the design phase the distinction between class and instance is blurred. In describing the classes from Chapter 1, for example, there might be a card that is at times viewed as representing Flo, an individual florist, and at other times as the category Florist in general.

The upper-left corner of each CRC card contains the name of the class being described. The selection of meaningful class names is extremely im-

---

[1]That is, examination of *paradigms* in the original sense of the word.

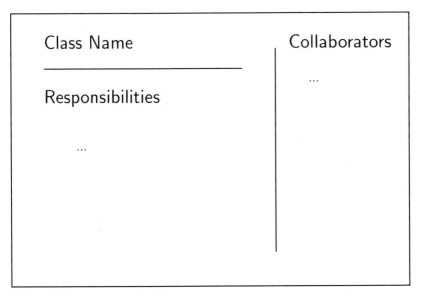

Figure 2.1   A class responsibility collaborator (CRC) card.

portant, as the class names create the vocabulary with which the design will
be formulated. Shakespeare could claim that a change in the name of an object will not alter the physical characteristics of the entity so denoted,[2] but it
is certainly not the case that all names will conjure up the same mental images in the listener. As government bureaucrats have known for a long time,
obscure and idiomatic names can make even the simplest operation sound in-
timidating. In a banking-machine design, for example, describing a device as a
"user-identification processor and authentication facilitator" will probably elicit
much less intuition as to the devices's purpose than will naming the same device
a "card reader." Names should be internally consistent, meaningful, preferably
short, and evocative in the context of the problem at hand. Often, people spend
a considerable amount of time finding just the right set of terms to describe the
objects being manipulated. Far from this being a barren and useless exercise,
the proper selection of names early in the design process greatly simplifies and
facilitates later steps.

The following general guidelines for developing useful names have been
suggested [Keller 90]:

- Use pronounceable names. As a rule of thumb, if you cannot read a name
  out loud, it is not a good name.

- Use capitalization (or underscores) to mark the beginning of a new word
  within a name, such as in "CardReader" or "Card_reader," rather than
  Cardreader.

---

[2]Romeo and Juliet, Act II, Scene 2.

- Examine abbreviations carefully. An abbreviation that is clear to one reader may be confusing to the next. Is a TermProcess a terminal process, something that terminates processes, or a process associated with a terminal? Clearly, this rule should not be construed to eliminate all abbreviations, since some are clearly so widely used as to be unambiguous. Using ID for "identification number," for example, is likely to be acceptable.

- Do not use digits within a name. Digits are easy to misread (0 and O, 1 and l, 2 and Z, S and 5, and so on).

- Name variables and functions that maintain Boolean values so as to describe clearly the interpretation of a true or false value. For example, printerIs-Ready clearly indicates that a true value means the printer is working, whereas printerStatus is much less precise.

Immediately below the class name on the CRC card, the responsibilities of the class are listed. Responsibilities describe the problem to be solved. Responsibilities should be expressed by short verb phrases, each containing an active verb. Responsibilities should describe *what* is to be done, and should avoid detailed specifications of *how* each task is to be accomplished. The responsibilities section can be viewed as a contract. Like real contracts, the responsibilities section should describe a *quid pro quo* — if you use the object in this manner, this will be the result. Similarly, like some contracts it describes only the most essential details, leaving incidental information to be filled in later.

The constraints of a 4-inch by 6-inch card are a good measure of appropriate complexity — a class that is expected to perform more tasks than can fit easily in this space is probably too complex, and you should expend further effort to find a simpler solution (perhaps by moving some responsibilities elsewhere, or by dividing the task between two or more separate objects). Once again, time spent finding short, concise, and meaningful descriptions of responsibilities will yield rewards later in the development process.

The third component of the CRC card is a list of collaborators. Few objects can perform useful operations entirely on their own. Almost all stand in some relationship to several others, either as providers or as requesters of a service or facility. The list of collaborators should include all classes of which the class being described needs to be aware. It should certainly include classes that provide services needed to meet the responsibilities of the class being described. It could also, but need not, include classes that require services provided by the described class. The decision whether to list another class as a collaborator is based on the degree of connection or cooperation. A special type of Window may be tied symmetrically to the data being displayed, and thus would be considered a collaborator. A data structure such as a stack, on the other hand, may not care at all to whom it is providing services, and thus need not list its caller as a collaborator (although the caller should list the stack as a collaborator).

2.2 DISCOVERING CLASSES

One of the first decisions that must be made in creating an object-oriented application is the selection of classes. Classes in object-oriented programming can have several different types of responsibilities, and thus not surprisingly there are different types of classes. The following categories, however, cover the majority of cases.

- **Data Managers, Data,** or **State** classes. These are classes whose principle responsibility is to maintain data or state information of one sort or another. For example, in Chapters 3 and 10 we will develop an abstraction of a playing card. The class Card will hold the rank and suit of the card. Data manager classes are often recognizable as the nouns in a problem description and are usually the fundamental building blocks of a design.

- **Data Sinks** or **Data Sources.** These are classes that generate data, such as a random number generator, or accept data and then process them further, such as a class performing output to a disk or file. Unlike a data manager, a data sink or data source does not hold the data for a period of time, but generates it on demand (for a data source), or processes it when called upon (for a data sink).

- **View** or **Observer** classes. An essential portion of most applications is the display of information on an output device, such as a terminal screen. Because the code for performing such activity is often complex, frequently modified, and largely independent of the actual data being displayed, it is good programming practice to isolate display behavior in separate classes from those classes that maintain the data being displayed. For example in our playing card abstraction we will create a second class, CardView, to take care of writing a card image on a terminal screen. Often the base data (for example the Card class) is called the *model*, while the display class (CardView) is called the *view*.

    Because we separate the model from the view, the design of the model is usually greatly simplified. Ideally, the model should neither require nor contain any information about the view. This facilitates code reuse, since a model can then be used in several different applications. It is not uncommon for a single model to have more than one view. For example, financial information could be displayed as bar charts, pie charts, or tables of figures, all without changing the underlying model.

    Occasionally interaction between a model and a view is unavoidable. If the figures in the financial table just described are permitted to change dynamically, for example, the programmer might wish the view to be instantly updated. Thus it is necessary for the model to alert the view that the model has been changed and that the corresponding view should be updated. Some programmers refer to such a model as a *subject*, in order to distinguish it from a model with no knowledge of use.

- **Facilitater** or **Helper** classes. These are classes that maintain little or no state information themselves but assist in the execution of complex tasks. For example in displaying our playing card image we will use the services of a facilitater class that handles the drawing of lines and text on the display device. Another facilitater class will help maintain linked lists of cards.

These categories are intended to be representative of the most common uses of classes, and hence useful as a guide in the design phase of object-oriented programming, but the list is certainly not complete. Most object-oriented applications will include examples of each of these categories, as well as some that do not seem to fit into any group.

If a class appears to span two or more of these categories, it can often be broken up into two or more classes. For example, the first design of the playing card abstraction had only one class, called Card. This was then split into the data class and the view class.

2.3   DESIGNING FROM SCENARIOS

Designing with CRC cards follows neither the traditional "top-down" nor the "bottom-up" models of software development [Fairley 85]. Instead, the design might be said to progress from the known to the unknown. The design process should begin with only the most obvious classes, and the classes necessary to handle the beginning of an application. The designer(s) then proceed by playing "what if" — by simulating scenarios that illustrate expected use.

The CRC cards can play a concrete role in this simulation process. If several individuals are working together on a design, each person is responsible for one or more classes. As each class becomes relevant to the scenario, it is held up during the period that it is "executing." The passing of "control" (run-time execution) can then be quite visibly seen as a movement from one card to another, or from one designer to another. Cards that are related in some manner, such as being close collaborators with one another, can be grouped together, whereas those that are independent of one another can be kept physically separated.

As each action in the scenario is identified, it is assigned as a responsibility to a specific object. The responsibility is then listed on the card corresponding to that object. Different scenarios (including exceptional or error conditions) are then tried, and more responsibilities are generated. Designers should be encouraged to work with the immediate problem at hand, and not to attempt to anticipate potential future requirements that have not yet been encountered. Often, responsibilities will move from one object to another as the design evolves under pressure from different scenarios. The advantage of index cards is that they are inexpensive, readily replaceable, and changeable. If a card becomes too messy, it can be redrawn; if it becomes too complex, it can be split into new classes.

The scenario technique naturally encourages an experimental approach to design. Since the cards are modified so easily, different designs can be evaluated quickly. The task becomes one of developing a clear description and an understanding of each component of the system. By working from scenarios, you can ensure that the design contains all the information necessary for the completion of a task (since it contains only features that the designer has experienced directly) and avoids unnecessary functionality. The physical nature of the cards seems to encourage a more visceral understanding of responsibilities for the designers; when a designer holds up a card and says "To do *this*, I must tell you to do *that*," and points to another member of the design team, she produces an impression that is difficult to duplicate using only textual symbols.

A Case Study — A Teller Machine

In this section, we will describe how we might proceed with an object-oriented design when faced with the problem of developing software for an automated teller machine. It is important to note that the design we present here is not the only design possible, nor is it even likely to be the best design possible. The problem was originally posed in [Beck 89], in the paper that introduced the idea of CRC cards, although the solution we describe here differs from that discovered by Beck and Cunningham. This example has been used in various courses, and participants have presented many different variations. An alternative formulation can be found in [Wirfs-Brock 90].

Our design starts with the first component that the user approaching the automated teller will encounter — namely, the card reader (Figure 2.2). The first responsibility of the CardReader is to display a welcoming message; it then waits for the insertion of a card. Once a card has been inserted, the CardReader decodes the account information from the magnetic strip, and passes this number to the PinVerifier (Figure 2.3). The PinVerifier will return either a true value, in which case processing will continue, or a false value, in which case the card will be ejected, the welcome window will be redisplayed, and the cycle will be repeated.

The PinVerifier first passes the account number to the AccountManager (Figure 2.4), verifying that the account is valid and requesting the PIN (personal identification number) that is registered with the bank. A window is then displayed requesting the user to enter the digits of the PIN number. If these two values agree, the PinVerifier returns a true value; otherwise, it returns a false value.

Presuming the PIN step is successfully completed, the CardReader then passes control to the ActivitySelector (Figure 2.5). The user selects one item from a menu of available actions. We will assume this menu includes at least a deposit, a withdrawal, and terminate activity. The last of these returns control to the CardReader, which releases the card and redisplays the welcome window (Figure 2.2). The other options pass control to specialized managers (Figure 2.6), which request the appropriate information from the user and verify the legitimacy of the transaction with the AccountManager. A separate system (Figure 2.7) controls the drawer, which is used either to accept the deposit from the user or

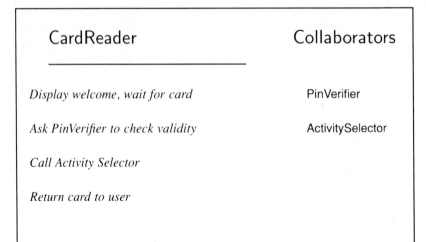

Figure 2.2   Responsibilities of the card reader.

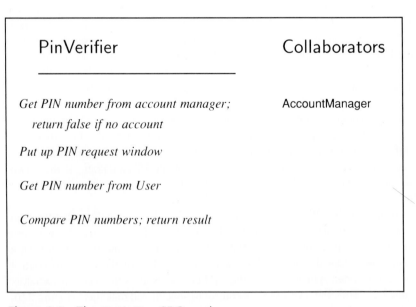

Figure 2.3   The PinVerifier CRC card.

AccountManager

Check validity of account;

 return PIN number

 Check withdraw/deposit info

Figure 2.4   The AccountManager CRC card.

ActivitySelector   Collaborators

Display activity menu   DepositManager

Wait for user selection   WithdrawManager

Call appropriate transaction manager

Figure 2.5   The ActivitySelector CRC card.

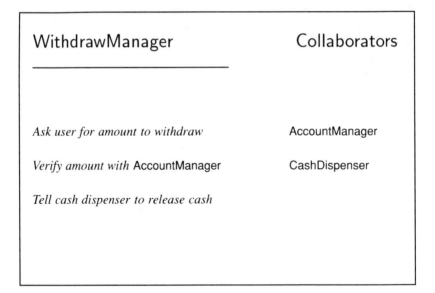

Figure 2.6   Activity-specific managers.

to dispense cash. Following successful completion of each task, or the abortion of the task by either the system or the user, the specialized task managers return to the activity selector.

Data Managers

The development of an actual software system from a design based on the CRC card approach is a process of iterative refinement. Once the high-level structure of the design is agreed on, each step (that is, each responsibility) is examined in turn, and more detailed specifications are generated. Eventually, the detail of the specification exceeds the point at which English seems natural as a medium of expression, and the design lapses into code.

The next step in the process of refining the specification emphasizes the management of data values. We cannot stress too strongly that this step should be taken only *after* an acceptable collection of responsibilities has been established. The task of the first part of the design process using CRC cards is to define *what* responsibilities are assigned to each class. It is only after these are established that we can talk about *how* those responsibilities are to be achieved.

Clearly, information (that is, actual data values) will be dispersed throughout the entire design, according to the needs of the individual classes. It is important to distinguish between long-lived data — that is, those values which must be maintained for a significant period of time or used by a large number of individuals — and short lived data values. An example of the former in our banking-machine design might be the account balance. An example of the

ElectronicDrawer	Collaborators
Issue cash	WithdrawManager
Issue time-stamped deposit envelope	DepositManager
Retrieve deposit envelope	

Figure 2.7   ElectronicDrawer manager.

latter is the particular character typed by the user in selecting from a menu. The following principle can be described as basic to responsible data management:

> Any value that will be accessed or modified widely, or that will exist for a significant period of time, should be *managed*. That is, one and only one class should have responsibility for the actions taken to view or alter the values. All other classes that need to obtain the values must pass requests to the manager for such actions, rather than accessing the data themselves.

The upholding of this principle involves wrapping any data access inside a procedure call (the message to the manager). To some programmers, this seems to be an unnecessary inefficiency. For the benefit of those individuals we note the following points:

- Any such inefficiencies are more than offset by the reduced coupling between classes. This reduction results in more understandable and thus more easily maintainable code.
- The actual inefficiencies involved are small, and in some languages and in certain cases can be eliminated altogether (by the use of an inline function in C++, for example).

To make the connection between data and data manager explicit, we add a fourth field to each CRC card, which describes the data values managed by the class. These values can be described on the back of each CRC card, which is appropriate since the values are in a sense hidden inside the class. Each responsibility is then examined to determine what data values are needed

to carry out the assigned task. Usually, this step will result in new responsibilities being generated, as one class needs to request values from another
class.

The following guidelines can be used in this process (compare these with
Parnas' principles, described on page 12).

- Access to data should be restricted as much as possible. If a class does not
  absolutely need access to a certain bit of information to carry out its tasks,
  it should neither seek nor have such access.

- A class should have access to all and only the data values it needs to perform
  its given responsibilities.

Let us illustrate these points by considering several of the data items manipulated in our banking-machine design. The first data item we encountered was
the account number. This was retrieved by the CardReader from the magnetic
strip on the card. Although the CardReader has responsibility for the discovery
of this number, thereafter it seems irrelevant to the actions of that class. Thus,
the CardReader should not be the manager of this value. The account number
is important, however, to most of the actions associated with the AccountManager. Thus, it seems reasonable that the account number should be passed by the
CardReader to the AccountManager, and thereafter the account manager should
be considered to be the *manager* for this data item.

Next, consider the PIN number. Since the CardReader is already com-
municating with the AccountManager, a programmer might be tempted to have
the CardReader request the recorded PIN number from the AccountManager,
and then to pass this value on to the PinVerifier. Once more, however, the
question to be asked is whether the PIN number has anything to do with the
future actions of the CardReader. Since the answer is no, there is no reason
for the CardReader to have any interest in the PIN number. Thus, the Pin-
Verifier requests the recorded PIN number from the AccountManager and the
entered PIN number from the user, and no other class needs access to these
values.

The account balance clearly should be managed by the AccountManager.
This implies the actions of the DepositManager and WithdrawalManager cannot
involve direct changes to this value. The WithdrawalManager does not subtract a
certain amount from the balance, but instead asks the AccountManager whether
it is possible to make a withdrawal of a given size. It is the responsibility
of the AccountManager to check the size of the withdrawal against the current
account balance, and to return either an agreement to the given change or an
indication that insufficient funds remain in the account to cover the request.
Figures 2.8 and 2.9 illustrate an appropriate and an inappropriate dialogue when
the user has requested a withdrawal of $200 from her account. In addition to
centralizing the information (the balance) in one place, this technique of data
management also permits a more modular approach to adding new functionality. For example, many banking systems do not permit multiple withdrawals

WithdrawalManager   AccountManager

What is the current balance?   *The current balance is $1737.17*

(Hmm. If I subtract $200
from that number I still
get a positive value. OK.)
Please reset the balance to $1537.17

Figure 2.8   An inappropriate discussion between managers.

WithdrawalManager   AccountManager

Can the client withdraw $200?   *(Hmm. If I subtract $200*
                                     from the balance I still
                                     get a positive value.)
                                     Yes.

OK. Then please record
the withdrawal

Figure 2.9   An improved discussion between managers.

within a certain period; for example, they may permit no more than one withdrawal every 24 hours. This additional functionality would be easy to add to a system structured like that in Figure 2.9, but would be more difficult to add to one structured like that in Figure 2.8.

2.4   DISCOVERING INHERITANCE

Once the management of data values has been established, there is yet another step in the design process. As we noted in Chapter 1, object-oriented programming emphasizes the reuse of existing code, and the development of general-purpose tools. We have purposely avoided discussing these issues in our description of the CRC process because we believe that these are secondary concerns, and should not be part of the initial design process. Nevertheless, once the initial design is agreed on, the recognition of commonality can facilitate further development. (We can state this another way by saying that inheritance is a useful *implementation* technique, but not a *design* technique).

Two relationships are of fundamental importance to this second stage of object-oriented design. These two relationships are known colloquially as the *is-a* relationship and the *has-a* (or *part-of*) relationship.

The *is-a* relationship holds between two concepts when the first is a specialized instance of the second. That is, for all practical purposes the behavior

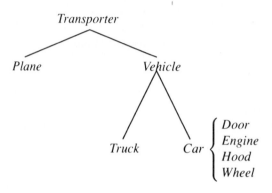

Figure 2.10　*Is-a* and *has-a* relationships.

and data associated with the more specific idea form a subset of the behavior
and data associated with the more abstract idea.[3]　For example, a Florist *is-a*
Shopkeeper, since general facts about shopkeepers are applicable to florists. To
test for the *is-a* relationship, we consider the assertion that "*X* is a *Y*," where
X and *Y* are the concepts being investigated. If the assertion is correct — that
is, if it is in accordance with our other knowledge — then we judge *X* and *Y* to
have the *is-a* relationship.

The *has-a* relationship, on the other hand, holds when the second concept is
a component of the first, but when the two are not in any sense the same thing, no
matter how abstract the generality. For example, a Car *has-a* Engine, although
clearly it is the case neither that a Car *is-a* Engine nor that an Engine *is-a* Car.
A Car, however, *is-a* Vehicle, which in turn *is-a* Transporter (Figure 2.10).

Most of the time, the distinction is clear-cut.　Sometimes, however, the
difference may be subtle, or may depend on circumstances. A symbol table in
a compiler, for example, may be implemented as a special type of linked list.
Should we say that a symbol table *is-a* linked list, or that a symbol table *has-a*
linked list?　Arguments can be made for both relations, yet the latter seems
preferable since it delays a design decision that we may want to revise later.
(For example, we may later want to change the symbol-table structure to use
hash tables).

The *is-a* relationship defines class–subclass hierarchies, whereas the *has-a*
relationship describes data to be maintained within a class. In searching for code
that can be reused or made more general, we place emphasis on the recognition
of these two relationships.

We start by examining classes already available in libraries associated with
whatever programming language is being used for the application. The Smalltalk
system, for example, provides an exceedingly rich set of classes designed to be
extended for user purposes. Similar libraries are becoming available in C++

---

[3] Although, as with Phyl the platypus in Chapter 1, we must eventually have ways of handling the
(we hope rare) exceptions.

and Object Pascal. (Pointers to some of these libraries are given in Chapter 20.) Windows, for example, are commonly provided in existing software libraries. The activity menu put up by the ActivitySelector (Figure 2.5) is a special type of window. Depending on the system, we may be able to access a great deal of functionality for free simply by making the ActivityMenu a subclass of an existing class.

Finding existing classes that can be reused is a more or less top-down approach (that is, top-down in the sense of the class hierarchy). A bottom-up approach attempts to find commonality in the descriptions of the classes, promoting common features to a new abstract superclass. For example, the CardReader, the PinVerifier, the ActivitySelector, and the activity-specific managers of Section 2.3 all display information in a window and wait for a response from the user. It is likely that much of the code to perform these actions would be similar or identical. If so, then generating a new abstract class (such as DialogManager) would probably be useful.

Next, individual classes can be examined to see if their behavior can be split into components with independent utility. For example, in our playing card abstraction we will eventually want both to display the card on a terminal and to maintain the card on a linked list. Since the former is independent of the latter (we can think of the card being used in a set, or in some other data structure), it is reasonable to isolate the two functions. We do this by creating a class CardView to manage the display function, and a subclass CardLink, which adds the linked-list functionality. Other subclasses could be defined to use the card in other situations.

Finally, we examine *has-a* relationships to see whether the values being maintained can be represented using existing tools. For example, most object-oriented languages provide basic classes for common data structures, such as linked lists and sets. Reusing existing tools can make development easier and faster.

Making effective use of inheritance is a complicated topic; we will return to it later in Chapter 6.

2.5   COMMON DESIGN FLAWS

The following are some of the more common design flaws that occur when people design systems using CRC cards.

- *Classes that make direct modifications to other classes.* Responsibilities that lead to the modification of data contained in another class are a violation of the encapsulation inherent in responsibility-driven design. This violation leads to unnecessary hidden links between classes.

- *Classes with too much responsibility.* Classes with too much responsibility need to learn to delegate some of their responsibility to subordinate or helper classes. If a class cannot be described easily on a 4-inch by 6-inch card, then it is probably too complex. Often a portion of the class behavior can be abstracted out and assigned to a helper class.

- *Classes with no responsibility.* Often, people equate physical existence with logical existence as classes. Although this equality is often the case — for example both the CardReader and ElectronicDrawer classes correspond to actual devices — it is not always the case. In our basic design, money was not an object, because money did not have any behavior. A class with no responsibility serves no function, and usually can be eliminated in a manner that improves the design.

- *Classes with unused responsibility.* This flaw is usually the result of an attempt to design a class in isolation, without regard to its participation in a scenario. Often, anticipated future needs turn out not to exist, and their presence on the list of responsibilities complicates the design unnecessarily.

- *Misleading names.* You should avoid using names that are not descriptive of the responsibilities attached to the class, or that mislead the reader into making assumptions that are not being satisfied.

- *Unconnected responsibilities.* This flaw occurs when a class has a collection of responsibilities that are not connected by data, functionality, or any other obvious binding.

- *Inappropriate use of inheritance.* This flaw occurs when the designer uses inheritance when the relationships between class and superclass is not *is-a*, or when the class can inherit no useful behavior from the superclass.

- *Repeated functionality.* This flaw occurs when code is duplicated in two or more classes, instead of being abstracted into a common superclass.

Exercises

1. Add to the automated-teller machine design of Section 2.3 the facility to generate a receipt summarizing the transactions performed. Multiple transactions for the same customer (such as a deposit and a withdrawal) should appear on the same receipt.

2. Describe the responsibilities of an organization that comprises at least six types of individuals. Examples of such organizations are a school (students, teachers, principal, janitor), a business (secretary, president, worker), and a club (president, vice-president, member). For each class of individual, describe the responsibilities and the collaborators.

3. Take a common game, such as the card games solitaire or twenty-one. Describe a software system that will interact with the user to play the game. Example components include the deck, and the discard pile.

4. Describe an intelligent kitchen manager. The system should manage a database of recipes, and keep an inventory of the foodstuffs on hand. With the aid of a user, the system should design a menu for 1 week at a time, producing a grocery list of items not already available.

5. For each of the following pairs, tell whether the relationship is *is-a* or *has-a*:

    house — roof
    janitor — employee
    digital mouse — input device
    menu — window
    set — collection

3
Classes and Methods

Although the terms they use may be different, all object-oriented languages have in common the concepts of classes, instances, message passing, methods, and inheritance. As we have noted already, the use of different terms for similar concepts is a rampant problem in the field of object-oriented programming languages. We will use a consistent and, we hope, clear terminology for all languages, and will note in language-specific sections the various synonyms for our terms. You should also refer to the glossary in Appendix E for explanations of unfamiliar terms.

In this chapter, we will illustrate the bare mechanics of how the programmer goes about declaring a class and defining methods associated with instances of that class. In Chapter 4 we will examine the process of creating instances of classes, and of passing messages to those instances. We will defer an explanation of the mechanics of inheritance until Chapter 6. This decision is in keeping with our premise that inheritance is a secondary concern, and is not a basic concept of object-oriented programming.

3.1 ENCAPSULATION

In Chapter 1, we noted that object-oriented programming, and objects in particular, can be viewed from many different perspectives. In this chapter, we wish to view objects as examples of abstract data types.

Programming by making use of data abstractions is a methodological approach to problem solving where information is consciously hidden in a small part of a program. In particular, the programmer develops a series of abstract data types. Each abstract data type can be viewed as having two faces, similar to the dichotomy in Parnas' principles (page 12). From the outside, a client (user) of an abstract data type sees only a collection of operations that together define the behavior of the abstraction. On the other side of the interface, the programmer defining the abstraction sees the data variables that are used to maintain the internal state of the object.

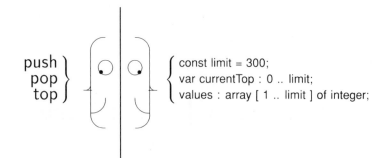

Figure 3.1   The interface and implementation faces of a stack.

For example, in an abstraction of a stack data type, the user would see only the description of the legal operations — say, push, pop, and top. The implementor, on the other hand, would need to know the actual concrete data structures used to implement the abstraction (Figure 3.1). The concrete details are encapsulated within a more abstract framework.

We have been using the term *instance* to mean a representative, or example, of a class. We will accordingly use the term *instance variable* to mean an internal variable maintained by an instance. Each instance will have its own separate collection of instance variables. These values should not be changed directly by clients, but rather should be changed only by methods associated with the class.

A simple view of an object is then a combination of state and behavior. The state is described by the instance variables, whereas the behavior is characterized by the methods. From the outside, clients can see only the behavior of objects; from the inside, the methods provide the appropriate behavior through modifications of the state.

3.2   EXAMPLE: A PLAYING CARD

We will use a software abstraction of a common playing card to illustrate the various object-oriented programming languages we will consider in this book. In Chapter 10, we will use this class in the development of a program to play the card game solitaire. The class Card itself, however, like a real playing card, has little knowledge of its intended use, and can be incorporated into any type of card game.

Figure 3.2 shows a CRC card that describes the behavior of a card. The responsibilities of the class Card are very limited. Basically a card is simply a data manager, holding and returning the rank and suit values. In particular, the base class Card has no ability to display itself. A view class, called CardView, is created to handle display-related tasks. A CRC card for class CardView is shown in Figure 3.3. By isolating the display of the card from the data for the card itself, we isolate the major device and environmental dependencies from the

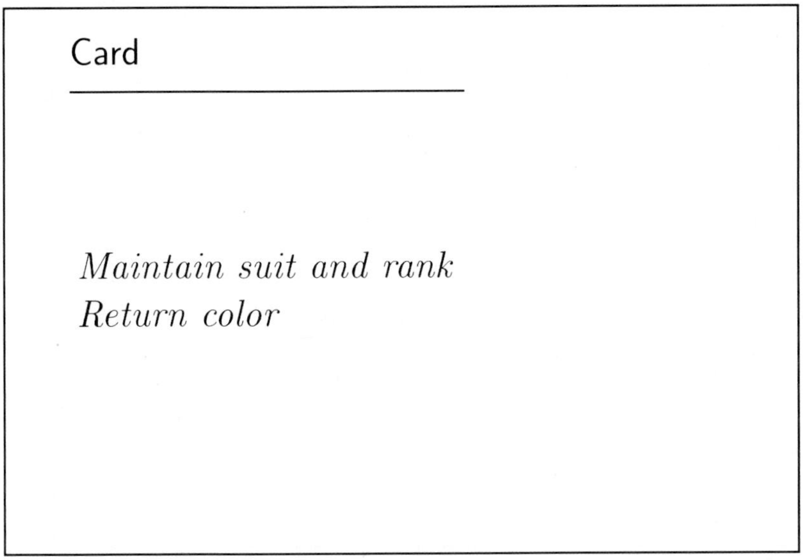

Card

Maintain suit and rank
Return color

Figure 3.2 A CRC card for class Card.

CardView

Draw card on playing surface
Erase card image
Maintain face-up or face-down status
Maintain location on playing surface
Move to new location on playing surface

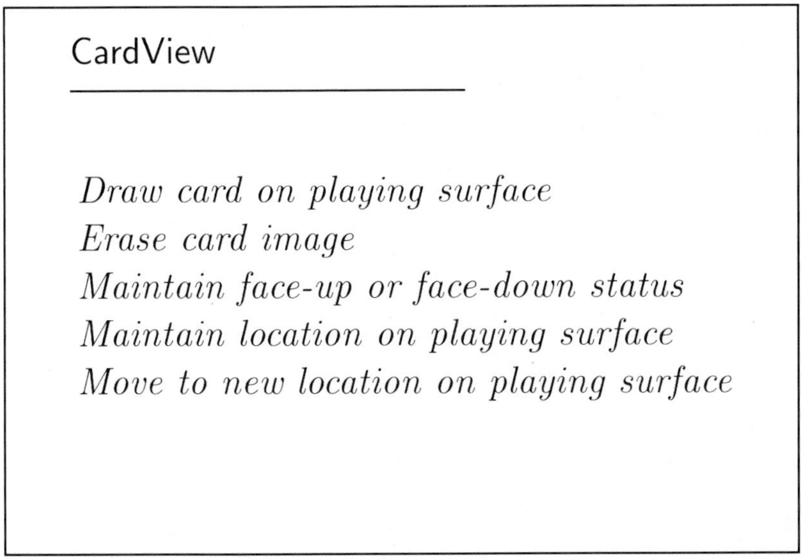

Figure 3.3 A CRC card for class CardView.

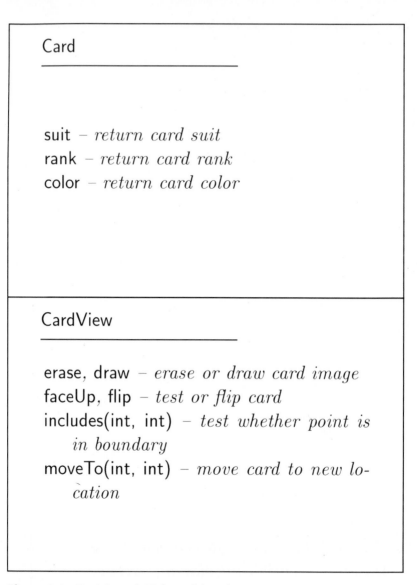

Figure 3.4   Revision of CRC card for class Card.

less dependent structures. For instance, the ability to draw the card will depend very heavily on the windowing package we will use in Chapter 10. If we were to change to a different system, only the view class would need to be altered.

Deciding in which class behavior belongs is not always clear cut. Having separated the data management tasks from the display tasks, it is easy to decide that the method color belongs in class Card, and that the method display should be found in class CardView, but what about the methods flip and faceUp? Is

---

CardView – data values

---

theCard – *(type Card) the card value*
up – *(boolean) face-up or down status*
locx, locy – *location on playing surface*

Figure 3.5   Data values maintained by class Card.

the face-up or face-down status of a card an intrinsic property of the card itself, or merely a property of how the card is displayed? One could argue this point either way, but we have decided to place this behavior in the class CardView. (One point to consider is whether there are uses for the class Card which do not require knowledge of the face-up status. If so, then the Card abstraction should not be charged with the maintenance of this information.)

As we noted in Chapter 2, CRC cards are refined and redrawn, slowly evolving from a natural-language description to a more code-like form. The next step in this process would be to provide names and argument lists to each method. Often at this step the length of the description can exceed the size of a card, and several cards can be stapled together. Figure 3.4 shows this next step in refinement. Notice that even when the responsibilities require nothing more than returning a value (such as deciding whether a card is face up or face down, or discovering the suit or rank) we have nevertheless defined a function to mediate the request. There are practical as well as theoretically important reasons for doing so, which we will return to in Chapter 15.

As we suggested in Section 2.3, at this point the data values to be maintained by each instance of the class can be identified and recorded on the back side of the CRC card, as shown in Figure 3.5. The next step is to translate the behavior and state described on the front and back of the CRC card into executable code. We will consider this step after first exploring the dichotomy between description and definition.

> **1.** A class definition must provide the intended user with all the information needed to manipulate an instance of the class correctly, and with *nothing more*.
>
> **2.** A method must be provided with all the information needed to carry out its given responsibilities, and with *nothing more*.

Figure 3.6   Parnas' principles applied to objects.

3.3   INTERFACE AND IMPLEMENTATION

In Chapter 1, we traced some of the evolution of the ideas of object-oriented programming, noting that they build on and extend earlier concepts of modularization and information hiding. In the course of this evolutionary process, some ideas and concepts are discarded when they prove to be at odds with object-oriented design, and other notions are retained and even extended. In particular, Parnas' principles are as applicable to object-oriented techniques as they were to modules. Figure 3.6 gives a rephrasing of Parnas' ideas in terms of objects.

Parnas' principles divide the world of an object into two spheres. On the one hand, there is the world as seen by the user of an object (or, more precisely, by the user of the services provided by an object). We will call this view the *interface* part, since it describes how the object is interfaced to the world at large. The second view, the view from within the object, we will call the *implementation* part. The user of an object is permitted to access no more than what is described in the interface. The implementation describes how the responsibility promised in the interface is achieved.

With the exception of Smalltalk, all the languages we are considering support to one degree or another the division into interface and implementation. We will describe the mechanics of this division in the sections specific to each individual language. Note that this separation of interface and implementation is not exactly the same as the encapsulation of data discussed in Section 3.1. The latter is an abstract concept, whereas the former is an implementation mechanism. Another way to phrase this idea is to say that modules can be used in the process of implementing objects or abstract data types, but a module by itself is not an abstract data type.

3.4   CLASSES AND METHODS

In this section we describe the mechanics involved in defining classes and methods in each of the four languages we are considering.

Classes and Methods in Object Pascal

The language Object Pascal was defined by Larry Tesler of Apple Computer
[Tesler 85]; thus, it is not surprising that the module facilities of the language
build on the existing module facilities of Apple Pascal. In this language, a
module is called a *unit*. Unlike in C++ and Objective-C (which we will describe
shortly), the unit is maintained in a single file, rather than being split into two
separate files. Nevertheless, the unit is divided into an interface component
and an implementation component. Units can import other units, a process that
makes available to the importer the features described in the interface section
of the imported unit.

A unit for the classes Card and CardView is shown in Figure 3.7. The body
of the interface section is similar to a function body in Pascal, and can contain
const, type, and var sections, including declarations of non–object-oriented data
types, such as the enumerated types suits and colors.

The description of a class is similar to a record description, only it can
contain procedure and function headings as well as data fields. A name cannot
denote both a data field and a method, and thus we use the name suitValue for
the data field, which is distinct from the function suit that returns this value.
Multiple classes can be defined in a single unit.

The declaration of a class will be examined by clients, in order to discover
how a class is manipulated, much more frequently than the actual code is examined. For this reason, comments should be used to help facilitate the rapid
retrieval of information. The data declarations should be separated from the
declaration of methods. Methods should be grouped, and labeled, according to
more abstract classifications of behavior. Within each group, methods should
be listed in alphabetical order. Tab stops should be used to line up each method
name, so the names can be scanned quickly as a table.

Although judicious use of comments can improve readability, the programmer should avoid overuse. Assuming methods are provided with meaningful
names, there is no reason to comment every method declaration, for example.
Too many comments can complicate, rather than simplify, the readability of
the code.

Notice in the data section of the class description for CardView that a field
of type Card is declared. It is important to point out that this declaration does
not actually create a new instance of class Card, but merely sets aside space for
a pointer to this value. Variables or fields declared with an object type, such as
the instance variable theCard, can contain either value data or, as with variables
declared to be of type pointer in Pascal, the special value nil. It will be the
responsibility of the initialization code for class CardView to ensure that this
field is properly established.

The implementation section of a module, like the interface section, can
contain const, type, and var sections, as well as function and procedure bodies.
Any types and variables declared in the implementation section are useful only
within the unit. Figure 3.8 shows a portion of the implementation unit for the

```
unit card;
  interface
    type
      suits = (Heart, Club, Diamond, Spade);

      colors = (Red, Black);

      Card = object
          suitValue :      suits;       (* data fields *)
          rankValue :      integer;

            (* initialization *)
          procedure   setCountAndSuit (c : integer,
                                        s : suits);

          function   color : colors;    (* current state *)
          function   rank : integer;
          function   suit : suits;
        end;

      CardView = object
          theCard :     Card;
          up :          boolean;
          xcoord :      integer;
          ycoord :      integer;

          function  card : Card;   (* data access *)
          function  faceUp : boolean;
          function  x : integer;
          function  y : integer;

          procedure   flip;       (* modification *)
          procedure   moveTo(x, y : integer);

          procedure   draw;       (* display *)

          function   includes(x, y : integer) : boolean;
        end;
  implementation
      ...
end.
```

Figure 3.7   The interface portion of a unit in Object Pascal.

```
implementation
  const
    CardWidth = 65;
    CardHeight = 75;

  function Card.color : colors;
  begin
    case suit of
      Diamond:  color := Red;
      Heart:    color := Red;
      Spade:    color := Black;
      Club:     color := Black;
    end
  end

  . . .

  function CardView.includes ( x, y : integer) : boolean;
  begin
    includes := (x >= xcoord) and (x <= xcoord +
                                        CardWidth) and
        (y >= ycoord) and (y <= ycoord + CardHeight);
  end

  . . .
end.
```

Figure 3.8   The implementation portion of a unit in Object Pascal.

classes Card and CardView. Unlike procedure names in conventional languages, method names need not be unique and the same method name can be used in several different classes, even in the same module. Thus, when a method is defined, a special syntax is needed to indicate the class for which the definition of the method is being provided. In Object Pascal, this syntax is the class name, followed by a period, followed by the method name.

Classes and Methods in Smalltalk

An explanation of the Smalltalk language is almost inextricably tied up with at least a simple understanding of the Smalltalk user interface. Thus, an explanation of how new classes are created in Smalltalk must necessarily begin with an explanation of the *browser*. We will present a superficial explanation of some basic features of the browser. Anything more complex than this discussion is beyond the scope of this book. The interested reader should consult a text specifically intended to help people understand the user interface, such as [Goldberg 84].

Graphics	Array	insertion	add:
Collections	Bag	removal	addAll:
Numerics	Set	testing	———-
System	Dictionary	printing	

message selector and argument names
    ˝ comment stating purpose of message˝
    | temporary variable names |
    statements

Figure 3.9 A view of the Smalltalk browser.

To the user, the view of a browser is that of a window divided into five
separate panes — four small panes over one large pane (Figure 3.9). Each of
the upper panes scrolls over lists of textual material. The bottom pane is used
for displaying and editing information. The browser is manipulated by means
of a mouse, which must have three separate buttons. The left button is used to
indicate editing operations and selection; the middle and right buttons are used
to produce menus of various permissible operations.

Classes in Smalltalk are grouped together into categories. The first pane
scrolls over all the categories known to the Smalltalk system. Although it is
possible to create a new category, it suffices for our purposes to select an existing
category and to create our new class in it. Selecting the category "Graphics"
in the first pane causes two actions. The first is to display, in the second pane,
the list of all the classes currently organized under the selected category. The
second action is to display, in the large editing pane under the four upper panes,
the text of a message used to create new classes.

Using a point-and-click editor, the user can change the message so that it
appears as shown in Figure 3.10. For the moment, we will treat this as merely
a descriptive device that indicates the class Card is to be made a subclass of
the class Object. (All classes in Smalltalk must be subclasses of at least one
other class. The class Object is the most common class used for this purpose.)
Instances of the class Card will each maintain two data values. Notice that the
names of these values are not tied to any particular data type. The Smalltalk

```
Object subclass: #Card
  instanceVariableNames: 'suit rank'
  classVariableNames: ''
  poolDictionaries: ''
  category: 'Graphics-Primitives'
```

Figure 3.10 The description of a Smalltalk class.

```
setSuit: s  rank: c
  " set the suit and rank instance variable values "
  " also other initialization "
  suit ← s.
  rank ← c.
  up ← false.
  x ← y ← 0
```

Figure 3.11   The method setSuit:rank: in Smalltalk.

language does not have any type-declaration statements, and variables can take on any value whatsoever. We will have more to say about typed versus untyped languages when we discuss message passing in the next chapter. There are neither class variables nor pool variables associated with our class. (Class variables and pool variables are advanced topics. The former will be introduced in Chapter 18; the latter is beyond the scope of this book.)

The pound (#) sign in front of the word Card identifies the item as a *symbol*. The most important property of a symbol is the one-to-one correspondence between symbol values and symbol names; that is, each named symbol will have a different value, but every symbol with the same name will share the same value. Thus, symbols are used commonly as keys and placeholders for categories.

Having correctly defined the characteristics of the new class, the user selects the **accept** operation from a menu of possibilities.[1]   The new class having been entered, the third pane describes groups of permitted operations. Using the middle button, the user can enter categories of operations, such as *values*, *location*, *manipulation* and so on.

Selecting a group pane brings into play the final pane of the upper group, which selects individual methods. As with the category pane, when a group pane is selected, the existing methods in the group are displayed in the fourth pane, while simultaneously a template that can be edited to generate new methods is displayed in the bottom window. This edit template is as shown in Figure 3.9.

To create a new method, the user edits this template, and selects the **accept** item from a menu when complete. For example, Figure 3.11 shows the method used to initialize the suit and rank of a card. In Smalltalk, arguments are separated by keywords, which can be recognized because they end in a colon, whereas identifiers cannot do so. Thus, the name of the method being defined in Figure 3.11 is setSuit:rank:, which takes two arguments that are known to the method as s and c. Notice also that the assignment arrow is a single character, ←, and that the period is used as a statement separator (it is optional on the last statement of the method).

Access to instance variables from outside of the methods associated with a class is not permitted in Smalltalk. Therefore, to provide such access we

---

[1] The **accept** option is found in the menu provided by the middle mouse button.

```
suit
  " return the suit of the current card "
  ↑ suit
```

Figure 3.12   The method suit in Smalltalk.

must define explicit accessor functions. The method suit, shown in Figure 3.12, returns the value of the instance variable suit. The up arrow, ↑, is used to indicate that the following value is to be returned as the result of executing the method. Notice that methods can have the same name as instance variables, and no confusions can arise (at least to the system — we will say nothing of the programmer).

Although integers between 1 and 13 would be the logical values to use for the rank field, the programmer can use symbols for the suit value. Similarly, a method such as color can return a symbol as a result. Figure 3.13 shows the method color. Notice that conditional statements in Smalltalk are written as though they were messages sent to the conditional part. The open braces create what are known as *blocks*, and can be thought of in this circumstance as being similar to the **begin-end** pairs of Pascal.[2]

Classes and Methods in Objective-C

Objective-C is an object-oriented extension of the imperative programming language C. This being the case, much of the structure and the use of the language is inherited from C. In particular, the implementation of modules is based on the common C convention that divides files into two categories; interface files (normally given a ".h" extension) and implementation files (in C normally given a ".c" extension, which in Objective-C is changed to a ".m" extension). The assumption is that a user of a class (the first person in Parnas' dichotomy) needs to see only the interface file.

An interface file for our cards example is shown in Figure 3.14. The interface file serves two purposes. To the programmer, it is an important aid in documenting the purpose and functionality of a class. To the system, the interface file conveys information such as types and storage requirements. Occasionally these two uses are in conflict with each other. For example, in Objective-C, as in Smalltalk, users of a class are not permitted access to the instance information, the internal state, of the object. Only the methods associated with a class can access or modify the instance data. Nevertheless, to determine storage requirements, the system must know the size of each object. Thus, instance variables are described in the interface file, not for the benefit of the user (although they may provide some descriptive information, they are nevertheless inaccessible), but rather for the benefit of the compiler.

---

[2]The reality is slightly more subtle, but is unimportant to our discussion here. An explanation of what blocks are and of and how blocks and message passing can be used to provide control flow, can be found in Chapter 2 of [Budd 87].

```
color
  " return the color of the current card "
  (suit = #diamond)    ifTrue: [ ↑ #red ].
  (suit = #club)       ifTrue: [ ↑ #black ].
  (suit = #spade)      ifTrue: [ ↑ #black ].
  (suit = #heart)      ifTrue: [ ↑ #red ].
```

Figure 3.13   The method color in Smalltalk.

The first several lines of the interface file consist of code that would be the same in C or in Objective-C. The "import" directive is similar to the "include" directive in C, except that it ensures that the file is included no more than once. In this case, the file being imported is the interface description of the class Object. The "define" directives construct several symbolic constants, which we will use for the suits and the colors.

The at sign (@) indicates the beginning of Objective-C specific code. In this case, the code describes the interface to objects of class Card. It is possible to place interfaces for several classes in the same interface file, although commonly each class has a separate file. In Objective-C, as in Smalltalk, every class must be a subclass of an existing class, with the class Object serving as the most common value.

The list enclosed in set braces that follows the class indication represents the declaration of the instance variables (data) that will be associated with the class. Each instance of the class will have a separate data area. Objective-C distinguishes between conventional C values — such as integers, reals, structures, and the like — and objects. The latter are declared as the data type id. As in Object Pascal, a variable declared as type id (such as the instance variable theCard) can contain either a legal value or the special value Null.

The lines following the data description give the definition of the methods that will be associated with this class. Each method description begins with a minus sign (−) in the first column. This character can then be followed by an optional type expression, similar to a cast expression in C. This expression indicates the type of value the method will return; an object type (id) is the default assumption used if no explicit alternative is given. Thus, the method suit (notice that methods can have the same name as instance values) returns a value of type integer, whereas the method card returns an object. The method flip is described by the type void, which is the C way of indicating it returns no value; that is, it is a procedure and not a function. Once again, tab stops, comments, and alphabetic ordering can be used to improve the readability of the description.

Methods that take arguments, such as the method to move a card or to test a point for inclusion within the area bounded by a card, are written in the Smalltalk fashion with keywords separating the arguments. Unlike in Smalltalk, however, each argument must be given a declaration of type, with the object type id being assumed if no alternative is provided. This declaration is given in the same cast-like syntax used to indicate the result type.

```
/* interface description for class Card */
# import <objc/Object.h>
# define Heart        0
# define Club         1
# define Diamond      2
# define Spade        3
# define Red          0
# define Black        1

@interface Card : Object
{
  int    suit;
  int    rank;
}

- (void)    suit: (int) s      /* initialization */
            rank: (int) c;


- (int)    color;                  /* current state */
- (int)    rank;
- (int)    suit;
@end

@ interface CardView : Object
{
  id   theCard;
  int    up;
  int    x;
  int    y;
  id    link;
}
-        card;
- (void)    draw;
- (int)    faceUp;
- (void)    flip;
- (int)    includesX: (int) testx y: (int) testy;
- (void)    moveTo: (int) newx and: (int) newy;
- (int)    x;
- (int)    y;
@end
```

Figure 3.14   An interface file in Objective-C.

```
/* implementation of class Card */

# import "card.h"

# define cardWidth 68
# define cardHeight 75

@implementation Card
- (int) color { return suit % 2; }

- (int) rank { return rank; }

- (int) suit { return suit; }

- (void) suit: (int) s rank: (int) c
  { suit = s; rank = c; up = 0;}
@ end

@implementation CardView
- card { return theCard; }

- (int) faceUp { return up; }

- (void) flip { up = ! up; }

- (int) includesX: (int) testx y: (int) testy
  { if ((testx >= x) && (textx <= x + cardHeight) &&
      (testy >= y) && (testy <= y + cardWidth)) return 1 ;
    else return 0; }

- (void) moveTo: (int) newx and: (int) newy;
  { x = newx; y = newy; }

- (int) x { return x; }

- (int) y { return y; }
@end
```

Figure 3.15 The implementation of class Card in Objective-C.

The implementation file for the class Card is shown in Figure 3.15. The file begins by importing the interface file. Once more, Objective-C code can be freely intermixed with ordinary C code; in this case, the next two lines define symbolic constants for the length and width of our playing card.

The implementation directive is used to define the actual code for the methods associated with a class. Both the parent-class name and the instance-variable definitions can be omitted from the implementation part; they then will be taken from the interface description.

It is not necessary for the order of methods in the implementation section to match the order in which methods were defined in the interface section. To simplify the task of finding a specific method body, we often define methods in alphabetic order.

The method headings are repeated, just as in the interface file, only they are now followed by the body of the methods. This body is enclosed in curly braces, as in C.

Classes and Methods in C++

The language C++, like Objective-C, is an object-oriented extension of the imperative programming language C. As in C, it is useful in C++ to distinguish between interface files (conventionally given a ".h" extension) and implementation files (the suffix varies across systems).

An interface file for the classes Card and CardView is shown in Figure 3.16. As in Objective-C, an interface file can contain descriptions of more than one class, although usually this is done only if the classes are closely related. Since C and C++ do not support the import keyword, the conditional inclusion facilities can be used to the same effect; the first time the file Card is included, the symbol cardh (which presumably does not occur elsewhere) will not have been defined, and thus the ifndef statement will be satisfied and the file will be read. On all subsequent readings of the file within the module the symbol will be known, and the file will be skipped.

Class descriptions begin with the keyword class. In C++, as in Object Pascal, a class description is much like a structure definition, only it is permitted to have procedure headings as well as data values. The keyword private precedes those portions that can be accessed only by the methods in the class itself, whereas the keyword public indicates the true interface — those elements that are accessible outside the class. As in Objective-C, the description of the private instance variables is given only for the benefit of the compiler, so that the compiler can determine the memory requirements for an object. To a user of a class, these fields remain inaccessible.

Because users are most often interested in the public interface, it should always be listed first. Similarly, comments, tab stops, grouping, and alphabetizing should be used to make the declaration more meaningful.

The keyword const is used to describe quantities that will not alter, and can be applied to instance variables, arguments, or other names. In this case, the card width and card height are constant values. (The form we use here has the disadvantage of creating a separate constant for each instance of CardView. We will later, in Chapter 18, see how to declare constant members so that only one constant value is constructed.)

Notice the declaration for the theCard field in the class CardView. The language C++ does not hide the distinction C makes between an object and a pointer to an object, whereas in Smalltalk, Objective-C, and Object Pascal, all objects are represented internally as pointers, although the user never sees

```
// interface description for class Card

# ifndef cardh
# define cardh // include this file only once

class Card
{
public:
  int setSuitAndCount (int, int);      /* initialization */
  int    suit ();                /* current state */
  int    color ();
  int    rank ();
private:
  int    s;
  int    r;
};

class CardView
{
public:
  const int CardWidth = 68;
  const int CardHeight = 75;

  Card *   card();
  void     draw ();
  void     erase ();
  int      faceUp ();
  void     flip ();
  int      includes (int, int);
  int      x ();
  int      y ();
  void     moveTo (int, int);
private:
  Card *   theCard;
  int      up;
  int      locx;
  int      locy;
};
# endif
```

Figure 3.16   An interface file in C++.

these. The issues of implicit versus explicit pointers are tied to questions of storage-allocation techniques and the meaning of assignment, and are sufficiently complex and subtle that we defer further discussion to a later point (Chapter 11).

The keyword void indicates, as in Objective-C, the absence of a type. When used as the return type for a method, it means the method is used in a procedure-like fashion for its side effect, and not for a functional result.

```
// implementation of the class CardView

# include "card.h"

int CardView::includes(int a, int b)
{
  if ((a >= x()) && (a <= x() + CardHeight) &&
    (b >= y()) && (b <= y() + CardWidth)) return 1;
  return 0;
}
...
```

Figure 3.17   An implementation file in C++.

The methods setSuitAndCount, moveTo, and includes illustrate the declaration of parameter types as part of the declaration of a function. This style of function declaration is known as a *prototype*, and has now been adopted as part of the ANSI standard C language. Notice that the prototype is similar to an argument list, although the arguments are provided with types, and names are optional.

Since methods are treated simply as special types of fields in an object, and are otherwise not distinguished from data fields, it is not possible to have a method and data field share a common name. Thus, the field s stores the value representing the suit of the card, whereas the method suit returns this value. Similarly r and rank store and return the rank field, respectively.

An implementation file for a class must provide definitions for the methods described in the interface file. The beginning of such a file is shown in Figure 3.17. The body of a method is written as a conventional C function, with the exceptions that the class name and two colons precede the method name, and that instance variables (fields) within a class can be referenced as variables.

In order to encourage programmers to make use of the design principles of abstraction and encapsulation, C++ provides the ability to define inline functions. An inline function looks to the caller exactly the same as a non–inline function, using the same syntax for parameters and arguments. The only difference is that the compiler can choose to expand inline functions into code directly at the point of call, avoiding the overhead of procedure call and return instructions. (As is the case with the register directive, the inline directive is a suggestion to the compiler. The compiler is free to ignore the directive if it wishes).

The use of abstraction and encapsulation often encourage the creation of a large number of functions that perform little work and thus have small function bodies. By defining these as inline functions programmers can maintain the benefits of encapsulation, while avoiding some of the run-time costs of function invocation. Although we have previously dismissed an over concern with effi-

```
class Card
{
  public:

  int    color ();
  int    rank ();
  int    suit ();

  private:
  int s;      // suit value
  int r;      // rank value
};

inline int Card::rank () { return r; }

inline int Card::suit () { return s; }

inline int Card::color() { return suit() % 2; }
```

Figure 3.18   An interface file with inline functions.

ciency as being detrimental to the development of reliable code,[3] programmers are often justly uneasy when a function body consists of perhaps only a single return statement, and thus the execution time overhead of the procedure call may be larger than the execution time of the procedure body. By use of an inline function these problems can be avoided.

As the name suggests, an inline function will be expanded into direct code when called, and thus the overhead of a procedure call is eliminated. On the other hand, multiple copies of the function body can be created, so the feature should be used only with those functions in which the function body is very small or that are called very rarely. Although they provide an efficiency advantage over conventional procedures, inline functions continue to enforce the protection policies of the class designer. For example, clients cannot have direct access to data that are declared private.

Figure 3.18 illustrates a declaration of several inline functions. When extensive use is made of inline functions, it is not uncommon for the implementation file to be shorter than the interface file. (Indeed, in this case there is no implementation file component for the class Card as all functions are defined inline.)

You can also write inline definitions by defining the body of the method directly in the class definitions. An example of this form is shown in Figure 10.10 (page 145). However, such use tends to make the class definition more difficult to read, and should be employed only when there are very few methods and the method bodies are very short. In addition, some compilers (AT&T C++ 2.0, for example) require that inline functions be defined before they are used. By sep-

---

[3]The following quote from an article by Bill Wulf provides some apt remarks on the importance of efficiency: "More computing sins are committed in the name of efficiency (without necessarily achieving it) than for any other single reason — including blind stupidity" [Wulf 72].

arating the body of the inline function from the class definition, methods can be listed in a logical order for exposition in the class definition, and a different order constrained by the implementation in the text following the class definition.

Exercises

1. Suppose you were required to program a project in a non–object-oriented language, such as Pascal or C. How might you simulate the notion of classes and methods?

2. In Smalltalk and Objective-C, methods that take multiple arguments are described using a keyword to separate each argument; in C++ and Object Pascal, the argument list follows a single method name. Describe some of the advantages and disadvantages of each approach; in particular, explain the effect on readability and understandability.

3. A digital counter is a bounded counter that turns over when its integer value reaches a maximum value. Examples include the numbers in a digital clock, or the odometer in a car. Define a class description for a bounded counter. Provide the abilities to set maximum and minimum values, to increment the counter, and to return the current counter value.

4. Refine the automated-teller machine example from Chapter 2, describing the various classes and methods needed to construct the software system.

5. Consider the following two different combinations of class and function. Explain the difference as the user would see it.

```
class example {
  public:
    int i;
};
int addi(example x, int j) { return x.i + j; }
class example {
  public:
    int i;
    int addi(int j) { return i + j; }
};
```

6. In both the C++ and Objective-C versions of the card abstraction the modular-division instruction is used to determine the color of a card based on the suit value. Is this a good practice? Discuss a few of the advantages and disadvantages. Rewrite the methods to remove the dependency on the particular values associated with the suits.

7. Both C++ and Objective-C use separate files for the interface and implementation parts of a module, whereas Object Pascal uses a single file. What are some of the advantages and disadvantages of each approach? Consider a commercial software vendor that wishes to keep its software proprietary by distributing only binary versions.

8. Contrast the encapsulation provided by the class mechanism with the encapsulation provided by the module facility. How are they different? How are they the same?

C H A P T E R

4
Messages, Instances, and Initialization

In Chapter 3, we described how new classes can be defined by the programmer. In this chapter, we continue the exploration of the mechanics of object-oriented programming by examining how new instances of classes are created and manipulated, and how the user describes the process of passing a message, or request, to an object. In Section 4.1, we will explore the mechanics of message passing. We will then investigate the tasks of creation and initialization. By *creation* we mean the allocation of memory space for a new object, and the binding of that space to a name. By *initialization* we will mean not only the setting of initial values in the data area for the object, similar to the setting of fields in a record, but also the more general process of establishing the essential initial conditions necessary for the manipulation of an object. The degree to which this latter task can be largely hidden from clients who make use of the services provided by an object in most object-oriented languages is an important aspect of encapsulation, which we have already identified as one of the principle advantages of object-oriented techniques over other programming styles.

4.1 MESSAGE-PASSING SYNTAX

We are using the term *message passing* to mean the process of presenting an object with a request to perform a specific action. Although the concept is central to object-oriented programming, the terms used in the various languages, and the syntax employed to represent the ideas vary widely. In the following sections, we will describe the features particular to each of the various languages we are considering.

Message Passing in Object Pascal

A *message* in Object Pascal is simply a request sent to an object to invoke one
of the latter's methods. As we noted in Chapter 3, a method is described in
an object declaration in a manner similar to a data field in a record declaration.
In an analogous fashion, the conventional dot notation used to represent access
to a data field is extended to mean invocation of a method. The message
selector — the text that follows the dot — must match one of the methods
defined in the class (or inherited from a superclass; we will explore inheritance
in Chapter 6). Thus, if x has been declared to be an object of class CardView
(Figure 3.7, page 44), then the following command instructs the card to move
to the location given by the coordinates (25,37):

```
x.moveTo(25,37);
```

The object to the left of the period is known as the *receiver* for the
message. Notice that, with the exception of the designation of a receiver, the
syntax used for a message is identical with the syntax used in a conventional
function or procedure call. If no arguments are specified, the parenthetical list
is omitted. For example, the following message instructs the card x to flip
itself over:

```
x.flip;
```

If the method specified is declared as a procedure, then the expression must
be used as a procedure. Similarly, if the method is declared as a function, it
must be used as a function.

The pseudo-variable self used in the body of a method indicates the receiver
for the message to which the method is reponding. This variable is not declared,
but can be used as an argument or as the receiver in further messages. For
example, the method color, which returns the color of a card, could be written
as follows:

```
function Card.color : colors;

begin

   if (self.suit = Heart) or (self.suit = Diamond) then

     color := Red

   else

     color := Black;

end;
```

Here, the method suit is being invoked twice to obtain the suit value, rather
than the method using direct access to the instance value.

Message Passing in C++

As we noted in Chapter 3, although the *concepts* of methods and messages are applicable to the language C++, the *terms* are seldom used in C++ texts. Instead, a method is described in C++ literature as a *member function*, and the process of passing a message to an object is referred to as *invoking a member function*.

As in Object Pascal, the syntax used to indicate invoking a member function is similar to that used to access data members (what we are calling instance variables). The notation describes the receiver, followed by a period, followed by the message selector (which must correspond to a member-function name), finally followed by the arguments in a parenthetical list. If x is declared as an instance of class CardView (Figure 3.18, page 55), the following statement tests whether the location given by the coordinates (25,37) lies within the area currently covered by the card:

```
if ( x.includes(25,37) ) { ... }

else { ... }
```

Even when no arguments are required, a pair of parentheses is still necessary to distinguish the invocation of a member function from the accessing of member data. Thus, the following code might be used to determine whether the card x is face up:

```
if ( x.faceUp() ) { ... }

else { ... }
```

A member that is declared to yield a value of type void can be used only as a statement — that is, as a procedure call. Member functions that yield other values can be used, in C fashion, as either statements (in a procedure-like fashion) or functions (in the fashion of a function call).

As in Object Pascal, in C++ there is a pseudo-variable associated with every method that holds the receiver for the message that invoked the method. In C++, however, this variable is called this, and it is a *pointer* to the receiver, not the receiver value itself. Thus, pointer indirection ($\rightarrow$) must be used to send subsequent messages to the receiver. For example, the method color shown in Figure 3.18 could have been written in the following fashion to avoid direct access to the private field maintaining the suit value:

```
int Card::color() { return ( this->suit() % 2); }
```

Within the body of a method, the call on another method without the receiver is interpreted using the current receiver. Thus the method color could (and would, usually) be written as follows:

```
int Card::color() { return ( suit() % 2); }
```

Message Passing in Smalltalk

The syntax used to represent a message in Smalltalk is different from the syntax used in C++ or Object Pascal. It is still the case that the first part of the message-passing expression describes the receiver. Instead of this part being followed by a period, a space is used to separate the receiver from the message selector. As in C++ or Object Pascal, the selector must match one of the methods defined in the class. Thus, for example, if x is a variable of class CardView (Figure 3.10, page 46), the following instructs x to flip itself over:

```
x flip
```

As we noted in Chapter 3, arguments to methods are indicated by keyword selectors. Each keyword is followed by a colon, and a keyword must precede each argument. The following would be used to request card x to move to the locations given by the coordinates 25 and 37:

```
x moveTo: 25 and: 37
```

In Smalltalk, even binary operators, such as + and *, are interpreted as messages, with the receiver being taken from the left-hand value and the argument being represented by the right-hand value. As with keyword and unary messages (messages with no arguments), classes are free to provide whatever meaning they want to associate with binary messages.[1] There is a precedence ordering, with unary messages having highest precedence, binary messages having next-highest precedence, and keyword messages having lowest precedence.

As in Object Pascal, in Smalltalk the pseudo-variable self is used to indicate the receiver of a message within a method. Thus, the method color, shown in Figure 3.13, could be rewritten as follows to avoid direct access to the instance variable suit:

```
color
    "return the color of the current card "

    (self suit == #diamond)    ifTrue: [ ↑ #red ].
    (self suit == #club)       ifTrue: [ ↑ #black ].
    (self suit == #spade)      ifTrue: [ ↑ #black ].
    (self suit == #heart)      ifTrue: [ ↑ #red ].
```

---

[1]C++ provides a similar ability to overload the meaning of binary operators, such as +, *, <=, or even the assignment operator. Discussion of this topic is beyond the scope of this book, although we will briefly mention the overloading of assignment in Chapter 11.

Message Passing in Objective-C

The syntax and terminology for message passing used in Objective-C follows closely the Smalltalk model. Thus, there are keyword and unary messages; however, classes cannot redefine binary operators.

Message passing can occur in Objective-C programs only within *message expressions*. A message expression is an expression enclosed in a set of square brackets [...]. For example, if x is an instance of class CardView, the following message instructs x to flip over. Note the use of the semicolon to end the statement.

```
[ x flip ];
```

The Smalltalk syntax is used for messages that take arguments. For example, the following directs x to move to the location given by the coordinates (25,36):

```
[ x moveTo: 25 and: 36 ];
```

It is necessary to surround only the message-passing expression. If the message-passing expression results in a value to be used with an assignment statement, the assignment operator must be placed outside the brackets. Thus, the following expression assigns to the variable y a copy of the card x:

```
y = [ x copy ];
```

Message-passing expressions can be used anywhere that ordinary C expressions are legal. Thus, for example, the following C statement is testing whether the card x is face up:

```
if ( [ x faceUp ] ) ...
```

As in Object Pascal and Smalltalk, Objective-C uses the name self to refer to the receiver from within a method. Unlike the others, however, self is a true variable. It can be modified by the user, for example. We will see when we discuss *factory methods* that such modification can be useful.

4.2   CREATION AND INITIALIZATION

Before offering detailed explanations of the mechanics of creation and initialization in each of the programming languages we are considering, we first examine in an abstract fashion the issues associated with this topic. By examining the various orthogonal axes in the design space, you will become better prepared to appreciate the features that have and have not been selected in each language.

Stack Versus Heap Storage Allocation

The question of stack versus heap storage allocation is concerned with how storage for variables is allocated and released, and what explicit steps the programmer must perform as part of these processes. We can distinguish variables

```
program ptrexample;
type
  shape : record
      form : (triangle, square, circle);
      side: integer;
    end;
var
  x :  ^ shape;
begin
  new(x);
  ...
  dispose(x);
end.
```

Figure 4.1   Allocation of dynamic variables in Pascal.

that are *automatic* from those that are *dynamic*. The essential difference between automatic and dynamic variables is that storage for an automatic variable
is created when the procedure (or block) containing the variable declaration is
entered, and is released (again automatically) when the procedure (or block) is
exited. Many programming languages use the term *static* to describe variables
allocated automatically on the stack. We will use the alternative term *automatic*
both because it is more descriptive and because *static* means something (in fact
several things) quite different in C and C++. At the time the space is created for
a variable, the name and the created space are linked, and they cannot change
during the time the variable is in existence.

Now consider *dynamic* variables. In Object Pascal, as in Pascal, a dynamic
variable is created using the system-provided procedure new(x), which takes as
argument a variable declared as a pointer (Figure 4.1). The newly created space
is allocated, and, as a side effect, the value of the variable argument is changed
to point to this new space. Thus, the process of *allocation* and *naming* are
tied together.

In C++, dynamic allocation is usually provided by means of the operation
new. For example, Figure 4.2 illustrates the creation of a new instance of class
Card and an assignment of this storage to the variable c.

The essential difference between stack-based and heap-based storage allocation is that storage is allocated for an automatic (stack-resident) value without
any explicit directive from the user, whereas space is allocated for a dynamic
value only when requested.

Memory Recovery

When heap-based storage-allocation techniques are employed some means must
be provided to recover storage that is no longer being used. Generally, languages
fall into two broad categories.Languages such as Pascal, C, C++, and Object

```
Card *c;
    ...
c = new Card;
    ...
dispose c;
```

Figure 4.2   An example of dynamic allocation in C++.

Pascal require the user to keep track of values, to determine when they are no longer useful, and explicitly to free their space by calling a system-supplied library routine. This routine is called dispose in both Object Pascal and C++, and is shown in Figures 4.1 and 4.2.

Other languages, such as Lisp and Smalltalk, can detect automatically when values are no longer accessible, and hence can no longer contribute to any future computations. Such values are then collected, and their space is recovered and recycled in future memory allocations. This process is known as *garbage collection*. There are several well-known algorithms that can be used to perform such recovery. The description of these algorithms is beyond the scope of this book; a good overview is given in [Cohen 81]. As with the arguments against and in favor of dynamic typing, the arguments for and against garbage collection tend to pit efficiency against flexibility. Automatic garbage collection can be expensive, and necessitates a run-time system to manage memory.

On the other hand, in languages in which the programmer is required to manage the dynamic memory area, the following errors are common:

- Memory that is allocated dynamically is never released; this problem is known as a *memory leak*.

- An attempt is made to use memory that has been already freed.

- Memory is freed by two different procedures, leading to the same memory location being freed twice.

To avoid these problems, it is often necessary to ensure that every dynamically allocated memory object has a designated owner. The owner of the memory is responsible for ensuring that the memory location is used properly and is freed when it is no longer required. In large programs, as in real life, disputes over the ownership of shared resources can be a source of difficulty.

Lifetimes of Values

By the *lifetime* of a value, we mean the portion of execution time when the computer must retain the space allocated to the value. The concept of lifetime for values is often confused with notion of the scope of a variable that contains a value. By a variable *scope* we mean the textual portion of a program in which the occurrence of the variable identifier can appear. The reason for this confusion is probably that in most ALGOL-like or Pascal-like languages, almost all variables are automatic, as we noted in an earlier section. That is, the lifetime of a variable extends from when the procedure (or block) containing the variable is entered until it is exited. Although this property is important for providing efficient implementations of such languages, it is certainly not the only possibility. Even in Pascal, the space allocated to a dynamic variable can outlive the procedure in which it is created. In many object-oriented languages, such dynamic behavior is even more frequent.

Pointers

Pointers are an efficient and effective means of dealing with dynamic information, and are therefore used in almost all implementations of object-oriented languages. Whether pointers represent an abstraction suitable for use by most programmers is a topic of considerably more debate in the programming-languages community, and this debate is reflected in the fact that not all object-oriented languages provide them. In some languages (such as Smalltalk and Object Pascal), objects are represented internally as pointers, but are never used as pointers by the programmer. In other languages (such as C++), explicit pointers are used frequently. In Objective-C, variables declared as id are in fact pointers, but this fact is hidden from the user. When objects are declared with an explicit class in Objective-C, it is necessary for the programmer to distinguish between objects and explicit pointers to objects.

Immutable Creation

In Chapter 3, we presented a description of the class Card, and noted one property we would like our card abstractions to possess; namely, that the values associated with the suit and rank of the card would be set once, and thereafter would not be altered. Variables, such as the suit and count instance variables, that do not alter their values over the course of execution are known as *single-assignment* values, or *immutable* variables. An object for which all instance variables are immutable is in turn known as an immutable object.

Immutable values should be distinguished from program constants, although in large part the distinction is one of scope and binding time. A constant in most languages (Object Pascal, for example), must be known at compile time, has global scope, and remains fixed. An immutable value is a variable that can be assigned, but only once. The value is not determined until execution time, when the object containing the value is created.

Immutable objects, of course, can always be constructed by convention. For example, we can provide the message to set the suit and count value for our card abstraction, and simply trust that the client will use this facility only once during the process of initializing a new object, and not subsequently to alter the values of an existing object. More cautious object-oriented developers prefer to not leave themselves dependent on the good will of their clients, and prefer linguistic mechanisms that ensure proper use. The languages we are examining differ in the degree to which they provide such services.

4.3 MECHANISMS FOR CREATION AND INITIALIZATION

We have described some of the possible options in the design of mechanisms for creation and initialization in programming languages; in this section, we will outline the exact mechanisms used in each of the programming languages we are considering.

Creation and Initialization in C++

C++ follows C (and Pascal and other ALGOL-like languages) in having both automatic and dynamic variables. An automatic variable is assigned space when the block containing the declaration is entered, and space is freed when control exits from the block. One change from C is that a declaration need not appear at the beginning of a block; it must appear merely prior to the first use of the declared variable. Thus, declarations can be moved closer to the point where the variables are used.

```
...

Complex a;

a.real = 3;

...

Complex b;

b.imag = ...
```

An illustration of the loose coupling between variables and values in C++ is the introduction of the *reference* declarations. A reference declaration, indicated by the ampersand symbol (&) prior to the declared name, establishes a single-assignment variable — that is, a variable that is set once and cannot thereafter be changed. It binds a name as an *alias*, or alternative, to an expression. This is most often used to implement call-by-reference parameter passing. Consider the following declarations:

```
void f(int& i)
{ i = 1; }

main() {
   int j = 0;
   f(j);
   printf("%d\n", j);
}
```

```
class Complex
{
  public:
    float real;
    float imag;
    Complex ();
    Complex (float rp );
    Complex (float rp, float ip);
    ...
};

Complex::Complex()
{   real = imag = 0.0;  }

Complex::Complex (float rp )
{    real = rp; imag = 0.0;  }

Complex::Complex (float rp, float ip)
{   real = rp; imag = ip;  }
```

Figure 4.3   Example constructors in C++.

Inside the procedure f, the parameter i will point to the same location as the variable j. Thus, changes to i will in effect be changes to j as well, and the value printed will be 1 and not 0. The distinction between references and pointers, and the proper use of each, are topics that are somewhat subtle in C++. For a good explanation of the use of references, see the article by Andrew Koenig [Koenig 89a].

Implicit initialization is facilitated in C++ through the use of object *constructors*. A constructor is a method with the same name as the object class. This method is invoked any time an object of the associated class is created. This is typically when a variable is declared, although it will also occur with objects created dynamically with the new operator. For example, the class definition shown in Figure 4.3 contains a constructor function (the method named Complex) that will automatically assign a value of 0 to the real and imaginary parts of a complex number when an identifier is declared. By means of constructors, a programmer can ensure that immutable fields, such as the count and suit fields of our Card abstraction, are assigned values only during the process of creation (see Exercise 1).

The mechanism of constructors is made considerably more powerful when combined with the ability in C++ to overload functions. A function is said to be overloaded when there are two or more function bodies known by the same name. In C++, overloaded functions are disambiguated by differences in parameter lists. We can use this feature to provide more than one style of initialization. For example, we might want to initialize a complex number sometimes by providing only the real part, and sometimes by providing both a real and an imaginary value. The class description shown in Figure 4.3 provides this functionality by defining three different versions of the constructor function. The constructor function selected would depend on the arguments provided by the user as part of the creation process. The following example illustrates the use of the third form of constructor, automatically assigning the real part the value 3.14159 and the value 2.4 to the imaginary part:

```
Complex *c;

...

c = new Complex(3.14159, 2.4);
```

The alternative forms can also be used in declaration statements. The following illustrates the declaration of three variables, each using a different constructor:

```
Complex x, y(4.0), z(3.14159, 2.4);
```

Default initializers can frequently be used to reduce the necessity for overloading. For example, all three constructors shown in Figure 4.3 can be replaced by the single procedure shown in Figure 4.4. A default initializer provides a value to be used in place of an argument should the user not provide a value. Thus, if the user provides no arguments, the default values for the parameters rp and ip will be 0 if the user provides one value, the default for ip will still be 0 and if the user provides two values, neither of the default values will be used. Notice that the default initializers appear in the class declaration, but not in the subsequent function body.

Default initializers can be used on any function, not simply on constructors. The default initializers work positionally; it is not possible to provide a value for the second argument without first providing a value for the first argument.

Although less commonly needed, it is also possible to define in C++ a function that is invoked automatically wherever memory for an object is released. This function is called the *destructor*. For automatic variables, space is released when the procedure containing the declaration for the variable is exited. For dynamic variables, space is released when the delete operator is applied. The destructor function is written as the name of the class preceded by a tilde ($\sim$). The destructor function does not take any arguments, and is seldom directly invoked by the user. An example destructor, which merely prints the value of the complex number being released, is shown in Figure 4.4.

Automatic storage can be allocated and freed in C++ in any compound statement, and not simply at the entrance and exit from a procedure. We can use this fact, and combine it with the destructor feature, to make a simple mechanism for tracing the flow of control in a program during debugging. Consider the class definition shown in Figure 4.5. The class Mark defines a constructor that, as a side effect, prints a message on the standard output. The associated destructor also prints a message. We can surround any section of code we wish to investigate with a compound statement in which we declare an instance of

```
class Complex
{
  public:
    float real;
    float imag;
      // use zero for missing arguments
    Complex (float rp = 0.0, float ip = 0.0);
    ...
    ~Complex();
};

Complex::Complex (float rp, float ip)
{  real = rp; imag = ip;  }

Complex::~Complex()
{  printf("releasing complex %g %g\n", real, imag);  }
```

Figure 4.4   An example use of default initializers.

class Mark. Even if we do nothing else with the value (and, in truth, there
is nothing else we can do with the value), the output will be produced at the
beginning and end of the compound statement.

The statements shown in the body of the procedure marktest in Figure 4.5
will, for example, produce the following output:

```
entered marktest

output 1

entered inner block

output 2

exit inner block

output 3

exit marktest
```

Creation and Initialization in Object Pascal

In Object Pascal, all objects are dynamic, and must be created explicitly using the
system function new. However, the argument to new can be an object identifier,
instead of a pointer (Figure 4.6). Similarly, the system routine dispose is used to
reclaim the space occupied by an object when the latter is no longer needed. It
is up to the user to manage storage using new and dispose; the system provides
only minimal support. A run-time error occurs if there is insufficient memory
available to honor a request for allocation.

```
class Mark
{
  char *text;
public:
  Mark(char *c);
  ~Mark();
};

Mark::Mark(char *c)
{  text = c; printf("entered %s\n", text);}

Mark::~Mark()
{  printf("exit %s\n", text);}

...

int marktest() {
  Mark xx("marktest");
  ..
  printf("output 1\n");
  {  Mark yy("inner block");
    ...
    printf("output 2\n");
    ...
  }
  ...
  printf("output 3\n");
  ...
};
```

Figure 4.5 Using constructors and destructors for debugging.

Notice that the dereferencing operator (↑) is not needed, despite the dynamic nature of objects. That is, references to objects, although they are dynamic, are not indicated by explicit pointers.

Object Pascal differs from other object-oriented languages in providing no support for implicit object initialization. Instead, once an object is created (using new), it is common to call an explicit initialization method. Figure 4.6 illustrates this behavior, with the message initial.

Support for protection is weak in Object Pascal. For example, there is no way to prevent direct access to the fields rp and ip in an instance of Complex, and there is no way to ensure that the initial message is not invoked more than once.

```
type
  Complex : object
    rp : real;
    ip : real;
    procedure initial(r, i : real);
    ...
    end;
var
  P : Complex;

procedure Complex.initial(r, i : real)
begin
  rp := r;
  ip := i;
end;

begin
  new(P);
  P.initial(3.14159, 2.4);
  ...
  dispose(P);
end.
```

Figure 4.6   Creation and initialization in Object Pascal.

Creation and Initialization in Smalltalk

Smalltalk variables are dynamically typed. Thus, a variable can potentially hold a value of any class. An instance of a given class is created by passing the message new to the *class object* associated with the class. We will discuss class objects in more detail in Chapter 18; for now, it suffices to say that a class object is simply an object that encapsulates information about a class, including how to create new instances.

This value returned by the class object exists independently of any name, but is usually almost immediately assigned a name either through assignment or through being passed as an argument. The following, for example, creates a new instance of our class Card:

```
d ← Card new.
```

The user does not take explicit action to deallocate memory in Smalltalk. Values that are no longer accessible to the running program are recovered automatically by a garbage-collection system. A run-time error occurs if, after garbage collection has been performed, it is not possible to honor a request for storage allocation.

Smalltalk provides several mechanisms to assist in object initialization. *Class methods* are methods that can be associated with a specific class object. We will discuss class objects and class methods in more detail in Chapter

```
r: rp   i: ip | n |
  n ← Complex new. " create the new number"
  n real: rp imag: ip. " assign it coordinates "
  ↑ n
```

Figure 4.7   A class method in Smalltalk.

18; for the moment, it is sufficient merely to state that class methods can be used only as messages to a class object, and are thus used in place of the message new. Frequently, these methods invoke new to create the new object, then perform some further initialization code. Since class methods cannot directly access instance variables, they must typically invoke instance messages to perform initialization. For example, a class method r:i: is shown in Figure 4.7. It creates a new Complex object, storing the latter in a temporary variable called n. It then calls the method real:imag: (presumably defined as a method in class Complex) to establish the values of the instance variables. To create a new complex number using this method, the user would type the following:

```
c ← Complex r: 3.14159 i: 2.459
```

We declare temporary variables by simply listing their names between vertical bars between the method heading and the method body. This is true for both class methods and normal methods. The scope of temporary variables includes only the method in which they are declared.

Smalltalk provides no direct mechanism for initializing immutable fields. Frequently, methods, such as the real:imag: method used in Figure 4.7, will be marked as "private." The understanding is that private methods should not be invoked directly by clients, but this limitation is honored only by convention, and no enforcement is attempted.

Another technique useful for initializing objects in Smalltalk is the *cascaded message*. A cascaded message is handy when multiple messages are to be sent to the same receiver, as is frequently the case during initialization. The cascaded message is written as the receiver, followed by the list of messages separated by a semicolon. For example, the following expression creates a new Set and initializes it with the values 1, 2, and 3. The result assigned to the variable x is the new set. The use of cascades often eliminates the need for temporary variables:

```
x ← Set new add: 1 ; add: 2 ; add: 3.
```

Initialization in Little Smalltalk.   Little Smalltalk is a simplified subset of the Smalltalk-80 language. The system, described in [Budd 87], uses a nongraphical interface, but maintains the dynamic nature of the language. Initialization in Little Smalltalk differs slightly from the procedures used in Smalltalk-80.

Class methods are not supported in Little Smalltalk. Instead, the method new defined in class Class (the method executed when the user passes the message new to a class object) examines the instance methods for each newly created object, and, if a method named new is found, that method is executed using the newly created object as the receiver. Thus, initialization can be accomplished simply by provision of a method called new in the class description.

The syntax for cascades is also slightly different in Little Smalltalk. In Smalltalk-80, there is no semicolon separating the receiver from the first message in a cascade; thus, to find the receiver for the remaining messages in the cascade, we must "strip off" the first message. In Little Smalltalk, the receiver for all the messages, as well as the result of the cascaded expression, is always the expression to the left of the first semicolon. Thus, the cascaded expression in the last section would be written in Little Smalltalk as follows:

```
x ← Set new ; add: 1 ; add: 2 ; add: 3.
```

Creation and Initialization in Objective-C

Objective-C basically combines Smalltalk syntax and C declarations. Typically, objects are declared to be instances of id, and thus more precise type information may not be known until run time. The actual object allocation is performed, as in Smalltalk, by passing of the message new to a class object. (Note that id is defined using a typedef, and, in fact, a variable of type id is a pointer to the actual object.)

As we saw in Chapter 7, it is possible to declare Objective-C variables using a class name directly. Such variables are allocated space on the stack, and are released when the enclosing procedure is exited.

Variations in initialization in Objective-C are provided through the use of *factory methods*. Factory methods, like Class methods in Smalltalk, define functionality for a specific class. (As opposed to normal methods, which define functionality for *instances* of a class. One of the more difficult aspects of object-oriented programming is differentiating between attributes of instances and attributes of classes. We will return to this in a later chapter.)

The message new is used to create a new instance of a class, as in Smalltalk; an example is shown in Figure 4.8. A method definition preceded by a plus sign (+) is called a *factory method*, whereas methods preceded by a minus sign (−) are *instance methods*. There can be many factory methods defined in a class. For example, Figure 4.8 illustrates the creation of a factory method that creates and initializes in one step a new complex number. This value can be used in an assignment; for example:

```
id x; \\

x = [ Complex r: 3.14159 i: 2.4567 ]; \\
```

The Objective-C compiler does not issue any warning when instance variables are used within factory methods. If such references are made, it is assumed (although this fact is not checked) that the value of the variable self is a valid instance of the class. Since normally, in a factory method, self refers to the class itself, and not to an instance, the user must first alter the value of self before

```
@implementation Complex : Object {
  int realpart;
  int imagpart;
}

+ r: (int) rp i: (int) ip {
  self = [ Complex new ];
  realpart = rp;
  imagpart = ip;
  return self; }

- (int) real { return realpart; }

- (int) imag { return imagpart; }
@end
```

Figure 4.8   An example of factory methods in Objective-C.

referencing instance fields.[2] Thus, the method shown in Figure 4.8 first uses new to create a new instance of the class Complex, and then assigns this value to self. It is only after self has been changed that references to the instance variables realpart and imagpart will refer to the correct locations.

Although objects are allocated dynamically in Objective-C, the system does not perform automatic storage management. The user can alert the system that storage for an object is no longer being used by means of the message free, which is defined in class Object and thus is understood by all objects:

```
[ myObject free ];
```

Exercises

1. Write a constructor for the C++ class Card shown in Figure 3.16 (page 53). Explain why we can now remove the method setSuitAndCount, and why the fields suit and count are now immutable. What values should be passed in the argument list for the constructor associated with class CardView?

2. Write the method copy for the class Card of Chapter 3; copy should return a new instance of class Card with the suit and count fields initialized to be the same as the receiver.

3. In a language, such as Object Pascal, that does not provide direct support for immutable instance variables, how might you design a software tool that would help to detect violations of access? (*Hint:* The programmer can provide directives in the form of comments that instruct your tool which variables should be considered immutable.)

---

[2]The fact that the type of self is not checked for validity before references are made to instance variables can be a source of subtle errors in Objective-C programs.

4. We have seen two different mechanisms used to describe the invocation of methods (functions). The approach used in C++ and in Object-Pascal is similar to a conventional function call. The Smalltalk and Objective-C approach separates arguments with keyword identifiers. Which do you think is more readable? Which is more descriptive? Which is more error-prone? Present short arguments to support your opinions.

5. Write a short (two-paragraph or three-paragraph) essay arguing either for or against automatic memory-management (garbage-collection) systems.

6. Explain why the following program will produce the output "17" as the value of the instance variable two:

```
@implementation One : Object

{ int one; }

+ (void) foo: x

   { self = x; one = 17; }

@end


@implementation Two : Object

{ int two; }

- printit

   { printf("two is %d\n", two); }

@end


main() {

id x;


x = [ Two new ];

[ One foo: x ];

[ x printit ];

}
```

5
A Case Study:
Eight Queens

The purpose of this chapter is to present the first of several case studies of programs developed in an object-oriented fashion. In this chapter, the programs will be rather small, so that we can present versions in each of the languages we are discussing in this book. Later case studies will be presented in only one language.

After first describing the problem, we will describe how an object-oriented solution would differ from a solution developed in another manner. The chapter then concludes with a solution in each language. The complete programs can be found in Appendix A.

5.1 THE EIGHT QUEENS PUZZLE

In the game of chess, a queen piece can attack any other piece that lies on the same row, on the same column, or along a diagonal. The eight queens puzzle is simply the task of placing eight queens on a chess board such that no queen can attack any other queen. One solution is shown in Figure 5.1; the solution is not unique. The eight queens puzzle is often used to illustrate problem-solving or backtracking techniques [Griswold 83, Budd 87, Berztiss 90].

The essence of our object-oriented solution will be to create the queens and to provide them with such powers that they themselves discover the solution. In the computing-as-simulation view of Chapter 1, we establish the initial conditions of a model universe and then set that universe in motion; when the activity of the universe stabilizes, the solution is found.

How might we define the behavior of a queen so that the queen can find a solution on its own? The first observation to make is that, in any solution, no two queens can occupy the same column, and consequently no column

Figure 5.1 A solution to the eight queens puzzle.

can be empty. We can therefore assign a specific column to each queen at the start, and reduce the problem to giving each queen the task of finding an appropriate row.

A solution to the eight queens puzzle results when the queens stand in certain relationship to one another. Thus, it is clear that the queens will need to communicate. Realizing this, we can make a second important observation that greatly simplifies our programming task. Namely, each queen needs to send messages only to her neighbor on one side. More precisely, each queen needs to know about only the queen to her immediate left. Thus, the data maintained by each queen consist of three values; a column value, which is immutable (set once and never altered); a row value, which is altered in pursuit of a solution; and the neighbor queen to the immediate left.

Let us define an *acceptable solution for column n* to be a configuration of columns 1 through n in which no queen can attack any other queen in those columns. Each queen will be charged with finding acceptable solutions between her and her neighbors on her left. We will find a solution to the entire puzzle by asking the rightmost queen to find an acceptable solution. A CRC card description of the class Queen, including the data managed by each instance (description on the back side of the card), is shown in Figure 5.2.

As with many similar problems, the solution to the eight queens puzzle involves two interacting steps of *generating* possible partial solutions, and *filtering* out solutions that fail to satisfy some later goal. This style of problem solving is sometimes known as the generate and test paradigm [Hanson 78, Berztiss 90]. Let us consider the filter step first, as it is easier. For the system to test a potential solution, we will see, it is sufficient for a queen to take a coordinate (row–column) pair and produce a Boolean value that indicates whether that queen, or any queen to her left, can attack the given location. A pseudocode algorithm that checks to see whether a queen can attack a given position is

---

Queen

_____

first – *initialize row, then find first ac-*
    ceptable solution for self and neigh-
    bors
next – *advance row and find next accept-*
    able solution
canAttack – *see whether a position can*
    be attacked by self or neighbors

Queen – data values

_____

row – *current row number (changes)*
column – *column number (fixed)*
neighbor – *neighbor to left (fixed)*

Figure 5.2   Front and back sides of the queen CRC card.

shown in Figure 5.3. The procedure canAttack uses the fact that, for a diagonal motion, the differences in rows must be equal to the differences in columns.

In generating a solution, the actions that must take place to produce the first solution often are slightly different from those needed to produce subsequent solutions. For example, in our problem, the first solution involves initializing the row value, whereas subsequent solutions involve updating this value. For this reason, it is convenient to divide the generation task into two messages;

```
function canAttack(r, c)
  if  r = row then
    return true
  cd := column - c
  if (row + cd = r) or (row - cd = r) then
    return true
  return neighbor.canAttack(r, c)
end
```

Figure 5.3   Filtering out invalid solutions in the eight queens puzzle.

the message first, which produces an initial solution, and the message next, which produces a subsequent solution. An object that implements both of these messages is known as a *generator* [Budd 87]. As is common with generators, the first and next messages will turn out to have a common subpart after some initial differences.

When a queen in column n is asked to produce her first acceptable solution, the first step is to ask her neighbor to produce an acceptable solution for column $n-1$. At this level of analysis, we leave unspecified the actions of the leftmost queen, who has no neighbor. We will explore various alternative actions in the actual programs. Having found a solution for the earlier columns, the queen tries each row in turn, starting with row 1, using the procedure described in Figure 5.3. One of two outcomes results: either an acceptable solution is found, or the queen tries all positions without being able to find a solution. In the latter case, the queen asks her neighbor to find another acceptable solution, and the queen again starts testing potential row values.

A possible pseudocode description of this algorithm is shown in Figure 5.4. Although this solution is workable, when we develop the code for the next message, we will see that, by exploiting the commonality of the algorithms and the recursive nature of the solution, a considerably shorter solution is possible.

```
function first : boolean;
  if not neighbor.first
    return false
  repeat
    for  row := 1 to 8 do begin
      if not neighbor.canAttack(row, column) then
        return true
      end
  until not neighbor.next
end
```

Figure 5.4   Finding the first solution to the eight queens puzzle.

```
function testOrAdvance : boolean
  if neighbor.canAttack(row, column) then
    return self.next
  else
    return true;
end

function next : boolean
  if row = 8 then begin
    if not neighbor.next then
      return false
    row := 0
  end
  row := row + 1
  return self.testOrAdvance
end

function first
  if not neighbor.first then
    return false
  row := 1
  return self.testOrAdvance
end

procedure print
  neighbor.print;
  write row, column
end
```

Figure 5.5 Computing new position in the eight queens problem.

When a queen is asked to find another solution she simply advances her row number and checks with her neighbors, assuming she was not already in the last row. If she was already in the last row, she has no choice but to ask a neighbor for a new solution and to start the search from the first row once more. We can simplify the code for these actions, as well as the code for finding the first solution, if we introduce a new auxiliary procedure, testOrAdvance, which tests a position and advances if the latter is not a satisfactory solution. The function testOrAdvance is shown in Figure 5.5; it is defined recursively in terms of the procedure next. Similarly, next can be defined in terms of testOrAdvance. Finally, the code for first can be simplified by using testOrAdvance.

The one remaining task is to print out the solution. This is most easily accomplished by a simple method print that is rippled down the neighbors (Figure 5.5), although more dramatic techniques are certainly possible (Exercise 3).

```
type
  Queen = object
    row : integer;
    column : integer;
    neighbor : Queen;
    procedure initial(col: integer, ngh : Queen);
    function canAttack(r, c : integer) : boolean;
    function first : boolean;
    function testOrAdvance : boolean;
    function next : boolean;
    procedure print;
  end;
```

Figure 5.6   The Object Pascal class definition for Queen.

5.2   EIGHT QUEENS IN OBJECT PASCAL

The class definition for the eight queens puzzle in Object Pascal is shown in Figure 5.6. A subtle but nevertheless important point to note is that this definition is recursive; it defines a field of Queen type. This by itself is sufficient to tell the observant reader that declaration and storage allocation are not necessarily linked in Object Pascal, since otherwise it would appear that an infinite amount of storage would be necessary to hold any Queen value. We will contrast this with the situation in C++ when we discuss that language, and will consider the relationship between declaration and storage allocation in more detail in Chapter 11.

The pseudocode presented in the last section is sufficiently close to Pascal that we need not repeat the code here. There are two major sources of dif-

```
function Queen.next : boolean;
begin
  if row = 8 then
    if neighbor = nil then
      next := false
    else if not neighbor.next then
      next := false
    else begin
      row := 1;
      next := self.testOrAdvance;
    end
  else begin
    row := row + 1;
    next := self.testOrAdvance;
  end;
end;
```

Figure 5.7   The function next in Object Pascal.

```
begin
  neighbor := nil;
  for i := 1 to 8 do begin
    new(lastQueen);
    lastQueen.initial(i, neighbor);
    neighbor := lastQueen;
  end;
  if lastQueen.first then
    lastQueen.print;
end;
```

Figure 5.8 The main program in Object Pascal.

ferences. The first is the lack of a return statement in Pascal, and the second the necessity to test first whether a queen has a neighbor before passing a message to that neighbor. The function next, shown in Figure 5.7, illustrates these differences; this function should be compared to the earlier version shown in Figure 5.5.

The main program allocates space for each of the eight queens, initializes the queens with their column number and neighbor value, then passes the message first to the most recently created queen. The code to do this is shown in Figure 5.8; here, neighbor and i are temporary variables used during the course of initialization, and lastQueen is the most recently created queen.

5.3 EIGHT QUEENS IN C++

The eight queens program in C++ is in many ways similar to the one in Object Pascal. An important difference involves the use of pointers, both in the recursive definition of the class Queen and in the initialization of the eight queens that compose the solution universe. The class definition and the main program are shown in Figure 5.9. The use of a constructor eliminates the need for both the initialization method, and the temporary variable neighbor in the main program, since initialization is combined with creation of the new queen, and thus the old value of neighbor can be passed as argument to the constructor before the variable is overwritten by the assignment.

The use of an explicit return statement and the guaranteed short-circuit evaluation of the "and" and "or" conjunctives (&& and ||, respectively) simplifies the code considerably. Compare the code for the method next in Figure 5.9 to that in Figure 5.7, for example. Note also that the methods canAttack and testOrAdvance are used only internally (by first and next), and thus are not part of the public interface.

```
class Queen {
public:
  Queen(int c, Queen * ngh);

  int    first();
  int    next();
  void   print();

private:
  int    row;
  int    column;
  Queen *  neighbor;

  int    canAttack(int r, int c);
  int    testOrAdvance();
};

int Queen::next()
{
  if (row == 8) {
    if (!(neighbor && neighbor->next()))
      return 0;
    row = 0;
    }
  row = row + 1;
  return testOrAdvance();
}

main() {
  Queen *lastQueen = 0;

  for (int i = 1; i <= 8; i++)
    lastQueen = new Queen(i, lastQueen);
  if (lastQueen->first()) lastQueen->print();
}
```

Figure 5.9   The class description for Queen in C++.

5.4   EIGHT QUEENS IN OBJECTIVE-C

For the solution in Objective-C, we will make use of a programming technique that is frequently useful when linked lists (such as our linked lists of Queens) are being manipulated. This technique is the use of *sentinel* values. A sentinel value is simply a special value used to indicate the end of the list. The value **nil** is often used as a sentinel value in Pascal programs, for example. With object-oriented techniques, we can extend the concept of a sentinel value by giving behavior to the sentinel.

```
@implementation NullQueen : Object
{ }
- (int) first { return 1; }
- (int) next { return 0; }
- (int) checkrow: (int) r column: (int) c { return 0; }
- (int) print {  };
@end
```

Figure 5.10   The sentinel class NullQueen in Objective-C.

Consider, for example, the messages passed by each queen to her neighbor queen. There are four such messages: first, next, canAttack, and print. Now consider how these messages are used by the leftmost queen — the queen that normally has no neighbor. That is, we want to define the behavior for the sentinel value such that the leftmost queen produces the correct results. First, we would like the message first always to succeed, so that the leftmost queen will never be terminated prematurely. The message next, on the other hand, should always fail, since there is no alternative once the leftmost queen has exhausted all positions. Similarly, the message canAttack should always fail, since, if no preceding queen can attack a position, then that position is safe. Finally, the message print needs to provide no actions.

The sentinel is defined as an instance of class NullQueen, with the behavior shown in Figure 5.10. Note that we have here an implementation section for

```
- (int) testOrAdvance
{   if ( [neighbor checkrow: row column: column])
      return [ self next ];
    return 1;
}

- (int) first
{   row = 1;
    if ([ neighbor first ])
      return [ self testOrAdvance ];
    return 0;
}

- (int) next
{   if (row == 8) {
      if (! [ neighbor next ]) return 0;
      row = 0;
      }
    row = row + 1;
    return [ self testOrAdvance ];
}
```

Figure 5.11   Searching for a solution in Objective-C.

```
next
  (r = 8) ifTrue:
    [ (neighbor next) ifFalse: [ ↑ false ]. row ← 0 ].
  row ← row + 1.
  ↑ self testOrAdvance
```

Figure 5.12   The method next in Smalltalk.

the class NullQueen without a corresponding interface section. This omission is legal, although the compiler will provide a warning since it is somewhat unusual.

The use of a sentinel allows the methods in class Queen for first and next to pass messages to their neighbors without worrying whether they are the leftmost queen. Consider the methods shown in Figure 5.11, for example, and contrast them with those presented earlier.

5.5   EIGHT QUEENS IN SMALLTALK

The solution in Smalltalk is similar to the solution in Objective-C, including use of a sentinel. The only major difference is one of syntax. The method next, for example, is shown in Figure 5.12. A solution without the sentinel was described in [Budd 87].

Exercises

1. Modify any one of the programs to produce all possible solutions, rather than just a single solution. How many possible solutions are there for the eight queens puzzle? How many of these are rotations of other solutions? How might you filter out rotations?

2. Suppose we generalize the eight queens problem to the m N-queens problem, where the task is to place m N queens on an m N by m N chessboard. How would the programs need to be changed?
   It is clear that there exist values for m N for which no solution exists (consider m N = 2 or m N = 3, for example). What happens when your program is executed for these values? How might you produce more meaningful output?

3. Using whatever graphics facilities your system has, alter one of the programs to display dynamically on a chessboard the positions of each queen as the program advances. What portions of the program need to know about the display?

C H A P T E R

6
Inheritance

Once the basic philosophy of designing in terms of responsibilities and behavior is accepted, the next step in learning how to program in an object-oriented manner involves acquiring knowledge of how to make effective use of classes organized into a hierarchical structure based on the concept of inheritance. By *inheritance*, we mean the property that instances of a child class (or subclass) can access both data and behavior (methods) associated with a parent class (or superclass). Inheritance is always transitive, so a class can inherit features from superclasses many levels away. That is, if class Dog is a subclass of class Mammal, and class Mammal is in turn a subclass of class Animal, then Dog will inherit attributes both from Mammal and from Animal (Figure 1.2, page 7).

Let us return to Flo the florist from Chapter 1. There is certain behavior we expect florists to perform, not because they are florists but simply because they are shopkeepers. For example, we expect Flo to request money for the transaction, and in turn expect to be given a receipt. These activities are not unique to florists, but rather are common to bakers, grocers, stationers, toy-store owners, car dealers, and other merchants. Mentally, it is as though we have associated certain behavior with the general category Shopkeeper, and as florists are a subclass of shopkeepers, the behavior is automatically associated with the subclass.

Inheritance means that the behavior and data associated with child classes are always an extension (that is, strictly larger set) of the properties associated with parent classes. A subclass must have all the properties of the parent class, and others as well. On the other hand, since a child class is a more specialized (or restricted) form of the parent class, it is also, in a certain sense, a contraction of the parent type. This tension between inheritance as expansion and inheritance as contraction is a source for much of the power inherent in the technique, but at the same time for much of the confusion as to its use. We will use these opposing views when we establish heuristics for when to use inheritance and classes, in Section 6.3.

This inheritance of attributes extends to both data (instance variables and fields) and behavior (methods) in object-oriented languages.[1] A precise definition of inheritance can be made in terms of scope — something along the lines of the scope of a component identifier (instance variable or field) extending over the domain of the descendant class. However, as the exact details differ from language to language, we will let the intuitive notion suffice. The following sections will describe in more detail some of the considerations associated with the mechanism of inheritance.

6.1   THE BENEFITS OF INHERITANCE

In the early chapters of this book, we downplayed the importance of inheritance, in favor of concentrating on the notion of designing in terms of responsibilities, services, contracts, and behavior. Nevertheless, there are many important benefits that can accrue from the proper use of inheritance. In this section, we will briefly note some of these.

Software Reusability

When behavior is inherited from another class, the code that provides that behavior does not have to be rewritten. This may seem obvious, but the implications are important. Many programmers spend a large percentage of their time rewriting code that they have written many times before — for example, to search for a pattern in a string or to insert a new element into a table. Using object-oriented techniques, these functions can be written once and reused.

Other benefits of reusable code include increased reliability (the more situations in which code has been reused, the greater will have been the opportunities for discovering errors), and the decreased maintenance cost because of sharing by all users of the code.

Code Sharing

Code sharing can occur on several levels using object-oriented techniques. On one level, many separate users or projects can use the same classes. We can refer to these as software components. (Cox calls these software-ICs, in analogy to the integrated circuits used in hardware design [Cox 86]). Another form of sharing occurs when two or more different classes developed by a single programmer as part of a project inherit from a single parent class. For example, a Set and an Array may both be considered a form of Collection. When this happens, it means

---

[1]This statement is a slight overgeneralization. We have already seen the use of the private keyword in C++ to restrict methods to being used only within a class, and, in Chapter 15, we will examine ways in which, in some object-oriented languages, programmers can have more complete control over the accessibility of information defined in one class from within another class.

two or more different types of objects will share the code that they inherit. This code needs to be written only once, and will contribute only once to the size of the resulting program.

Consistency of Interface

When multiple classes inherit from the same superclass, we are assured that the behavior they inherit will be the same in all cases. Thus, it is easier to guarantee that interfaces to similar objects are in fact similar, and that the user is not presented with a confusing collection of objects that are almost the same but behave and are interacted with very differently. (This benefit assumes that inheritance takes place without overriding. Overriding, which we will discuss in Chapter 9, permits the programmer to change the meaning of any method arbitrarily.)

Software Components

In Chapter 1, we noted that inheritance will permit us to construct reusable software components. Already, several such libraries have become commercially available [Gorlen 90, Cox 86, Linton 89, Wilson 90], and we can expect many more specialized systems to appear in time.

Rapid Prototyping

When a software system can be constructed largely out of reusable components, development time can be concentrated on understanding the portion of the system that is new and unusual. Thus, software systems can be generated more quickly and easily, leading to a style of programming known as *rapid prototyping* or *exploratory programming*. A prototype system is developed, users experiment with it, a second system is produced based on experience with the first, further exploration takes place, and so on for several iterations. Such a style of programming is particularly useful in cases where the goals and requirements of the system are only vaguely understood when the project begins.

Polymorphism

Software produced in a conventional manner is generally written in a bottom-up fashion, although it may be *designed* in a top-down fashion. That is, the lower-level routines are written, and on top of these slightly higher abstractions are produced, and on top of these even more abstract elements are generated, and so on. This process is like building a wall, where every brick is laid on top of the underlying bricks (Figure 6.1).

Normally, code portability decreases as one moves up the levels of abstraction. That is, the lowest-level routines may be used in several different projects, and perhaps even the next level of abstraction may be reused, but the

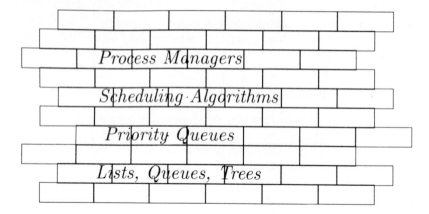

Figure 6.1 Software viewed as layers of abstraction.

higher level routines are intimately tied to a particular application. The lower level pieces can be carried to a new system and generally make sense standing on their own; the higher-level components generally make sense (because of declarations or data dependencies) only when they are built on top of specific lower-level units.

Polymorphism in programming languages permits the programmer to generate high-level reusable components that can be tailored to fit different applications by changing their low level parts. It is as though the upper levels of the wall shown in Figure 6.1 can be carried away and placed on new foundations to create a totally different type of structure.

We will have much more to say about polymorphism in Chapter 13, but to illustrate this point, and to provide a presentiment of the issues we will discuss later, consider the following algorithm:

```
function search ( x : key ) : boolean;

var pos : position;

begin

  pos := initialPosition(x);

  while not exhausted(pos, x) do

    if found (pos, x) then

      return true

    else

      pos := nextPosition(pos, x);

  return false;

end;
```

With suitable replacement of the functions initialPosition, exhausted, found, and nextPosition, this algorithm can represent linear search, binary search, hashing, binary tree search, and more. The algorithm itself is high level, and we can specialize it by replacing the low-level functions on which it is built.

Information Hiding

When a programmer reuses a software component, he or she needs only to understand the nature of the component and its interface. It is not necessary for the programmer to have detailed information concerning such matters as the techniques used to implement the component. Thus, the interconnectedness between software systems is reduced. We earlier identified the interconnected nature of conventional software as being one of the principal causes of software complexity. A few object-oriented languages provide an even greater degree of control over information flow. We will discuss this topic in more detail in Chapter 15.

6.2   THE COST OF INHERITANCE

Although the benefits of inheritance in object-oriented programming are great, it is true that there is almost nothing that is without cost of one sort or another. Thus, it is only honest for us to consider the cost of object-oriented programming techniques, and in particular the cost associated with the use of inheritance.

Execution Speed

It is seldom possible for general-purpose software tools to be as fast as carefully hand-crafted systems. Thus, inherited methods, which must be prepared to deal with arbitrary subclasses, are often slower than specialized code.

Concern about efficiency, however, often is misplaced. For one, the difference is often small. For another, the reduction in the speed of execution may be balanced by an increase in the speed of software development. Finally, most programmers actually have little idea how execution time is being used in their programs. It is far better to develop a working system, then to monitor it to discover where execution time is being used and to improve those sections, than to spend an inordinate amount of time worrying about efficiency early in a project. (See the remarks on execution speed in the footnote on page 55.)

Program Size

The use of any software library frequently imposes a size penalty over the use of systems especially constructed for a specific project. Although this expense may in some cases be substantial, it is also true that, as memory costs decrease, the size of programs is becoming less important. Containing development costs and producing high-quality error-free code rapidly are now more important than is limiting the size of programs.

Message-Passing Overhead

Much has been made out of the fact that message passing is, by its nature, a more costly operation than is simple procedure invocation. As with the question of overall execution speed, however, over concern about the cost of message passing is frequently penny-wise and pound-foolish. For one, the increased cost is often marginal; perhaps two or three additional assembly-language instructions and a total time penalty of 10 percent. (Timing figures vary from language to language. The overhead of message passing will be much higher in dynamically bound languages, such as Smalltalk, and much lower in statically bound languages, such as C++.) This increased cost, like others, must be weighed against the many benefits of the object-oriented technique.

A few languages — notably C++ — make available to the programmer a number of options that can reduce the message-passing overhead. These include eliminating the polymorphism from message passing (qualifying invocations of member functions by a class name, in C++ terms), and expanding inline procedures.

Program Complexity

Although object-oriented programming is often touted as a solution to the problem of software complexity, overuse of inheritance can often, in fact, simply replace one form of complexity with another. Understanding the control flow of a program that uses inheritance may require several multiple scans up and down the inheritance graph. This is what is known as the *yo-yo* problem; we will discuss this problem in more detail in the next chapter.

6.3   HEURISTICS FOR WHEN TO SUBCLASS

Just as many novice object-oriented programmers are unsure how to recognize classes in a problem description, many are also uncertain when one class should be made a subclass of another, and when use of other mechanisms is more appropriate.

The most fundamental rule is that, for a class to be related by inheritance to another class, there should be some relationship of functionality between the two classes. In Section 2.4 we described the *is-a* rule to capture this relationship. By saying that a subclass *is-a* superclass, we are saying that the functionality and data we associate with the child class (or subclass) form a superset of the functionality and data associated with the parent class (or superclass). Within this general framework, however, there is room for many variations. The following sections describe the most common situations.[2]

Specialization

By far the most common use of inheritance and subclassing is for specialization. Subclassing for specialization is the most obvious and direct use of the *is-a* rule. If you are considering two abstract concepts A and B, and the sentence "A is a B" makes sense, then you are probably correct in making A a subclass of B. For example, "a Dog is a Mammal" means that it probably makes sense for the class Dog to be a subclass of Mammal. "A Ford is a Car," "a Triangle is a Shape," and so on.

On the other hand, if the sentence "A has a B" makes more sense, then it is probably a better design decision to make objects of class B attributes (fields or instance variables) of class A. For example, "a Car has a Motor;" but it is not true either that "a Car is a Motor" or that "a Motor is a Car."

Another helpful question to answer is whether or not you wish subclasses, or instances of your class, to access data or behavior from the possible superclass. For instance, consider a Stack data type, which is implemented using a fixed-length array. In this case, the array is simply a useful storage area for the stack, and there is probably little functionality the Stack class could inherit from the Array class. Thus, using inheritance would be a mistake in this case, and maintaining the array as a field (or instance variable) inside of the Stack class would be a better alternative. That is, the fact that a Stack *is-an* Array is true only from the implementor's point of view, not from the user's. Since the user does not need to use any of the functionality of the class Array when using a Stack, then subclassing would be a mistake.

Sometimes, the rule is not as clear-cut, and may in fact be a matter of perspective. Consider a software system that allows the user to edit the contents of textual windows. If we think of this system as a "window editor," then it makes more sense to say that a window editor operates on a window, and thus the editor *has-a* window. On the other hand, if we reverse the situation and think of the system as an "editable window," then it makes more sense to say an editable window *is-a* type of window. There are advantages and disadvantages to both points of view, and neither can be said to be more "correct" than the other. In this case, questions such as how users will interact with the software (is there any behavior inherited from class Window that is useful for users of editable windows?) and other factors will influence the final decision. We will explore this idea further in Section 6.6.

---

[2]The categories described here are adopted from [Halbert 87], although I have added some new categories of my own. The editable-window example is from [Meyer 88a].

Specification

Another frequent use for inheritance is to guarantee that classes maintain a certain common interface; that is, that they implement the same methods. The parent class can be a combination of implemented operations and operations that are deferred to the child classes. Often, there is no interface change between the supertype and subtype — the child merely implements behavior described, but not implemented, in the parent.

This is actually a special case of subclassing for specialization, except that the subclasses are not refinements of an existing type, but rather are realizations of an incomplete abstract specification. Such a class is sometimes known as a *specification class*.

Subclassing for specification can be recognized when the superclass does not implement any actual behavior, but merely describes the behavior that will be implemented in subclasses. This form of subclassing is common in languages that make extensive use of virtual functions (Chapter 9).

Construction

A class can often inherit almost all of its functionality from a superclass, perhaps changing only the names of the methods used to interface to the class, or modifying the arguments in a certain fashion. For example, the Smalltalk class hierarchy implements a generalization of an array called a Dictionary. A Dictionary is a collection of key–value pairs, like an array, only the keys can be arbitrary values. (Such a data structure is also known as a table [Griswold 83, Pemberton 87].)

A *symbol table*, such as might be used in a compiler, can be considered to be a dictionary indexed by symbol names and in which the values have a fixed format (the symbol-table entry record). A class SymbolTable could therefore be made a subclass of class Dictionary, with new methods being defined that are specific to the use as a symbol table. Examples of such methods include adding a new symbol, and modifying a certain field in the symbol-table record associated with a symbol.

Because subclassing for construction is a common, and often misunderstood, use of inheritance we will discuss it in more detail in Section 6.6.

Generalization

Using inheritance to subtype for generalization is, in a certain sense, the opposite of subtyping for specialization. Here, a subtype extends the behavior of the supertype to create a more general kind of object. Subtyping for generalization is often applicable when you are building on a base of existing classes that you do not wish to modify, or cannot modify. For example, consider a graphics display system in which a class Window has been defined for displaying on a simple black-and-white background. You could create a subtype ColoredWindow that

Figure 6.2 Subclassing for generalization.

lets the background color be something other than white by adding an additional field to store the color and by overriding the inherited window display code so that the background is drawn in that color (Figure 6.2).

As a rule, subtyping for generalization should be avoided in favor of inverting the type hierarchy and using subtyping for specialization (Figure 6.3); however, this is not always possible.

Extension

While subclassing for generalization modifies or expands on existing functionality of an object, subclassing for extension adds totally new abilities. For example, in Chapter 10 we develop the class CardView, which provides for the ability to view a playing card on an output device. Later we want to make linked lists of these objects. We do so by adding, (1) a link field to each card view and, (2) associated methods to modify or access this field. Rather than alter the existing class CardView (which may have independent utility separate from the use on linked lists), we create a new subclass CardLink, which adds the linked list functions to those of the class CardView.

Subclassing for extension can be distinguished from subclassing for generalization in that the latter must override at least one method from the parent, and the functionality is tied to that of the parent, whereas extension simply adds

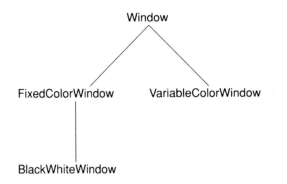

Figure 6.3 Restructured hierarchy for colored windows.

Mouse

Tablet

Figure 6.4   Subtyping for variance.

new methods to those of the parent, and the functionality is less strongly tied
to the existing methods of the parent.

Limitation

Subclassing for limitation is a specialized form of subclassing for specification,
where the behavior of the subclass is smaller or is more restricted than the
behavior of the superclass. Like subtyping for generalization, subclassing for
limitation occurs most frequently when a programmer is building on a base of
existing classes that should not, or cannot, be modified.

Suppose, for example, that an existing class library provides a double-
ended-queue, or *deque*, data structure. Elements can be added or removed from
either end of the deque. The programmer, however, wishes to write a stack
class, enforcing the property that elements can be added or removed from only
one end of the stack. In a manner similar to subclassing for construction, the
programmer can make the Stack class a subclass of the existing class, and can
modify or override the undesired methods so that they produce an error message
if used. It is the presence of these methods that override existing methods, and
that produce error messages if the methods are invoked, which characterizes
subclassing for limitation. (The process of overriding, by which a subclass
changes the meaning of a method defined in a superclass, will be discussed in
a subsequent chapter.)

Note that subclassing for limitation is an explicit violation of the *is-a* view
of inheritance. Thus, this technique should be avoided whenever possible.

PointingDevice

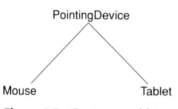

Mouse   Tablet

Figure 6.5   Restructured hierarchy for PointingDevice.

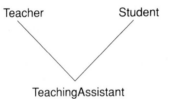

Figure 6.6 Subtyping for combination.

Variance

Subtyping for variance is useful when two or more classes have similar implementations, but there do not seem to be any hierarchical relationships between the concepts represented by the classes. The code necessary to control a mouse, for example, may be nearly identical to the code required to control a graphics tablet. Conceptually, however, there is no particular reason why either class Mouse should be made a subclass of class Tablet, or why class Tablet should be a subclass of class Mouse. One of the two classes can be selected arbitrarily as the parent, with the common code being inherited by the other and the device-specific code being provided as overridden methods (Figure 6.4).

Often, however, a better alternative is to factor out the common code into an abstract class, say PointingDevice, and to have both classes inherit from this common ancestor (Figure 6.5). As with subtyping for generalization, this choice may not be available if you are building on a base of existing classes.

Combination

One common situation occurs when a subclass represents a *combination* of features from two or more parent classes. A TeachingAssistant, for example, is both a Teacher and a Student and should logically behave as both (Figure 6.6). The ability of a class to inherit from two or more parent classes is known as *multiple inheritance*, and unfortunately is not provided in all the languages we are considering. We will discuss this feature in more detail in Chapter 12.

6.4 IF IT AIN'T BROKE

Sooner or later, an object-oriented programmer is sure to encounter the following problem. An existing class provides 80 percent of the functionality needed for a new application. The remaining functionality can be provided by just a few new methods. Should the programmer simply change the base class to provide the new functionality, or create a new class and use inheritance to gain access to the existing structure? Unfortunately, there are no hard and fast rules that provide an answer. There are only general guidelines that should be taken into consideration in individual cases.

Is the existing class being widely used in other applications? If so, then it is probably best to leave the class alone. As the saying goes, "if it ain't broke, don't fix it." This is almost certainly true if the proposed changes involve adding data fields to instances of the class, as there is no reason to penalize existing users to provide features for which they have no need. Similarly, changes to existing methods leave the programmer open to the very real risk that the modifications may introduce errors into other applications.

On the other hand, if the change is totally transparent (such as replacing one algorithm with a more efficient version), then a single change can have widespread, and probably welcome, benefits.

Deriving new classes to make minor changes to existing classes is also not always a wise choice. In a group situation, it can easily happen that each programmer extends a class in a different way, resulting in dozens of classes derived from a single base class. The plethora of classes makes understanding individual programs extremely difficult, instead of providing the simplification a nice neat inheritance tree should provide. The group should agree on a few common classes, providing the union of the functionality each programmer desires.

In providing new functionality to classes, a programmer must navigate carefully between the Scylla of runaway class hierarchies and the Charybdis of maintaining the integrity of existing classes.

6.5   TREE VERSUS FOREST

There are two alternative views regarding how classes as a whole should be structured in object-oriented languages. One view, reflected in languages such as Smalltalk and Objective-C, holds that classes should all be contained in a single large inheritance structure. Figure 6.7, for example, shows a portion of the inheritance class structure for Little Smalltalk. The advantage of this view is that functionality provided in the root of the tree, in class Object, is inherited by all objects. Thus, every object will respond to the message print, which displays a printable representation of the object, because this method is found in the abstract superclass Object. In such a language, every class defined by the user must be a subclass of some already-existing class — usually Object. We have seen this already in the example classes described in Smalltalk and Objective-C in Chapter 3.

The alternative view, represented by languages such as C++ and Object Pascal, holds that classes that are not logically related should be entirely distinct. The result is that the user faces a forest composed of several inheritance trees. An advantage of this approach is that the application is not forced to carry along with it a large library of classes, only a few of which may be used. The disadvantage is that there is no programmer-definable functionality that *all* objects are guaranteed to possess.

In part, the differing views of objects seem to be tied to the distinction between languages that use dynamic typing and those that employ static typing

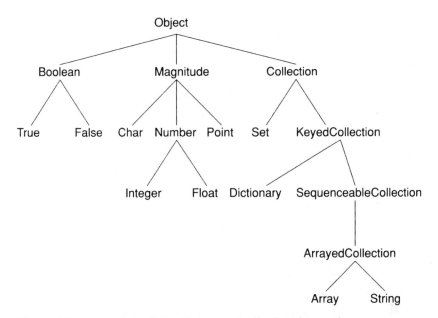

Figure 6.7   A portion of the Little Smalltalk class hierarchy.

(Chapter 7). In dynamic languages, objects are characterized chiefly by the messages they understand. If two objects understand the same set of messages and react in the same way, they are, for all practical purposes, indistinguishable, regardless of the relationships of their respective classes. Under these circumstances, it is useful to have all objects inherit a large portion of their behavior from a common base class.

6.6 COMPOSITION VERSUS CONSTRUCTION

A major difficulty the novice must overcome in learning how to program in an object-oriented manner involves discerning appropriate and inappropriate uses of the *is-a* relationship. In this section, we will illustrate an object-oriented solution to a simple problem — that of constructing a symbol table — using two different techniques. We will then contrast the two techniques using various measures, such as ease of development, code size, understandability, and utility. (The symbol-table example in the following discussion is adapted from [Taenzer 89].)

The task for our programmer is to construct a simple symbol table for string values. A symbol table is simply an associative list. Elements can be added to the symbol table, and the symbol table can be queried for the value associated with a symbol, returning an empty string if no current binding exists. In addition, we require our symbol-table abstraction to support the normal creation and deletion protocol embodied in the methods new and free.

Suppose our programmer chooses to work in the language Objective-C. The Objective-C library provides an existing data structure called a Dictionary,

```
@implementation SymbolTable : Dictionary
{
  /* no extra instance variables */
}

  /* add a value to the symbol table */
- add: (char *) key value: (char *) value
{
  /* convert the key and value into objects */
  /* then use self to add the string objects */
  /* to the dictionary */

  [ self atKey: [String str: key ]
         put: [ String str: value] ];
}

  /* look up the value associated with a key */
- (char *) lookup: (char *) symbol
{  id val;

  /* convert the key into a string object and */
  /* use self to send the message to the dictionary */

  val = [ self atKey: [ String str: key ] ];
  if ([val notNil]) return [ val str ];
  return ''; /* empty string */
}
@end
```

Figure 6.8   A symbol table built using inheritance.

based on the Smalltalk class of the same name. The class Dictionary provides an abstraction for a collection of key–value pairs, where the key and value elements can be any objects. The message atKey:put: is used to insert an object into the dictionary, whereas the message atKey: is used to extract the value associated with a key. In addition, the Objective-C library provides a String datatype that can be used to manipulate string values. The factory message str: in the class String is used to convert from a C-style string to an object string.

Recognizing that a symbol table can be viewed as simply a specialized type of dictionary, the first approach a programmer might try would be to make the class SymbolTable a subclass of Dictionary (Figure 6.8). It is necessary to define only two new methods, and both of these are rather trivial interfaces to the parent class. Because the class defines no new instance data, the inherited methods for new and delete can be used as they are.

An alternative technique our programmer could use would still use the existing Dictionary abstraction to perform the majority of the work, but would avoid using inheritance directly. Instead of inheriting from the class Dictionary, the class defines an instance variable to store the actual symbol-table data. The class SymbolTable is therefore simply a subclass of the class Object. Because this instance variable must be initialized and disposed of, it is necessary to override the creation messages new and free.[3] In place of translating the symbol-table insertion and deletion messages into further messages sent to self, the former messages are sent to the instance variable maintaining the data. The resulting program is shown in Figure 6.9. Notice that the method new uses the technique of changing the value self. This technique was described earlier in Chapter 4, Section 5.3.

Both of these solutions can legitimately be labeled "object-oriented," and neither can be said to be obviously "better" than the other. Nevertheless, the following advantages and disadvantages can be cited:

- The approach using inheritance for construction is shorter, since much of the administrative overhead in object creation and manipulation is inherited and need not be rewritten. Since the code is shorter, it may be easier to develop. Because of this reduced development time, the inheritance technique is often employed when software must be produced quickly, such as in a prototype system.

- The inheritance approach does not prevent users from manipulating a symbol table as though the latter were simply a dictionary. That is, since the behavior for the class SymbolTable is strictly larger than the behavior associated with class Dictionary, there is nothing to prevent a user from making use of the facilities provided by the superclass. Thus, the user can perform an at: operation, or even an atKey:put:, and bypass the symbol-table interface.

- In the composition approach, the fact that the class Dictionary is used is merely an implementation detail. Using this technique, it would be easy to reimplement the SymbolTable class to make use of a different technique (such as a hash table), with minimal impact on the users of the SymbolTable abstraction. If users counted on the fact that a SymbolTable is merely a specialized form of Dictionary, such changes would be much more difficult to implement.

- The composition approach, although longer and more difficult to develop, makes clear the interface to be used in manipulating the symbol table. Only the operations explicitly provided are permitted, and unauthorized access to the actual data structure holding the data is avoided.

- There are useful operations that might be desirable in a symbol table, that are provided free when the inheritance approach is used. For example, it might be useful to know how many entries there are in the symbol table.

---

[3]The presence of the keyword super in these methods is an indication that overriding is taking place. The detailed mechanics of overriding are not important for this discussion; we will discuss them in more detail in a subsequent chapter.

```
@implementation SymbolTable : Object
{
  id theDictionary;  /* the data dictionary */
}

+ new
{
  /* create the new dictionary */
  self = [ super new ];
  theDictionary = [ Dictionary new ];
  return self;
}

- free
{
  /* free the dictionary before freeing self */
  [ theDictionary free];
  return [ super free ];
}

- add: (char *) key value: (char *) value
{
  /* convert the key and value into objects */
  /* then add the string objects to the dictionary */

  [ theDictionary atKey: [String str: key ]
                   put: [ String str: value] ];
}

- (char *) lookup: (char *) key
{  id val;

  /* convert the key into a string object and */
  /* send the message to the dictionary */

  val = [ theDictionary atKey: [ String str: key ] ];
  if ([val notNil]) return [ val str ];
  return ''; /* empty string */
}
@end
```

Figure 6.9 A symbol table built using construction.

This information is provided automatically by the message size in the class Dictionary. If composition were used, a new method would have to be added to provide this functionality.

• The issues of understandability and maintainability are difficult to judge. The version using construction has the advantage of brevity of code, but not of protocol. The composition version, although longer, is the only code that another programmer needs to understand to use the symbol table. A programmer faced with understanding the version using inheritance would need to ask whether there was any behavior being inherited from the class Dictionary that is necessary for proper utilization of the symbol table.

Composition and construction are both useful object-oriented techniques. Unfortunately, the guidelines that dictate when one approach should be used in place of the other are vague, depending on such features as how long the software will be used and by how many people, the degree to which development time versus execution time is important, and more. A programmer making use of object-oriented languages should have a good understanding of both approaches, so that he or she can make an appropriate choice in any particular situation.

Exercises

1. This exercise builds on Exercise 1 in Chapter 3 (page 56). Suppose you were required to program a project in a non–object-oriented language, such as Pascal or C. How would you simulate the notion of classes and methods? How would you simulate inheritance? Can you support multiple inheritance? Explain your answer.

2. In Section 6.2, we noted that the execution overhead associated with message passing is typically greater than the overhead associated with a conventional procedure call. How might you measure these overheads? For a language that supports both classes and procedures (such as C++ or Object Pascal), devise an experiment to determine the actual performance penalty of message passing.

3. Contrast each of the uses of subclassing from Section 6.3 with each of the benefits of inheritance from Section 6.1, noting to what extent the technique promotes the benefit. For example, subtyping for construction promotes software reusability and rapid prototyping, but inhibits information hiding since the methods from the parent class are available for the user to access directly.

4. Develop a general rule for when the technique of inheritance should be used, and when the technique of construction should be employed (see Section 6.6).

5. Consider the three geometric concepts of a line (infinite in both directions), a ray (fixed at a point, infinite in one direction), and a segment (a portion of a line with fixed end points). How might you structure classes representing these three concepts in an inheritance hierarchy? Explain the reasoning behind your design.

6. Why is the example used in the following explanation not a valid illustration of inheritance?

> Perhaps the most powerful concept in object-oriented programming systems is inheritance. Objects can be created by inheriting the properties of other objects, thus removing the need to write any code whatsoever! Suppose, for example, a program is to process complex numbers consisting of real and imaginary parts. In a complex number, the real and imaginary parts behave like real numbers, so all of the operations ($+$, $-$, $/$, $*$, sqrt, sin, cos, etc.) can be inherited from the class of objects called REAL, instead of having to be written in code. This has major impact on programmer productivity.

7
Static and Dynamic Binding

Many properties of programming languages can be best understood in terms of *binding times*. A binding time is simply the time when an attribute of some portion of a program, or meaning of a particular construct, is determined. While the concept of binding times existed in earlier languages, object-oriented programming techniques bring the issue much more forcefully to the programmer's attention. Binding times can range from compile time (when the source of the program is first encountered), through linkage time (when the results of several compilations are combined), to execution time (when a program is finally run). Even during execution, we can distinguish among features that are bound when a program begins, those that are bound when a procedure or function is initiated, and those that are not bound until the statement containing the feature is executed. Among the attributes for which variations in binding times exist in the four languages we are considering are the matching of identifiers and types, and the resolution technique used to match a message to a method. As we shall see, subtle differences in binding-time mechanisms can nevertheless result in major differences in how a language is used.

7.1 STATIC AND DYNAMIC TYPING

If we are to understand the difference between static and dynamic typing, it is important that we distinguish among identifiers, types, and values. An *identifier* (or *variable*) is simply a name; it is the means by which the programmer denotes a quantity to be manipulated. The term *value* describes the current contents in the computer memory associated with a variable. A *type* can be associated, depending on the language, with either a variable or a value.

In statically typed languages, such as Object Pascal or C++, types are associated with variables. Types are matched to identifiers by means of explicit declaration statements. In these languages, the type serves, among other purposes, to denote the set or range of legal values that the variable can contain. An attempt to assign to a variable a value that is not in the set of legal quantities for the associated type will, if it can be detected by the compiler, produce an error message. For example, in the following Object Pascal fragment, an attempt is made to assign a character value to a variable declared to contain real values. Such an error would be detected and reported by the compiler.

```
var

   r : real;

begin

   r := 'x';

end;
```

Types are also used to determine the meaning of operations, such as addition, that have two or more interpretations. The expression

```
a + b
```

for example, will mean integer addition if the identifiers a and b have been declared as type integer, and real addition if they have been declared real.

To the run-time system, a variable is simply a box of bits. It is the static type of a variable that is used to give meaning to the bits. Sometimes, this meaning can be incorrect. For example, using variant records in Pascal or unions in C, it is possible to overlay two variables of different types. The same memory location can be assigned a value of one type (say a real number), and subsequently used as though it contained a value of a different type (say an integer). Languages in which this is not possible — in which it can be guaranteed at compile time that all expressions have the correct type — are said to be *strongly typed*.

Object-oriented languages introduce a new twist into the problem of matching identifiers and types. If classes are viewed as types (a connection that is not universally accepted, and to which we will return in Chapter 18), then class hierarchies, such as that shown in Figure 1.2 (page 7), represent hierarchies of types. The *is-a* relationship asserts that any instance of a child class is in all important respects a representative of a parent class; instances of the class Florist are instances of the class Shopkeeper, for example. Thus, a *value* of type Florist, such as my florist Flo, can be assigned to a *variable* declared to be of type ShopKeeper.

More precisely, any value of a specific class can be assigned to a variable declared as the given class, or any superclass of the class. The reverse situation, where variables declared to be instances of a superclass are assigned to variables of a subclass, is tied to what we will call the "container problem," which we will consider in the next section. In situations where the type (class) of a value does not match the class of a variable containing the value, the class of the variable is known as the *static class*, and the class of the value is known as the *dynamic class*.

In dynamically typed languages, types are bound not to identifiers, but rather to values. The distinction can be thought of informally as the difference between being known for an association ("Jennifer is a Yale graduate; you know how those Yalies are") versus being known for specific qualities ("You know Jennifer; she is 5 foot 4 inches tall, has brown eyes, and knows absolutely everything about Smalltalk"). In dynamically typed languages a variable cannot be said to *be* an integer, for example, but can be said only to *contain* an integer value currently.

We have seen, in the examples of Smalltalk and Objective-C code shown in Chapter 3, that variables are not declared with specific types (or they are declared with the general object type id in Objective-C). Thus, it is not possible to assign a variable an "illegal" value in these cases, as all values that represent legitimate objects are legal. Rather than a value simply being a box of uninterpreted bits, in a dynamically typed language every value must carry with it some identification, some knowledge that indicates the exact nature of that value. This identification tag is tied to the value, and is carried along by assignment. A single identifier, over the course of time, can be assigned values of many different types.

We will explore the ramifications of this difference between static and dynamically typed approaches to values using an example.

The Container Problem

Suppose we have defined a class Ball and two subclasses, BlackBall and White-Ball. Next, we have constructed the software equivalent of a box (Figure 7.1) into which we can drop two instances of class Ball, and one of those instances (selected randomly) will fall out and be returned. We drop a BlackBall and a WhiteBall into the box, and recover the result. Now certainly the resulting object can be considered a Ball, and thus can be assigned to a variable declared as that type. But is it a BlackBall? Can I assign it to a variable declared as class BlackBall? Can I even tell whether or not it is a BlackBall?

In a dynamically typed language, it is the ball itself that determines whether it is a BlackBall or a WhiteBall. The ball carries with it information necessary to know its class (color). Thus, for example, I can determine the color of the ball simply by asking to which class it belongs.

In a statically typed language, the ball itself may have no idea what color it is. That is, the ball value may not know to which class it belongs. Thus, it may not be possible to determine whether it is legal to assign the value of the result to a variable declared as type BlackBall.

Although the BlackBall and WhiteBall example may seem contrived, the underlying problem is quite common. Consider the development of classes for

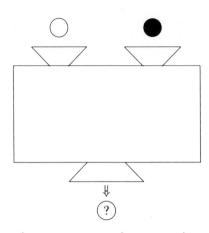

Figure 7.1   A Ball losing its identity.

frequently used data structures, such as sets, stacks, queues, lists, dictionaries, tables, and the like. Such data structures are used to maintain collections of objects. A touted benefit of object-oriented programming is the production of reusable software components. Surely collection containers, if anything, are candidates for such components.

A collection container, however, is in a certain respect exactly like the ball machine in Figure 7.1. If a programmer places two different objects into a set, and later takes out one, how does he know which type of object he will get?

These problems are not trivial, but they are solvable. We will in subsequent discussions (Chapters 14 and 17) present two different forms of container collections. In later, language-specific sections of this chapter we will outline some of the aspects of the container-class problem in each of the languages we are considering.

7.2   STATIC AND DYNAMIC METHOD BINDING

Related to the problem of how a language associates types with identifiers is the question of how a method is associated with a message. That is, if I send a message "draw" to a receiver, how is it determined which method will be used to respond to the message?

We will not describe the exact mechanics of message passing until the next chapter, and will not discuss inheritance in detail until Chapter 6. The intuitive notions developed in Chapter 1, however, can be used as a basis for our discussion here. In Chapter 1, we introduced the concept of *inheritance*. When inheritance is used, information (data and behavior) associated with a superclass is accessible to subclasses.

Thus, for example, imagine the following game. Alice holds a kitten in her arms, but shields it from Bill's sight. Alice tells Bill that she is holding a small mammal, and asks Bill whether the mammal has fur. Bill could then argue as follows — "no matter what type of animal (what class of object) it really is, I know it is a subclass of Mammal. All Mammals have fur. Therefore, the animal Alice is holding has fur."

Now suppose that Alice is holding Phyl, the platypus from Chapter 1. They play the same game, and Alice asks Bill whether female instances of the class of animals she is holding give birth to live young. If Bill argues as before, he will say yes. But, of course, he will be wrong, since in this situation the behavior common to all Mammals is overridden in the class Platypus.

To put this example in a computer-science framework, we can imagine a variable declared to be of class Mammal holding a value of type Platypus. Should the search for an appropriate binding for a method be based on the static class of the declaration (namely, Mammal) or on the dynamic class of the value (that is, Platypus)?

The first is known as *static binding*, since the binding of method to message is based on the static characteristics of the variable. The second option, where discovery of a method is based on the type of the value, and not on the type of the declaration, is known as *dynamic binding*.

Even when dynamic binding is used to match a method to a message, it is not uncommon for object-oriented languages that use static typing to decide whether or not a given message-passing expression is legal based on the static class of the receiver. That is, if fido is declared as an instance of class Mammal, it is not legal to pass to fido the message bark unless this message is understood by *all* instances of class Mammal. Even if I know that at run time fido will in fact always hold a value of class Dog, the compiler will not permit the message unless it is defined in the parent class.

Merits of Static Versus Dynamic Binding

Arguments concerning the relative merits of static typing versus dynamic typing, or static binding versus dynamic binding, invariably reduce to a discussion of the relative importance of efficiency versus flexibility. To put these points in succinct form, static typing and static binding are more efficient; dynamic typing and dynamic binding are more flexible.

As we saw in the discussion of the container problem, dynamic typing implies that every object keeps track of its own type. If we take the "rugged individualist" view of objects (namely, that every object must take care of itself, and not depend on others for its maintenance), then dynamic typing would seem to be the more "object-oriented" technique. Certainly, dynamic typing greatly simplifies problems such as the development of general-purpose data structures, but the cost involved is a run-time search to discover the meaning (that is, code to execute) every time an operation is used on a data value. Although techniques can be employed to reduce this cost (we will explore some of these in Chapter 19), the expense cannot be eliminated altogether. It is largely because these costs can often be quite substantial that most programming languages have used static typing.

Static typing simplifies a programming-language implementation, even if (as in Object Pascal and in some cases in C++) dynamic binding is used to match a method to a message. When static types are known to the compiler, storage can be allocated for variables efficiently. Similarly, efficient code can be generated for ambiguous operations (such as addition) if the types are known to the compiler. But there are costs associated with this decision. For example, static typing often (although not necessarily, as we will see when we subsequently discuss Object Pascal) means that objects lose their "self-knowledge." Thus, an object coming out of a container, like the ball coming out of the mechanism in Figure 7.1, may not know what type it is.

If static typing simplifies an implementation, static method binding simplifies the implementation even more. If a match between method and message can be discovered by the compiler, then message passing (regardless of the syntax used) can be *implemented* as a simple procedure call, with no run-time mechanism required to perform the method lookup. This is about as efficient as we can reasonably expect (although inline functions in C++ can even eliminate the overhead of procedure calling).

Dynamic method binding, on the other hand, always requires the execution of at least some run-time mechanism, however primitive, to match a method to a message. In languages that use dynamic typing (and thus must use dynamic binding of messages to methods), it is not possible to determine, in general, whether a message-passing expression will be understood by the receiver. When a message is not understood by the receiver, there is no alternative but to generate a run-time error message. The fact that many of these errors can be caught at compile-time in a language that uses static method binding is an important point in favor of such languages.

Another argument put forth in favor of using static typing and static binding instead of their dynamic counterparts involves error detection. These arguments mirror the debate about strong versus weak typing in more conventional programming languages. When static types are used, errors such as assignment of incompatible types, or illegal values passed as arguments to functions, can be detected at compile time and produce compiler warnings. When dynamic values are used, such errors often go undetected until catastrophic errors occur during program execution.

Thus, we are seemingly left to decide which is more important: efficiency or flexibility, correctness or ease of use? Brad Cox argues [Cox 90] that the answers to these questions depend on both what level abstraction the software represents and whether we take the point of view of the producer or of the consumer of the software system. Cox asserts that object-oriented programming will be the primary (although not only) tool in the "software industrial revolution." Just as the nineteenth-century Industrial Revolution was made possible only after the development of interchangeable parts, the goal of the software industrial revolution is the construction of reusable, reliable, high-level, abstract software components from which software systems will be fabricated.

Efficiency is the primary concern at the lowest level of construction — what Cox refers to as the gate-level abstractions, using an analogy from electronic components. As the level of abstraction rises, through chip-level and card-level components, flexibility becomes more important.

Similarly, performance and efficiency are often primary concerns for the developer of software abstractions. For a consumer interested in combining independently developed software systems in new and novel ways, flexibility may be much more important.

Thus, there is no single right answer to the question of which binding techniques are more appropriate in a programming language. A variety of schemes is available, and each technique is useful in some fashion.

7.3 BINDING IN OBJECT PASCAL

The Object Pascal language is statically typed: Every identifier must be declared. An identifier declared as an object type can hold values of that type, or of any type derived by inheritance from that type.

Although the *language* is statically typed, objects nevertheless carry with them knowledge of their own dynamic type. There is a system-defined predicate, Member, that can be used to determine whether an identifier is an instance of a specific class. The Member function takes an object-reference expression (usually a simple identifier), and a class name (or, to be accurate, an object type name in Object Pascal). It returns the value true if the object-reference expression has a value and the current value of the object-reference expression is an object of the given type; it returns false otherwise. For example, if we have a class Animal and we wish to determine whether a variable fido of type Animal is in fact an instance of the more specialized subclass Mammal, we can use the following test:

```
if Member(fido, Mammal) then

   writeln('fido is a mammal')

else

   writeln('fido is not a mammal');
```

Note that Member returns true even if fido is an instance of a more specialized class, such as Dog.

The Member function, when coupled with the ability to perform type casts, can be used to solve in part the container-class problem. When the ball is taken from the box in Figure 7.1, the programmer can use Member to determine whether the result is a BlackBall or a WhiteBall, and can cast the ball to the right type accordingly.

Although the language is statically typed, dynamic binding is always used to match a method to a message. Thus, if the method hasLiveYoung is defined in class Mammal and overridden in class Platypus, the subclass will be searched even when the receiver is declared as class (object type) Mammal.

Although the binding of methods is performed dynamically in Object Pascal, the legality of any message-passing expression is determined by the static class of the receiver. Only if this class understands the message being invoked will the compiler generate code to perform the message.

7.4   BINDING IN SMALLTALK

Smalltalk is a dynamically typed language. Instance variables, as we saw in the previous chapter, are declared only by name, and not by type. As in Object Pascal, in Smalltalk it is possible to inquire as to the class of any object. All objects respond to the message class by returning an object representing their class. Thus, if fido is a variable suspected of holding a value of type Dog, the test

```
( fido class == Dog ) ifTrue: [ ... ]
```

will tell us for sure whether our suspicions are correct. The test will fail, however, if we replace Dog with Mammal. Thus, in Smalltalk (and in Objective-C), there are two tests that can be used on objects. The first, isMemberOf:, takes a class name as argument and is equivalent to the test just shown. The second, isKindOf:, is similar to the Member function in Object Pascal. It tells us whether the receiver is an instance, either directly or by inheritance, of the argument class. Thus, if fido is a Dog, the following test would succeed, whereas the test with isMemberOf: would fail:

```
( fido isKindOf: Mammal ) ifTrue: [ ... ]
```

Often, we are interested less in the class of an object than in whether the object will understand a specific message. Thus, both Seal and Dog might implement a method bark. Given a particular object, say fido, we can use the following technique to determine whether the object will respond to the message bark:

```
( fido respondsTo: #bark ) ifTrue: [ ... ]
```

Notice that the method selector is represented by a symbol.

Since static types are not available, dynamic binding must always be used to match methods to messages. If a receiver does not understand a particular message, a run-time error diagnostic is produced.

The Smalltalk standard library (called the *standard image*) provides a rich set of container classes that makes extensive use of the late-binding features of the language. We will describe some of these classes in Chapter 14.

7.5   BINDING IN OBJECTIVE-C

Given the opinions of the developer of Objective-C, Brad Cox, it is not surprising that the language is heavily directed toward dynamic behavior. In large part, everything that we noted concerning Smalltalk in Section 7.4 holds as well for Objective-C, including the fact that all objects understand the messages class, isKindOf:, and isMemberOf:. Dynamic binding is always used when the receiver is a dynamically typed object.

To tell whether a given object understands a specific message, we use the system-provided routine @selector to convert the textual form of a message selector to an internal encoding, as in the following:

```
if ( [ fido respondsTo: @selector(bark) ] ) { ... }
```

An interesting feature of Objective-C is optional use of statically typed variables, in combination with dynamically typed quantities. In contradiction to what we asserted in Section 3.4, objects can be statically declared in one of two ways. Given a class declaration, such as Card (page 50), the declaration

```
Card aCard;
```

defines a new identifier called aCard and allocates space for it. Message passing will be static, based on the class Card. Alternatively, a declaration can be phrased in terms of explicit pointers. Such a declaration does not declare space for the object, and space must be allocated using the message new. However when static class names are used to define receivers, method binding, although still dynamic, will nevertheless be slightly faster.

```
Card *aCard;

aCard = [ Card new ];
```

Because of the late-bound nature of the language, it is relatively easy to write container classes in Objective-C; in fact, a large set of such data structures is provided as part of the standard Objective-C library.

7.6   BINDING IN C++

Two primary objectives in the design of C++ were space and time efficiency [Ellis 90]. The language was intended as an improvement over C for both object-oriented and non–object-oriented applications. A basic underlying tenet of C++ is that no feature should incur a cost (either in space or execution time) unless it is used. If, for example, the object-oriented features of C++ are ignored, the remainder of the language should execute as fast as conventional C. Thus, it is not surprising that most features in C++ are statically, rather than dynamically, bound. Variables are declared statically; however they can be assigned values derived from subclasses.

Unlike in the other three languages, there is no facility in C++ that can be used to determine the dynamic class of an object. That is, values have no self-knowledge of their associated type. This is in keeping with the philosophy that costs should be incurred only where they are necessary. This limitation would make the container-class problem very difficult to solve, were it not for the great flexibility C++ provides with regards to overloading and overriding methods. We will describe these features in more detail in a later chapter, and in Chapter 17 we will present a collection of general-purpose container classes in C++. Using these techniques, we can create *homogeneous* collections (collections where all the elements are the same type). The more general, *heterogenous* collections, are considerably more difficult to write in C++. Such collections are relatively easy to write in late-bound languages, such as Smalltalk and Objective-C.

C++ provides both static and dynamic method binding, and complex rules to determine which form is used. In part, dynamic binding depends on the use of the virtual keyword in a method declaration. We will describe the meaning of this term in Chapter 6. Even when the virtual keyword is given, however, static binding can still be used unless the receiver is used as a pointer or as a reference. We will defer further discussion on this point until we have developed a more complete presentation of the issues involved.

Even when dynamic binding is used to match methods and messages, the legality of any particular message-passing expression is tested, as in Object Pascal, based on the static type of the receiver.

Exercises

1. Object Pascal is a language that uses static typing, but that nevertheless uses dynamic binding. Explain why the converse is not possible; that is, explain why it is not possible to have a language use dynamic typing and static binding of messages and methods.

2. Discuss whether the error-checking facilities made possible by static typing are worth the loss in flexibility. How important is the container class problem?

3. Where does the analogy that Cox discusses between hardware and software systems break down? What prevents the development of interchangeable, reliable software components?

4. Consider the assertion that statically typed languages, such as C++ and Object Pascal, can detect argument–parameter type mismatch errors, whereas such errors are not detected automatically in dynamically typed languages, such as Smalltalk or Objective-C. By using the respondsTo: method and an assert facility, can we always achieve the same effect as static typing? Explain your answer. Which method is more powerful? Which is more costly at run time?

8
Case Study:
Mixed-Type Arithmetic

We will study how mixed-type arithmetic is performed in the language Smalltalk to illustrate various possible approaches to problem solving that use inheritance. We have noted that all values, including numbers, are objects in Smalltalk. Integers are instances of the class Integer, and floating-point quantities instances of the class Float. In addition, there are various other types of numbers, such as the class Fraction, and classes representing integers of unlimited magnitude. All are subclasses of the abstract superclass Number. In this chapter, we will simplify the discussion by considering only the classes Integer and Float.

By *mixed-type arithmetic* we mean the attempt to perform an arithmetic operation, such as addition or multiplication, using values from two different classes. The addition of an integer and a floating-point number would be one example. In this case, we would expect the result to be a floating-point value.

These operations are complicated in Smalltalk by the fact that the Smalltalk language provides no form of declarations. Thus, in general, it is not possible to determine, at compile time, the type either of a receiver for a message or of the arguments. All such determinations must be made at run time.

There are, in fact, two different techniques in common use for solving the problem of mixed-type arithmetic. We will compare and contrast these two approaches to illustrate issues involved in programming with inheritance.

8.1 COERCIVE GENERALITY

Coercive generality is the technique used by the Smalltalk-80 system described in the "blue book" [Goldberg 83], as well as by the Little Smalltalk system [Budd 87]. We will describe the approach used in Little Smalltalk. In this scheme, each type of number is assigned a generality index. The generality index provides a linear ordering of the degree of abstractness of the number.

```
10
 9
 8
 7 Float
 6
 5 Fraction
 4 InfinitePrecisionInteger
 3
 2 Integer
 1
```

Figure 8.1   Generality numbers in Little Smalltalk.

Thus, fractions are more general than integers, floating-point values more general than fractions, and so on (Figure 8.1). We can determine the generality index of any number by passing the number the message generality. Two numbers are assumed to be compatible if they have the same generality index. If not, the number with the lower generality index is modified (coerced) into being compatible with the number with the higher generality index.

Let us consider first the addition of an integer and another integer — for example, the addition of the numbers 7 and 12. Figure 8.2 shows various methods from the class Integer. When the message + is passed to the object 7, it will invoke the method shown in Figure 8.2.

```
isInteger
  " am I an integer? "
  ↑ true

+ aValue
  " perform integer addition "
  (aValue isInteger)
    ifTrue: [ ↑ < 60 self aValue > ]
    ifFalse: [ ↑ self coerceAdd: aValue ]

generality
  " return my generality number, "
  " used in mixed class arithmetic "
  ↑ 2

asFloat
  " convert myself into a float "
  ↑ < 51 self >
```

Figure 8.2   Arithmetic methods from class Integer.

```
isInteger
  " am I an integer? "
  ↑ false

isFloat
  " am I a float? "
  ↑ false

coerceAdd: aValue
  " coerce arguments and try addition again "
  ↑ (self maxgen: aValue) + (aValue maxgen: self)

maxgen: aValue
  " convert number with lower generality "
  " into being compatible with the other "
  (self generality > aValue generality)
    ifTrue: [ ↑ self ]
    ifFalse: [ ↑ aValue coerce: self ]
```

Figure 8.3   Arithmetic methods from class Number.

This method tests whether the argument is an integer, by passing the message isInteger to the argument value. Since 12 is also an integer, it will find the method isInteger shown in Figure 8.2, which will return the constant value true, and thus the primitive operation 60 will be performed on the two values. (Recall that in Chapter 1 we said that not all behavior could be described in object-oriented terms. A primitive can be thought of as a system call to the underlying run-time system. In this case, the primitive 60 adds two integer arguments, returning the object representing their sum.)

Now let us consider the addition of an integer and a noninteger value — say, the addition of 7 and the floating-point value 3.14159. As before, since the receiver is an integer, the addition method shown in Figure 8.2 will be executed. This time, however, since the argument is not an integer, the message isInteger will not find the method of Figure 8.2 from the class Integer; instead, the method from class Number (Figure 8.3) will be executed.

This time, the constant false is returned, and the false branch of the if statement in the addition method in class Integer is executed. The statement contained in that block (Figure 8.2) passes the argument along with the message coerceAdd:, which is implemented in class Number. This method, shown in Figure 8.3, converts one or the other of the arguments until they are (it is hoped) compatible with each other, when it tries the operation again.

To perform the conversion, the routine maxgen: compares the generality values of the two arguments, if necessary passing to the value with higher generality the message coerce: and the other argument. Since the floating-point value has higher generality, it will be asked to coerce the integer. The method coerce: from class Float is shown in Figure 8.4. The coerce: method achieves the con-

```
isFloat
  " am I a float?   "
  ↑ true

+ aValue
  " perform floating addition "
  aValue isFloat
    ifTrue: [ ↑ < 110 self aValue > ]
    ifFalse: [ ↑ self coerceAdd: aValue ]

generality
  " return my generality number,"
  " used in mixed class arithmetic "
  ↑ 7

coerce: aValue
  " convert the argument into a floating point number "
  ↑ aValue asFloat
```

Figure 8.4   Arithmetic methods from class Float.

version by passing to the integer the message asFloat. The asFloat method (Figure 8.2) invokes another primitive operation to convert the integer into a floating-point value, yielding the floating-point value 7.0. This conversion accomplished, the addition is retried with two floating-point values. This time, it is successful, and the expected result (the floating-point value 10.14159) is produced.

We have described the case for integer plus float. You should verify that the symmetric case of a floating-point number being passed an integer as argument will also produce the correct result.

A fuller explanation of coercive generality in Smalltalk-80 is given in [LaLonde 90a], which describes, for example, how quaternions and complex numbers can be added to the scheme.

8.2   DOUBLE DISPATCHING

In a 1986 paper presented at the first *OOPSLA* conference,[1] Daniel Ingalls described a technique for handling variation in several arguments [Ingalls 86]. In simple terms, we make use of the overloading mechanism implicit in message passing by making each argument, in turn, a receiver for a message, and encoding the types of the remainder of the arguments in the message selector. Thus, when a floating-point value receives the message +, it reverses the arguments,

---

[1]The complete title is the Conference on Object-Oriented Programming Systems, Languages and Applications. Ingalls called the technique multiple polymorphism. This term, however, is easily confused with *multiple inheritance*, which denotes an entirely different concept. The term *double dispatching* is more accurate, and has been the preferred term in subsequent literature.

```
+ aValue
  " perform floating addition"
  ↑ aValue addToFloat: self

addToFloat: aValue
  " types match, can do addition "
  ↑ < 110 aValue self >

addToInteger: aValue
  " convert and try again"
  ↑ (aValue asFloat) + self
```

Figure 8.5   Arithmetic methods for Float using double dispatching.

```
+ aValue
  " perform integer addition"
  aValue addToInteger: self

addToInteger: aValue
  " types match, can do addition"
  ↑ < 60 aValue self >

addToFloat: aValue
  " convert then add "
  ↑ aValue + (self asFloat)
```

Figure 8.6   Arithmetic methods for Integer using double dispatching.

passing to the argument that it received the message addToFloat (Figure 8.5). Each type of object that can be added to a floating-point number must know how to deal with this message. Figure 8.6, for example, shows how an integer performs the addition by converting the integer value into a floating-point value and retrying the operation.

As before, you should verify that the symmetric case — of a floating-point number being passed an integer argument — also produces the correct result.

8.3   A COMPARISON

The double-dispatching scheme requires no generality numbers; thus, it is not necessary for the types of numbers to form a linear hierarchy. This is important because, if we extend the range of objects with which we are dealing beyond the obvious number classes, a linear hierarchy becomes difficult to maintain. Is a polynomial more or less general than a complex number, for example? What about a matrix and a polynomial?

The double-dispatching method does not use inheritance, whereas the coercion technique requires messages to be sent to the abstract superclass Number. The coercion technique, indeed, requires the classes to be in a certain class–subclass relationship, whereas no such requirements exist for the double-dispatching technique.

On the negative side, double dispatching increases costs because each type of quantity must now have explicit information about how it interacts with each other type of quantity. Thus, although double dispatching may require fewer methods initially, the number of methods grows as the product of the number of operators and the number of different classes. When coercive generality is used, on the other hand, the number of methods grows as the sum of the operators and classes [Budd 91].

By appropriately restructuring the class hierarchy and using inheritance, we can reduce somewhat the number of methods required to implement double dispatching [Hebel 90]; however, the number is still larger than that required using the generality approach.

Despite the increased number of methods required for double dispatching, actual timings indicate that the technique is slightly faster in practice [Budd 91, Hebel 90]. The real bottom line, however, is that neither technique is in all respects superior to the other. They both have their advantages and disadvantages. A good object-oriented programmer is aware of both techniques, and is able to adapt either of them to new situations.

Exercises

1. Show that the expected result is produced using either coercive generality or double dispatching when the original receiver is a floating-point value and the argument is an integer.

2. For each of the two arithmetic techniques described in this chapter, trace the complete sequences of messages generated for the addition of an integer to an integer and for the addition of an integer to a float. Which technique generates fewer messages? Which do you think would be faster in practice? Explain your answer.

3. Consider the class Complex that we introduced in Chapter 4. Describe the methods you would need to write to incorporate complex values into the two arithmetic schemes defined in this chapter.

4. Consider the two classes Even and Odd, representing even and odd integers, respectively. Instances of these two classes should have the expected properties; the addition of two odd numbers should yield an even number, whereas the addition of an even and odd number should yield an odd number. Explain why it would not be easy to incorporate these classes into an arithmetic scheme based on coercive generality.

5. Consider the problem of displaying multiple graphical images (rectangles, ovals, text, and so on) on multiple display devices. Each graphical image and each display

device is represented by a different class. Show how the task of displaying the graphical images on each of the different output devices could be organized using double dispatching.

6. Is it necessary that an integer be returned as a result of the message generality? Suppose a class — for example, Integer — returned a floating-point value. What problems could this cause? Explain your answer.

9

Replacement
and Refinement

Up to this point, our intuitive model of inheritance has been one in which the set of data values and methods associated with a child class has always been *strictly* larger than the information associated with a parent class. That is, a subclass always simply adds new data or new methods to those provided by the superclass. Clearly, however, this model does not always hold. Remember Phyl and Phyllis, the platypuses described in Chapter 1? We noted in our discussion in that chapter that a basic bit of information we know about the class Mammal is that all mammals bear live young. Nevertheless Phyllis, while steadfastly possessing most of the other properties of a Mammal, gives birth by laying eggs.

We can characterize this situation by saying that the subclass (Platypus), does more than simply monotonically add to the set of information we know about the parent class (Mammal). Instead, the child class actually changes or alters some property of the parent class. To understand this situation, where a subclass changes the meaning of a method defined in a parent class, we must examine the notion of inheritance in more detail.

9.1 ADDING, REPLACING, AND REFINING

We have assumed, up to this point, that data and methods added by a subclass to those inherited by the parent class are always distinct. That is, the set of methods and data values defined by the child class is disjoint from the set of values and methods defined by the parent (and ancestor) classes. To describe this situation, we say that such methods and data values are *added* to the protocol for the parent class.

A different situation occurs when a child class defines a method by the same name as that used for the method in the parent class. The method in the child class effectively hides, or *overrides*, the method in the parent class. When

we search for a method to use in a given situation, we will discover and use the
method in the child class. This is analogous to the way in which my specific
knowledge of the class Platypus overrides my more general knowledge from the
class Mammal.

As we described in Chapter 1, when a message is sent to an object, the
search for a matching method always begins by examining the methods associated with the class of the object. If no method is found, the methods associated
with the immediate superclass of the object are examined. If, once again, no
method is found, the immediate superclass of *that* class is examined, and so on,
until either no further classes remain (in which case an error is reported) or an
appropriate method is found.

A method in a class that has the same name as a method in a superclass is
said to *override* the method in the parent class. During the process of searching
for a method to invoke in response to a message, the method in the child class
will naturally be discovered before the method in the parent class.[1]

A method defined in a child class can override an inherited method for
one of two purposes. A method *replacement* totally replaces the method in the
parent class during execution. That is, the code in the parent class is never
executed when instances of the child class are manipulated. The other type of
override is a method *refinement*. A refinement of a method includes, as part of
its behavior, the execution of the method inherited from the parent class. Thus,
the behavior of the parent is preserved, and is augmented.

Chapter 6 described the mechanics of adding a new method in a child class.
The remainder of this chapter will be devoted to describing the mechanics of
replacement and refinement in each of the languages we are considering.

9.2   REPLACEMENT

In Little Smalltalk (as in Smalltalk-80), integers and floating-point numbers
are objects; they are instances of class Integer and Float, respectively. Both of
these classes are, in turn, subclasses of a more general class Number (Figure 6.7,
page 97). Now suppose we have a variable x that currently contains a Smalltalk
integer, and we send to x the square-root-generating message sqrt. There is no
method corresponding to this name in class Integer, so class Number is searched,
where the method shown in Figure 9.1 is found. This method passes the message
asFloat to self, which, you will recall from Chapter 3, represents the receiver for
the sqrt message. The asFloat message results in a floating-point value with the
same magnitude as the integer number. The message sqrt is then passed to this
value. This time, the search for a method begins with class Float. It so happens

---

[1]Like most broad generalizations, this one is usually, but not always, true. C++ uses both the
declared and actual type of the receiver for a message to determine which method to invoke,
and various techniques are available in different languages to modify the search path used to find
methods. The explanation for these is complicated, and we will defer it until Chapter 11.

```
sqrt
   " convert to float then take square root "
   ↑ self asFloat sqrt
```

Figure 9.1   Overriding the sqrt method in Smalltalk.

that class Float contains a different method called sqrt, which for floating-point values overrides the method in class Number. That method (which is not shown here), computes and returns the expected floating-point value.

The ability to override the method sqrt means that numbers other than instances of class Float can all share the single default routine found in class Number. This sharing avoids having to repeat this code for each of the various different subclasses of Number. Classes that require a behavior different from the default can simply override the method and substitute the alternative code.

A major difficulty with overriding, both for refinement and replacement, is preserving the detailed features of the *is-a* relationship. That is, when a method is overridden, the user does not in general have any guarantee that the behavior exhibited by the child class will have any relationship to the behavior of the parent class. In the example just cited, the methods in both the class Float and class Number were tied only by their conceptual relationship to the concept "square root." Great havoc can ensue if the designer of a subclass alters the behavior of an inherited method in too radical a fashion — for example, by changing the sqrt method such that it computes logarithms. In some object-oriented languages (for example, Eiffel [Meyer 88a]), a programmer can attach input and output assertions to methods. These assertions are inherited by subclasses, and must be satisfied by any method that overrides an existing method.

There are several schools of thought as to how a programmer should document a method that is being overridden, either for replacement or refinement. Smalltalk and Objective-C require no indication at all that overriding is taking place. In C++, the base class (the superclass) must have a special indication that overriding can take place; while in Object Pascal, this indication is in the descendant or subclass.

The placement of some indication in the superclass generally makes the implementation easier, since, if overriding is not a possibility, message passing can be implemented by the more efficient process of procedure calling (that is, the dynamic lookup at run time can be avoided). On the other hand, removing the requirement that this marking be present makes the language more flexible, since it permits any class to be subclassed even if the author of the superclass has not foreseen the possibility. For example, one programmer may produce a class (say, a List) for a particular application. Later, a second programmer may want to make a specialization of this class (for example, OrderedList), overriding many of the methods in the original. In languages such as C++, this could require making textual changes to the original class in order to declare methods as virtual; in contrast, in a language such as Objective-C, no change to the base class description would be necessary.

Replacement in C++

Overriding in C++ is complicated by the intertwining of the concepts of over-riding, overloading, virtual (or polymorphic) functions, and constructors. Over-loading and virtual functions will be explored in more detail in subsequent chapters; we will here restrict ourselves to an explanation of simple replacement and overriding with constructors, which are by far the most common situations.

Simple replacement occurs when the arguments in the child class match identically in type and number the arguments in the parent class, and the virtual modifier is used in the declaration of the method in the parent class.

In an earlier chapter we introduced the C++ class Card, which represented an abstraction of a playing card. We hinted then that we would later be using this abstraction to write a card game; namely, a program to play solitaire. This program (which we will present in detail in Chapter 10) will make use of a class CardPile, which represents a pile of cards. In actual fact, however, there are several different types of piles in the game of solitaire. There is the pile of cards being built up in suits from aces to kings; the table pile, where most of the play takes place; the deck pile, from which cards are drawn; and the discard pile, where cards from the deck pile are placed if they cannot be played. Each of these piles is represented by a different subclass of the class CardPile.

A major portion of the game of solitaire consists of moving cards from one pile to another. In the solution we will outline in Chapter 10, each pile is responsible for deciding whether a given card can be moved onto it. The default action (from class CardPile) is "just say no" — no card can be legally moved. A SuitPile, representing the cards at the top of the playing surface that are being built up in suit from aces to kings, can take a card if either the pile is empty and the card is an ace, or the pile is not empty and the card is the next one in sequence. A tableau, or table pile (represented by the class TablePile) can accept a card if it is a king and the pile is empty, or if it can be played on the current topmost card of the pile. These three methods are shown in Figure 9.2.

There is a subtle difference in meaning for the C++ compiler depending on whether or not the method canTake is declared *virtual* in the class CardPile. Both are legal. For the method to work in what we are describing as an object-oriented fashion, the method should be declared virtual. The virtual modifier is optional as part of the declarations in the child classes; however, for the sake of documentation it is usually repeated in all classes. A portion of these class descriptions is shown in Figure 9.3; the complete source is given in Appendix B.

Were the virtual modifier not given, the method would still replace the simi-larly named method in the parent class; however, the binding of method to mes-sage would be altered. Nonvirtual methods are static, in the sense of Chapter 7. That is, the binding of a call on a nonvirtual method is performed at compile time, based on the declared (static) type of the receiver, and not at run time. If the virtual keyword was removed from the declaration of canTake, variables *declared* as CardPile would execute the method in class CardPile (regardless of

```
int CardPile::canTake(Card *aCard)
{  // just say no
   return 0;
}

int TablePile::canTake(Card *aCard)
{
   if (top == nilLink) {  // can take kings on an empty pile
      if (aCard->rank() == 13) return 1;
      return 0;
      }
   // see if colors are different
    if ((top->card())->color() == aCard->color()) return 0;
   // see if numbers are legal
   if (((top->card())->rank() - 1) == aCard->rank())
      return 1;
   return 0;
}

int  SuitPile::canTake(Card *aCard)
{
   if (top == nilLink) {  // we're empty, can take an ace
      if (aCard->rank() == 1) return 1;
      return 0;
      }
   if ((top->card())->suit() != aCard->suit())
      return 0;
   if (((top->card())->rank() + 1) == aCard->rank())
      return 1;
   return 0;
}
```

Figure 9.2 An example of overriding in C++.

the actual class of the value contained in the variable), and variables declared as TablePile or SuitPile would execute the method in their respective class.

This is in keeping with the C++ philosophy that features should incur a cost only when they are used. If virtual functions are not employed, then inheritance imposes absolutely no execution time overhead (which is not the case for the other languages examined in this book). However, the fact that both forms are legal, but differ in their interpretations, is frequently a source of subtle errors in C++ programs. The case study to be presented in Chapter 17 contains several instances of both virtual and nonvirtual replacement.

Figure 9.3 also illustrates how constructors are written when classes use inheritance. The class CardPile contains a constructor that takes two arguments, representing the coordinates of one corner of the card pile. For the class TablePile, we wish to add a third argument; namely, the column number of the

```
class CardPile
{
  protected:
  CardLink *top;   // first card in pile
  int  x;     // x location of pile
  int  y;     // y location of pile

  public:
  CardPile() { top = nilcard; }
  CardPile(int a, int b) { x = a; y = b; top = nilcard; }
  ...
  int  virtual canTake(Card *c);
  ...
};

class SuitPile : public CardPile
{
  public:
  int  virtual canTake(Card *c);
};

class TablePile : public CardPile
{
  int  column;   // our column number
  public:
  TablePile(int c, int a, int b)
    { x = a; y = b; column = c; }
  ...
  int  virtual canTake(Card *c);
  ...
};
```

Figure 9.3   A class declaration with a virtual method.

pile in the game table. As we have seen already, constructors are not like other methods. For example, they are invoked only indirectly when a new object is created. Another way in which constructors differ from other methods is that the name of the constructor in a subclass is necessarily different from the name of the constructor in the superclass. A third difference is that we usually want to extend, and not to override, the constructor of the base class. That is, we still want the initialization of the base class to be performed, but in addition we want to perform further actions.

A constructor such as that shown for class TablePile in Figure 9.3 will always invoke the constructor with no arguments in the base class prior to executing the body of the constructor given in the subclass. A compilation error will be given if there is no constructor in the parent class that takes no arguments. Notice that, in this case, it is necessary for the constructor in the class TablePile to duplicate some of the code contained in the two-argument constructor for class CardPile. We will describe a more sophisticated technique that avoids this duplication when we discuss refinement in Section 9.3.

Data members — that is, instance variables — also can be overridden in C++. Such fields are, however, never virtual. That is, distinct storage locations are assigned to each variable, and to access a specific variable the programmer must use a qualified name. This qualified name is formed by prepending to the identifier the name of the class in which the variable is defined.

Replacement in Object Pascal

In Object Pascal, a method can replace another method in a superclass only if (1) the method name is spelled identically to the identifier of the method in the superclass; (2) the order, types, and names of the parameters and the type of function result, if any, match exactly; and (3) the description of the method in the child class is followed by the keyword override.

Figure 9.4 illustrates a method being replaced. Here, Employee is a general description for employees in a firm, and SalaryEmployee is a subclass. The function pay in class Employee computes a result, presumably by multiplying the hours worked by the hourly rate. This function is changed in SalaryEmployee since, for a salaried employee, the amount of pay is usually independent of the hours worked. Consider now a variable emp declared to be of class Employee. As we have noted, such a variable can hold a value that is either an Employee or a SalaryEmployee. Regardless of the value, a call on pay will invoke the correct method for the type of employee. (We will discuss the second procedure, establish, when we describe the accessing of overridden methods).

Replacement in Objective-C and Smalltalk

In Smalltalk and Objective-C, a method having the same name as a method in a superclass will always override the superclass method automatically. There is no need for the user to indicate explicitly that a method is being replaced. However, for the purposes of good documentation, it is helpful for the programmer to indicate this fact in a comment.

9.3 REFINEMENT

A method is overridden by a child class as often to add increased functionality as to substitute new functionality. For example a method initializing a data structure may need to perform the initialization of the superclass, and then some additional initialization particular to the derived class. Since, in most object-oriented languages access to both data and methods is inherited in the child class, the addition of new functionality could be accomplished simply by copying the overridden code from the parent class. This approach, however,

```
type
  Employee = object
      name : alpha;
      wage : integer;
      function pay(HoursWorked : integer) : integer;
      function hourlyWorker : boolean;
      procedure establish;
    end;

  SalaryEmployee = object (Employee)
      salary : integer;
      function pay(HoursWorked : integer) :
                    integer; override;
      function hourlyWorker : boolean; override;
      procedure establish; override;
    end;

var
  emp, e : Employee;
  s : SalaryEmployee;
  p : integer;

begin
  new(e);
  emp := e;
  ...
  p := emp.pay(38);
  ...
  new(s);
  emp := s;
  ...
  p := emp.pay(46);
  ...
end
```

Figure 9.4   Overriding a method in Object Pascal.

violates several important principles of object-oriented design; for example, it reduces code sharing, blocks information hiding, and lessens reliability since errors corrected in the parent class may not be propagated to the child classes. Thus, it is useful if there is some mechanism from within an overriding method to invoke the same method in the superclass, and thus to "reuse" the code of the overridden method. When a method invokes the overridden method from the parent class in this fashion, we say that the method *refines* that of the parent class.

We have seen this problem already, in the SymbolTable class constructed in Objective-C in Section 6.6 (Figure 6.9, page 100). Here the method new was overriding the method found in class Object, but what we wanted to do was to add to, and not to replace, the method in the superclass. We accomplish the invocation of the method in the superclass by sending a message to the object super. This is one of two different approaches that are used to provide the ability to find a method from a superclass. This technique, used also in Smalltalk and Object Pascal, simply changes the starting class for method lookup from the class of the receiver to the superclass of the class of the method currently being executed. The second technique, used in C++, explicitly names the class from which a method is to be taken. This approach eliminates the run-time lookup mechanism altogether, permitting message passing to be implemented by procedure calling.

Performing explicit qualification is somewhat more tedious and less elegant than is using super, especially if some method is copied from one class to another, unrelated class. On the other hand, it can be more powerful. Methods from non immediate ancestors can be designated (even if they are overridden in intervening classes), and name conflicts among multiple superclasses can be disambiguated when multiple inheritance is used (as we will see in Chapter 12).

Other object-oriented languages, besides the four we are discussing in this book, have even more exotic techniques for dealing with refinement. In Simula [Birtwistle 79], method refinement is prohibited: It is not possible to access an overridden virtual method. In Beta [Kristensen 87], on the other hand, it is not possible to write a method to perform simple replacement. All overridden methods must, at some point, execute the code inherited from the parent class. In the Lisp-based language CLOS [Bobrow 88], it is possible to define "wrapper" methods that are executed either before or after the method inherited from the parent class. Other languages have similar facilities.

Refinement in C++

C++ uses the technique of qualified names to provide access to methods from parent classes in overridden methods. A qualified name is written as a class name followed by a pair of colons and the name of a procedure. The qualified name removes the virtual message-passing mechanism, and ensures that the method will be taken from the named class.

We shall use once more an example from our solitaire program; a Pile uses the method addCard to add a new card to the stack (assuming the legality of the move has been checked using the canTake method described already). The method in class CardPile takes care of the basic actions of linking the cards in a list, updating the value of the instance variable top, and so on. The class TablePile, representing the tableau, must in addition worry about the physical placement of the card on the playing surface. If the tableau pile is empty, the card is simply placed normally. If, on the other hand, the tableau pile has a face-up card and the argument card is being played on it, then the latter card should be moved down slightly so that the topmost card can still be seen. To

```
   // place a single card into a card pile
void CardPile::addCard(Card *aCard)
{
   if (aCard != nilcard) {
     aCard->setLink(top);
     top = aCard;
     top->moveTo(x, y);
     }
}


   // place a single card into a table pile
void TablePile::addCard(Card *aCard)
{   int tx, ty;

   // if pile is empty, just place it normally
   if (top == nilcard)
     CardPile::addCard(aCard);
   else {    // else we have to display it properly
     tx = top->locx();
     ty = top->locy();
     // figure out where to place the card
     if (top->faceUp() && top->next() != nilcard &&
       (top->next())->faceUp())
       ; // do nothing, place on top of top card
     else
       ty += 30;   // else move it down a bit
     CardPile::addCard(aCard);
     top->moveTo(tx, ty);
     }
}
```

Figure 9.5   An example of superclass access in C++.

conserve the table playing area, however, only the topmost and bottommost
face-up cards are displayed, with any intermediate face up cards being hidden
by the topmost face-up card. The methods that accomplish this placement are
shown in Figure 9.5.

We earlier noted that a constructor in a child class *always* invokes a constructor for the parent class. The technique outlined in Section 9.2 invoked
the constructor in the parent class that had noarguments, although this may be
only one of several different constructors defined by the parent class. We now
describe a technique that permits the class description of the child class to select
any constructor desired for the purposes of initializing the portion of the class
inherited from the parent.

Consider the class description shown in Figure 9.6 for the class TablePile,
and contrast the constructor with that shown in Figure 9.3. Note the colon following the closing parenthesis of the argument list in the body of the constructor.

```
class TablePile : public CardPile
{
  int  column;  // our column number
  public:
  TablePile(int, int, int);
  ...
};
...
TablePile::TablePile(int c, int x, int y) : CardPile(x, y)
{ column = c; }
```

Figure 9.6 Overriding a constructor in C++.

This colon is followed by an invocation of the constructor in the parent class. Thus, the two-argument constructor for class CardPile, shown in Figure 9.3, will be invoked just prior to execution of the body of the constructor shown here. By varying the types of values passed in this second argument list, the programmer can selectively choose which of several constructors from the parent class should be invoked.

Refinement in Object Pascal

In Object Pascal, the modifier "inherited" is used within a method to indicate access to a method contained in a superclass. When an inherited method is invoked, the method in the superclass will be executed.

Suppose, for example, that we write a method to prompt a user interactively for fields to initialize a database record for an employee, using the class descriptions shown in Figure 9.4. The method in class Employee prints out the prompts and reads in the values for the name and wage field. The wage field, however, is requested only if the method hourlyWorker returns true. This method is defined in class Employee and is redefined in class SalaryEmployee. The method in class SalaryEmployee should do the same actions as the method in class Employee, and, in addition, should prompt for the salary. These methods are shown in Figure 9.7.

Refinement in Objective-C and Smalltalk

We have already seen an example of how methods from a superclass can be invoked in an overridden method. The following method new is from the SymbolTable class described in Figure 6.9 (page 100).

```
+ new
{
  /* create the new dictionary */
  self = [ super new ];
```

```
    theDictionary = [ Dictionary new ];
    return self;
}
```

The method passes the message new to the pseudo-variable super, which, like the pseudo-variable self (which we have already encountered in Chapter 3), represents the receiver of the original message. However, when super is used as a receiver for a message, the search for a corresponding method will begin with the superclass of the class in which the current method is located. That is, since this method is defined in class SymbolTable, the search for a method to invoke when the new message is sent to super will begin in class Object, the parent class of SymbolTable.

The concept in Smalltalk is exactly the same, except for the syntax. For example, in version 3 of Little Smalltalk, the class String is a subclass of the class ByteArray. Instances of class ByteArray represent arrays of bytes — that

```
function Employee.hourlyWorker : boolean;
begin
  hourlyWorker := true
end.

procedure Employee.establish;
begin
  writeln("enter employee name:");
  readln(name);
  if self.hourlyWorker then begin
    writeln("enter wage");
    readln(wage)
  end
end;

function SalaryEmployee.hourlyWorker : boolean;
begin
  hourlyWorker := false
end.

procedure SalaryEmployee.establish;
begin
  inherited establish;
  writeln("enter salary: ");
  readln(salary)
end;
```

Figure 9.7 Accessing a method from the parent class in Object Pascal.

is, small integer values. The class String simply modifies the interpretation of these values, treating them as characters, rather than as integers.

To test for equality of two strings, the method in class String first tests to see whether the argument is itself another string, returning false if it is not so. If it is a string, the equality-testing message is passed to super, thereby invoking the more general testing method from class ByteArray. Here is the method in class String:

```
= value
" if argument is a string, see if values are equal "
(value isKindOf: String)
ifTrue: [ ↑ super = value ]
ifFalse: [ ↑ false ]
```

Exercises

1. This exercise builds on Exercise 1 in Chapter 6 (page 101). Suppose that you are required to program a project in a non–object-oriented language, such as Pascal or C. How might you simulate the notion of classes and methods? How will you simulate inheritance? How will you simulate virtual functions and overriding?

2. We have described overriding here only in terms of one method overriding a method in a parent class. Does the concept of overriding make sense for instance variables? Explain why it does or does not.

3. Recall the use of a sentinel value in the Smalltalk and Objective-C solutions to the eight queens puzzle in Chapter 5. Would it have made sense to make the class Queen a subclass of class NullQueen? Explain why it would or would not. Consider issues such as documentation, readability, and code sharing.

4. Modify either the C++ or Object Pascal version of the eight queens problem from Chapter 5 such that the class Queen is a subclass of class NullQueen, and the appropriate methods are marked as overridden.

5. Frequently while an instance of a subclass is being initialized, some code from the parent class must be executed, followed by some code from the child class, followed by more code from the parent class. In a windowing system, for example, the parent class might allocate some important data structures, the child class might then modify some fields (such as the name of the window and the window size) in these data structures, and then the parent class might finally map the window onto the display device.
Show how this sequence of calls might be generated in an object-oriented language. (Hint: You will probably need to split the initialization process into two or more messages.)

6. Consider the following class definitions and program in Objective-C. Determine which of the print statements will execute without error, and what values will be printed.

```
@implementation classA : Object
- (int) answer1: (int) x
  { return x; }
@end

@implementation classB : classA
- (int) answer2: (int) x
  { return [ self answer1: (x * 2) ]; }
@end

@implementation classC : classB
- (int) answer1: (int) x
  { return [ super answer1: (x * 3) ]; }
- (int) answer2: (int) x
  { return [ super answer2: x ]; }
@end

main() {
id iA, iB, iC;

  iA = [ classA new ];
  iB = [ classB new ];
  iC = [ classC new ];

  printf("%d\n", [ iA answer1: 1 ]);
  printf("%d\n", [ iA answer2: 1 ]);
  printf("%d\n", [ iB answer1: 1 ]);
  printf("%d\n", [ iB answer2: 1 ]);
  printf("%d\n", [ iC answer1: 1 ]);
  printf("%d\n", [ iC answer2: 1 ]);
}
```

10
Case Study: Solitaire

We will use a solitaire program, written in C++, to illustrate the utility and power of the mechanisms of inheritance and overriding. We have earlier (Chapters 3 and 9) examined portions of this program, specifically the abstraction of the playing card represented by class Card. The class CardPile represents our abstract notion of a pile of playing cards. Since moving cards from one pile to another is the major component of the game, the subclasses of class CardPile are the major data structures used in implementing the solitaire program. We will discuss the class CardPile in Section 10.2.

In implementing the user interface for our solitaire game, we make use of the InterViews library of classes [Linton 89]. InterViews is a collection of C++ classes that is built on top of the X windowing system [Scheifler 88]. The use of predefined classes greatly simplifies the task of producing a user interface. We will discuss object-oriented graphical user interfaces in Section 10.3.

10.1 THE CLASS CARD

In earlier chapters we discussed the abstraction represented by the classes Card and CardView; the complete source code for the class is given in Appendix B. Thus, here, it is sufficient merely to reiterate some of the important points about these classes.

Each instance of class Card maintains a suit and rank value. To prevent modification of these values, the instance variables maintaining the values are declared private, and access to the values is mediated through a pair of functions. In addition, the user can request the color of the card.

Each instance of class Card is matched with a corresponding instance of CardView. The view class is used to display the card on a graphical output device. Instances of class CardView have a location, and erase and redraw their images (Figure 10.1). In addition, they can be interrogated to determine if a specific point in the playing surface is within the bounds of the card.

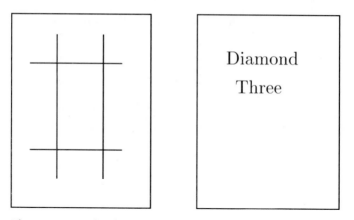

Figure 10.1   The face down and face up representations of a card.

As far as object-oriented programming concepts are concerned, the important fact to remember about playing cards is that each card is responsible for maintaining its own state and its own behavior. For example, each card is charged with remembering whether it is face up or down, and each card must know how to draw itself. The actual implementation of these drawing operations is tied to the InterViews system, and we will defer an explanation of this topic until we discuss the user interface.

In order to maintain cards on a linked list, link fields must be added to each instance of CardView. This is accomplished by subclassing, introducing a new class CardLink shown in Figure 10.2. Instances of CardLink inherit all the behavior of CardView, and in addition can be held on a linked list as part of a card pile.

10.2   INHERITANCE AND OVERRIDING

The version of solitaire we will describe is known as Klondike. The countless variations on this game make it probably by far the most common solitaire game; so when you say "solitaire," most people think of some version of Klondike. The version we will use is that described in [Morehead 49]; in the exercises we will explore some of the common variations.

The game is played with a single standard pack of 52 cards. The *tableau*, or playing table, consists of 28 cards in seven piles. The first pile has one card, the second two, and so on up to seven. The top card of each pile is initially face up; all other cards are face down.

The *foundations* — which we call the suit piles — are built up from aces to kings in suits. The foundations are constructed above the tableau as the cards become available. The object of the game is to build all 52 cards into the suit piles.

```
class CardLink : public CardView
{
  public:
  CardLink(int s, int c);
  CardLink(Card *c);
  CardLink *  next ();
  void     setLink (CardLink * aCard);

  private:
  CardLink *  link;
};

inline CardLink::CardLink(int s, int c) :
CardView(s, c) { ; }

inline CardLink::CardLink(Card * c) : CardView(c) { ; }

inline CardLink * CardLink::next() { return link; }

inline void CardLink::setLink (CardLink * aCard)
                                   { link = aCard; }
```

Figure 10.2   The class CardLink.

The remaining cards that are not part of the tableau are initially all in the *stock*, which we call the deck pile. Cards in the deck pile are face down. Cards are drawn one by one from the deck pile and are placed, face up, on the discard pile. From there, they can be moved onto either a tableau pile or a suit pile. Cards are drawn from the deck pile until the pile is empty; at this point, the game is over if no further moves can be made.

Cards can be built on a tableau pile only on a card of next-higher rank and opposite color. Cards can be built on a suit pile only if they are the same suit and next higher card, or the suit pile is empty and the card is an ace. Spaces in the tableau that arise during play can be filled only by kings.

The topmost card of each tableau pile and the topmost card of the discard pile are always available for play. In addition, an entire collection of face-up cards from a tableau (called a *build*) can be moved to another tableau pile, if the bottommost card of the build can be legally played on the topmost card of the destination. The topmost card of a tableau is always face up. If a card is moved from a tableau, leaving a face-down card on the top, the latter card can be turned face up.

From this short description, it is clear that the major portion of the game of solitaire involves manipulating piles of cards. In addition to the piles already described, a fifth pile type, called DealPile, is used to maintain the original unsorted deck of cards. To initialize a game, the deal pile is shuffled to create a new deck pile.

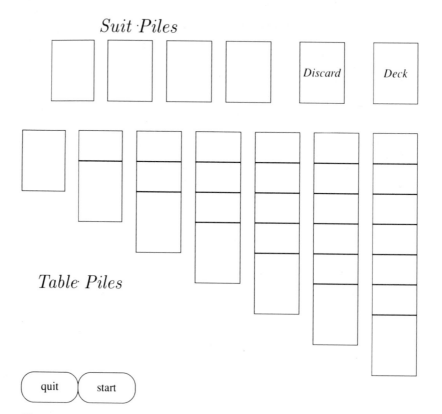

Figure 10.3 Layout for the solitaire game.

Much of the behavior we want to associate with a card pile is common to each of the several varieties of piles in the game. For example, each pile maintains a linked list of the cards in the pile, and the operations of inserting and deleting elements from this linked list are common. Other operations, although common in the abstract to each of the piles, differ in the details. For example, we need to be able to determine whether a specific card can be added to a pile. A card can be added to a suit pile only if the card is an ace and the suit pile is empty, or the card is of the same suit as and has the next-higher value than the current topmost card in the pile. A card can be added to a tableau pile, on the other hand, only if it is of the opposite color as the current topmost card in the pile and has the next lower value (Figure 10.3).

Figure 10.4 shows a CRC card that defines the basic behavior of the class CardPile. How this behavior is modified in the subclasses is shown by the CRC cards in Figures 10.5, 10.6 and 10.7.

The actions of the five virtual functions defined in class CardPile, and overridden in the subclasses, can be characterized as follows:

CardPile

---

addCard(Card *) – *Add a card to the pile. Changes coordinates of card to those of pile, but does not redraw pile.*
canTake(Card *) – *See whether pile can take card. Default: return no.*
contains(int, int) – *See whether card contains point.*

CardPile – page 2

---

display() – *Display pile. Default: display topmost card.*
initialize() – *Initialize pile.*
select(int, int) – *Button was pressed at position. Default: do nothing*
shuffleTo(CardPile *) – *Insert copies of current cardpile randomly.*

Figure 10.4 A CRC card description of class CardPile.

initialize Initialize the pile. The default action is to simply make a pile consisting of zero cards. This is overridden in class DeckPile to produce a shuffled deck containing all 52 cards. It is overridden in the class TablePile to draw a number of cards from the deck pile, all face down except the last. The number of cards drawn is equal to the column number of the table pile.

addCard Add a card to the pile. The default action simply adds the card to the linked list, and moves the card (without redrawing it) to the current

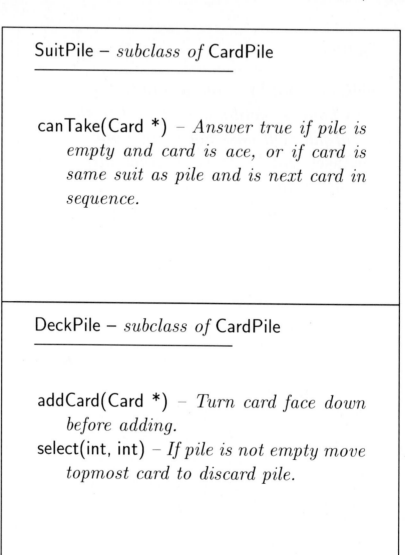

Figure 10.5 CRC cards for classes SuitPile and DeckPile.

coordinates of the pile. This is overridden in the class TablePile to position the card so that other face-up cards can still be seen. The addCard method is overridden in the discard class to ensure that the card is face up before it is added. Similarly, in the deck class, it is ensured that the card is face down.

display Display the card deck. The default method merely displays the topmost card of the pile. This method is overridden in the TablePile class so as to

TablePile – *subclass of* CardPile

---

addCard(Card *) – *Position card correctly on table after adding.*

canTake(Card *) – *Answer true if pile is empty and card is king, or if card can be legally added.*

copyBuild(CardDeck *) – *Copy an entire face-up build to another deck.*

TablePile – Page 2

---

display() – *Display all cards, not simply the topmost card.*

initialize() – *Draw correct number of cards from* DeckPile *to initialize column.*

select(int, int) – *Play selected card, if possible.*

Figure 10.6 CRC card for class TablePile.

display a column of cards. The top half of each hidden card is displayed. So that the playing surface area is conserved, only the topmost and bottom-most face-up cards are displayed (this permits us to give definite bounds to the playing surface).

select Perform an action in response to a mouse click. The select method is invoked when the user selects a pile by clicking the mouse in the portion

DiscardPile – *subclass of* CardPile

---

addCard(Card *) – *Turn card face up before adding.*
select(int, int) – *Play topmost card, if possible.*

DealPile – *subclass of* CardPile

ShuffleTo(Pile *) – *shuffle cards and assign to the argument pile*

Figure 10.7   CRC card for classes DiscardPile and DealPile.

of the playing field covered by the pile. The default action does nothing. This is overridden by the table, deck, and discard piles to play the topmost card, if that card can be played.

canTake Tell whether a pile can take a specific card. Only table and suit piles can take cards. Thus, the default action is simply to return no; this is overridden in the two classes mentioned.

	Suit	Table	Deck	Discard	Deal
initialize		X	X		
addCard		X	X	X	
display		X			
select		X	X	X	
canTake	X	X			

Table 10.1   Methods overridden in subclasses of class CardPile.

An examination of Table 10.1 illustrates one of the important benefits of inheritance and overriding. Given five operations and five classes, there are 25 potential methods we might have to define. By the use of inheritance, however, we need to implement only half of these. Furthermore, we are guaranteed that each pile will respond to similar requests in a similar manner.

The controlling code in the main program (found in file solitaire.cc in Appendix B) illustrates another use of inheritance. Each of the 13 piles is actually pointed to twice by the object that maintains the game window. The interface for this class is shown in Figure 10.8. Note that there are instance

```
class GameWindow : public MonoScene
{
public:
  CardPile *  discard;  // the discard pile
  CardPile *  deck;     // the unplayed card deck

  GameWindow();

  void      newGame();    // start a new game

  void        clearArea(int, int, int, int);
  int         suitCanAdd(Card*);
  CardPile *  suitAddPile(Card*);
  int         tableCanAdd(Card*);
  CardPile *  tableAddPile(Card*);

protected:
  CardPile *  allPiles[13];  // all piles
  CardPile *  suitPiles[4];  // the pile of suits
  CardPile *  table[7];  // the playing table

  void virtual   Handle (Event&);
  void virtual   Redraw(Coord,Coord,Coord,Coord);
};
```

Figure 10.8   The class description for the game manager.

```
//  start a new game
void GameWindow::newGame()
{   int i;

  // initialize all the piles
  for (i = 0; i < 13; i++)
    allPiles[i]->initialize();

  // then redraw the screen
  Draw();
}
```

Figure 10.9   Initializing a new game.

variables that permit each pile to be maintained by its use, such as a table pile or a suit pile. In addition, a second array of size 13 contains pointers to all piles.

This second array greatly simplifies many operations that must be performed on all piles, but for which we do not care to distinguish one pile from another. For example, to initialize a game it suffices to initialize each of the 13 piles, and then to display them. The code to accomplish this is shown in Figure 10.9.

10.3   OBJECT-ORIENTED USER INTERFACES

We have noted already that our user interface will be built with the aid of the InterViews collection of classes, which is in turn built on top of the X window system. We do not have space for more than a superficial description of InterViews; the interested reader is strongly encouraged to consult [Linton 89] and related material.

The advantage of using an existing package for user interfaces (or for any other task, for that matter) is that the majority of work in implementing the interface will have been done for you already. For example, our game will make use of two buttons invoked by the mouse. The first button starts a new game; the second button halts the program. The InterViews library includes a class called PushButton that takes care of displaying the button on the screen, tracking the mouse, inverting the image of the button when pressed, and all the other operations conventionally associated with graphical user interfaces. The constructor for this class takes three arguments; the text associated with the button, the initial state of the button (an instance of another InterViews class called ButtonState), and a Boolean value indicating whether the button is "active" (that is, can be legally pressed). When pressed, an instance of PushButton invokes the virtual method Press.

To provide the functionality we desire for our two buttons, we can create two new classes that are subclasses of PushButton. These classes are shown in

```
// The Quit button at the bottom of the screen halts game
class QuitButton : public PushButton
{
public:
  QuitButton() : PushButton("quit",
  new ButtonState(false), true) {}
  void virtual Press() { exit(0); }
};

// The Start button at the bottom of the screen starts game
class StartButton : public PushButton
{
public:
  StartButton() : PushButton("start",
  new ButtonState(false), true) {}
  void virtual Press() { game->newGame(); }
};
```

Figure 10.10   Creation of two new types of buttons using InterViews.

Figure 10.10. They each define only two methods: a constructor that merely invokes the constructor from the parent class, and a method that defines the behavior we desire when the button is pressed. By using inline definitions, we need to write only the class description (note that the body of the constructor is empty). All the other button-related activities will be taken care of for us by methods defined in the parent class PushButton.

```
//
//  the main program
//    create a new game window
//  map it onto the screen with two buttons at bottom
//  start it up
//

int main (int argc, char ** argv) {
  World *world = new World("solitaire", argc, argv);

  game = new GameWindow;

  world->InsertApplication( new VBox(game,
    new HBox(new QuitButton, new StartButton)));

  drawField = game->GetCanvas();

  world->Run();
}
```

Figure 10.11   The main procedure in the solitaire application.

```
static char *suits[ ] = {"Heart", "Club", "Diamond",
                                      "Spade" };

static char *ranks[ ] = {"blank", "Ace", "2", "3", "4",
  "5", "6", "7", "8", "9", "10", "Jack", "Queen", "King" };

void CardView::draw()
{
  // erase the card and redraw it
  erase();
  painter->Rect
    (drawField,  x(), y(), x()+CardWidth, y()+CardHeight);
  if (up) {  // draw the card face up
    painter->MoveTo(x()+12, y()+round(CardHeight*0.80));
    painter->Text(drawField, suits[theCard->suit()]);
    painter->MoveTo(x()+15, y()+round(CardHeight*0.60));
    painter->Text(drawField, ranks[theCard->rank()]);
    }
  else {  int n;  // draw the card face down
    n = x()+round(CardWidth*0.3);
    painter->Line(drawField, n, y()+5, n,
     y()+CardHeight-10);
    n = x()+round(CardWidth*0.7);
    painter->Line(drawField, n, y()+5, n,
     y()+CardHeight-10);
    n = y()+round(CardHeight*0.3);
    painter->Line(drawField, x()+5, n,
     x()+CardWidth-10, n);
    n = y()+round(CardHeight*0.7);
    painter->Line(drawField, x()+5, n,
     x()+CardWidth-10, n);
    }
}
```

Figure 10.12 The method display from class CardView.

A major task for any user-interface system is to determine the layout of
the various graphical components on the display screen. The InterViews system
simplifies this task by describing the layout in terms of horizontal and vertical
collections of boxes. In our case, the game is described as a vertical box containing the primary game board, which sits on top of a horizontal box containing
the two buttons. This initialization code is shown in Figure 10.11, which gives
the main program for our application. The size of the game window is specified
as part of the constructor for the class GameWindow.

Two classes are used to organize the graphics facilities in InterViews. The
class Canvas represents the actual area for the display, and the facilitator class
Painter is the means by which graphics are placed on the canvas. Every window

```
//
//  handle a mouse-down event in the game window
//
void GameWindow::Handle (Event& e)
{   int i;

    // we are only interested in mouse down events
    if (e.eventType != DownEvent) return;

    for (i = 0; i < 13; i++)
      if (allPiles[i]->contains(e.x, e.y)) {
        allPiles[i]->select(e.x, e.y);
        return;
        }
    return;
}
```

Figure 10.13   Determining which pile the user selected.

has an associated canvas. The canvas for our game window is placed in the global variable drawField as part of the initialization process (Figure 10.11). Similarly, a painter is created and is placed in a global variable as part of the process of creating a new game. As an illustration of how a painter and canvas are used, Figure 10.12 gives the method used by class Card to display either the face or back of a playing card.

Because we have made the game window a subclass of the InterViews-provided class MonoScene, tasks such as layout and tracking the mouse will be performed automatically. We will structure our interface so that the user can play the game entirely with the mouse. To move any specific card, the user simply moves the mouse over the card and clicks. When the user clicks in a MonoScene window, the virtual method Handle is invoked.[1] The game window overrides this method, so that, when the user clicks the mouse, the pile over which the mouse is placed is determined and the method select, which we described in the last section, is invoked. The code to do this is shown in Figure 10.13.

In addition to Handle, the only other virtual method overridden in the game class is the method Redraw. The procedure Redraw takes four arguments, which represent a portion of the screen that needs to be redrawn. Our application simply redraws the entire screen, by asking each pile to display itself. With the exception of the explicit call on Draw generated when a new game is initiated (Figure 10.9), the InterViews system automatically takes care of calling Redraw whenever the window is moved or occluded. Thus the constructor for our game

---

[1]A Handle method is also provided in the class PushButton, which is indirectly a subclass of MonoScene. However the class PushButton overrides the method so as to invoke the slightly simpler method called Press.

window and the two methods Handle and Redraw are the only interface-specific portions of code we need to generate.

Exercises

1. The following are common variations of Klondike. For each, describe what portions of the solitaire program would need to be altered to incorporate the change.

   a) If the user clicks on an empty deck pile, the discard pile is moved (perhaps with shuffling) back to the deck pile. Thus, the user can traverse the deck pile multiple times.

   b) The top card of a tableau cannot be moved to another tableau pile if there is another face-up card below it.

   c) Cards are drawn from the deck three at a time and are placed on the discard pile in reverse order. As before,only the topmost card of the discard pile is available for playing. If fewer than three cards remain in the deck pile, all the remaining cards (however many there may be) are moved to the discard pile.

   d) Any royalty card, not simply a king, can be moved onto an empty tableau pile.

2. The game "Thumb and Pouch" is similar to Klondike except that a card may be built on any card of next-higher rank, of any suit but its own. Thus, a nine of spades can be played on a 10 of clubs, for example, but not on a 10 of spades. This variation greatly improves the chances of winning. (According to Morehead [Morehead 49], the changes of winning Klondike are one in 30, whereas the chances of winning Thumb and Pouch are one in four.) Describe what portions of the program would need to be changed to accommodate this variation.

3. The game "Whitehead" is similar to Klondike, except that the entire tableau is dealt face up, and columns are built down in color (red on red, black on black, regardless of suit). A space may be filled by any available card or build. Describe what portions of the program would need to be changed to accommodate this variation. (Morehead [Morehead 49] gives the chances of winning a game of Whitehead as one in 20).

4. In the game "Spiderette" there are no suit piles; all building is performed on the tableau. The object is to build the tableau into four piles, from king to ace. A card can be played on any card of the next-higher rank, regardless of suit. A space made available by removing all cards can be filled by any available card or build. Describe what portions of the program would need to be changed to accommodate this variation.

5. Implement one or more of the variations described in the earlier problems.

6. Implement a new button that, when pressed, produces a window of "radio-button" alternatives. By means of these selections, the user can custom-tailor the game to produce any of the alternatives described in earlier exercises, or other variations. (This is a difficult exercise).

7. Using the extensive graphics facilities provided by InterViews and by the X window system [Scheifler 88, Linton 89], alter the program to draw more accurate images for the front and back of a card. How much of the program needs to know about these changes?

8. Add two new buttons to the solitaire game. The first, labeled "step," will when pressed perform any moves possible from the discard pile or the tableau. Thus, a user could play by simply turning over cards one by one and hitting the "step" button. The second button, labeled "play", will automatically turn over cards from the deck and will try to play them. If the user pushes this button, she will not play the cards at all, and the game will run itself automatically.

11
Inheritance and Types

In this chapter, we will examine some of the effects of inheritance on other aspects of object-oriented languages. We will examine in detail the type system, the meaning of operations such as assignment, the process of testing for equivalence, and storage allocation.

We have described the *is-a* relationship as a fundamental property of inheritance. One way to view the *is-a* relationship is as a means of associating a *type*, as in a type of a variable, with a set of *values* — namely, the values the variable can legally hold. If a variable x is declared as an instance of a specific class, say Window, then certainly it should be legal for x to hold values of type Window. If we have a subclass of Window, say TextWindow, since a TextWindow *is-a* Window, then it should certainly make sense that x can hold a value of type TextWindow.

Intuitively, it does makes sense. From a practical point of view, there are difficulties associated with implementing object-oriented languages in a manner such that this intuitive behavior can be realized. These difficulties are not insurmountable, but the way in which various language designers have chosen to address them differs from language to language. An examination of what these problems are and of how they affect the language serves also to illuminate the reasons for obscure features of languages over which the unwary programmer is likely to stumble.

11.1 MEMORY LAYOUT

Let us start by considering a seemingly simple question. The various answers that can be given to this question will then lead us in different directions. How much storage should we allocate to a variable that is declared to be of a specific class? To take a concrete example, how much storage should we allocate to the variable x that we earlier described as being an instance of class Window?

```
class Window {
   int height;
   int width;
   ...
public:
   virtual void oops();
};
class TextWindow : public Window {
   char *contents;
   int   cursorLocation;
   ...
public:
   virtual void oops();
};
```

Figure 11.1 Class definitions for window and textWindow.

It is commonly believed that variables allocated on the stack as part of the procedure-activation process are more efficient than are variables allocated on the heap (but see [Appel 87] for a dissenting opinion). Thus, language designers and implementors go to great lengths to make it possible for variables to be stack allocated. But there is one major problem with stack allocation — namely, the storage requirements must be determined statically, at compile time or at the latest at procedure entry time. These times are well before the values the variable will hold are known.

The difficulty is that subclasses can introduce data not present in a superclass. The class TextWindow, for example, probably brings with it data areas for edit buffers, locations of the current edit point, and so on (Figure 11.1). Should these data values be taken into consideration when space for x is allocated?

There would seem to be at least three plausible answers:

1. Allocate the amount of space necessary for the base class only. That is, allocate to x only those data areas declared as part of the class Window, ignoring the space requirements of subclasses.

2. Allocate the maximum amount of space necessary for any legal value, whether it be from the base class or from any subclass.

3. Allocate only the amount of space necessary to hold a single pointer. Allocate the space necessary for the value at run time on the heap, and set the pointer value appropriately.

All three solutions are possible, and two of them are found in the languages we are considering in this book. In the following sections, we will investigate some of the implications of this design decision.

```
Window x;
Window *y;
. . .
y = new TextWindow;
```

Figure 11.2 Static and dynamic values in C++.

Minimum Static Space Allocation

The language C was designed with run-time efficiency in mind, and thus, given the widespread belief that stack-based allocation of memory locations results in faster execution times than are possible with dynamic variables, it is not surprising that the successor language C++ chose to retain the concepts of both nondynamic variables and dynamic (run-time-allocated) variables.

In C++, the distinction is made in terms of how a variable is declared and, accordingly, whether or not pointers are used to access the values of the variable. In Figure 11.2, for example, the variable x is allocated on the stack. Space for the variable will be set aside on the stack when the procedure containing the declaration is entered. The size of this area will be the size of the base class alone. The variable y, on the other hand, contains only a pointer. Space for the value pointed to by y will be allocated dynamically when a new statement is executed. Since by this time the size of a TextWindow is known, there are no problems associated with allocating an amount of storage on the heap sufficient to hold a TextWindow.

What happens when the value pointed to by y is assigned to x? That is, the user executes the statement:

```
X = *Y;
```

The space allocated to x is only as large as is necessary to accommodate a Window, whereas the value pointed to by y is larger (see Figure 11.3). Clearly, not all of the values pointed to by y can be copied. The default behavior is to copy only the corresponding fields. (In C++, the user can override the meaning of the assignment operator, and provide any semantics desired. Thus, we refer here only to the default behavior observed in the absence of any alternative provided by the user.) Thus, clearly some information is lost (namely, the information contained in the extra fields of y). Some authors use the term *slicing* for this process, as the fields of the right hand side which are not found in the left hand side are sliced off during assignment.

Is it important that this information is lost? Only if the user can tell the difference. How might the user be able to notice? The semantics of the language ensure that only methods defined in the class Window can be invoked using x, rather than any methods defined in TextWindow. Methods defined in Window and implemented in that class cannot access or modify data defined in subclasses, so

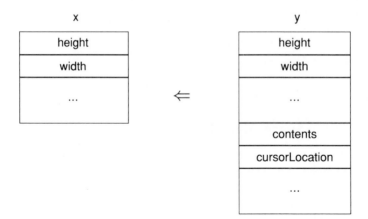

Figure 11.3   Assigning a larger value to a smaller box.

no access is possible there. But what about methods defined in class Window, but *overridden* in the subclass? Consider, for example, the procedures oops() shown in Figure 11.4. If the user executed x.oops() and the method from class TextWindow was selected, an attempt would be made to display the data value x.cursorLocation, which does not exist in x. This either would cause a memory violation or (more likely) would produce garbage.

The solution to this dilemma is to change the rules that are used to bind a procedure to the invocation of a virtual method. For objects allocated on the stack at procedure entry time, the binding for a call on a virtual procedure is taken from the static class (the class of the declaration) and not from the dynamic class (the class of the actual value).

More precisely, during the process of assignment the value is *changed* from the type representing the subclass to a value of the type represented by the parent class. This is analogous to the way an integer variable might be changed during the process of assignment to a real variable. Thus, it is possible to ensure that, for stack-based variables, the dynamic class is *always* the same as the static class. Given this rule, it is not possible for a procedure to access fields that are


```
void Window::oops()
{
  printf("Window oops");
}
void TextWindow::oops()
{
  printf("TextWindow oops %d", cursorLocation);
}
```

Figure 11.4   A possible memory protection violation.

not physically present in the object. The method selected in the call x.oops() would be that found in class **Window**, and the user would not notice the fact that memory was lost during the assignment.

This solution is produced, however, only at the expense of introducing a subtle inconsistency. Expressions involving pointers bind virtual methods in the manner that we have described in earlier chapters. Thus, these values will perform differently from those involving nondynamic values. Consider the following:

```
Window X;

TextWindow *Y, *Z;

. . .

Y = new TextWindow;

X = *Y;

Z = Y;

X.oops();

(*Z).oops();
```

Although the user is likely to think that x and the value pointed to by z are the same, it is important to remember that the assignment to x has transformed the type of the value. Because of this change, the first call on **oops()** will invoke the method found in class **Window** whereas the second will invoke that of TextWindow.

Maximum Static Space Allocation

A different solution to the problem of deciding how much space to allocate to a declaration for an object would be to assign the maximum amount of space used by any value the variable might possibly hold, whether from the class named in the declaration or from any possible subclass. This approach is similar to that used in laying out overlayed types in conventional languages, such as variant records in Pascal or union structures in C. On assignment, it would not be possible to assign a value larger than would fit in the target destination, so the picture shown in Figure 11.3 cannot occur, and the subsequent problems described in the last section do not arise. This would seem, indeed, to be an ideal solution were it not for one small problem: The size of any object cannot be known until an entire program has been seen. Not simply a module (unit in Object Pascal, File in C++), but rather the entire program, must be scanned before the size of any object can be determined. Because this requirement is so restrictive, no object-oriented language uses this approach.

```
type
  intBuffer : object
    value : integer;
    end;
var
  x, y : intBuffer;
begin
  new(x);
  x.value := 5;
  writeln(x.value);
  y := x;
  y.value := 7;
  writeln(x.value);
end;
```

Figure 11.5   A integer buffer class in Object Pascal.

Dynamic Memory Allocation

The third approach does not store the *value* of objects on the stack at all. When space for an identifier is allocated on the stack at the beginning of a procedure, the space is simply large enough for a pointer. The values are maintained in a separate data area, the heap, that is not subject to the first-in last-out allocation protocol of the stack. Since pointers all have a constant fixed size, no problem arises when a value from a subclass is assigned to a variable declared to be from a superclass.

This is the approach used in Object Pascal, Smalltalk and Objective-C. The user might have already guessed this fact by the close similarity of objects and pointers in the Object Pascal language. For both pointers and objects, it is necessary to invoke the standard procedure new to allocate space before the object can be manipulated. Similarly, it is necessary for the user to call free explicitly to release space allocated for the object.

Besides requiring explicit user memory allocation, another problem that occurs with this technique is that it is often tied to the use of *pointer semantics* for assignment.[1] When pointer semantics are used, the value transferred in an assignment statement is simply the pointer value, rather than the value indicated by the pointer. Consider the program shown in Figure 11.5, which implements a one-word buffer that can be set and retrieved by the user. Notice the two variables x and y declared to be instances of this class. In executing the program, the user might be surprised when the last statement prints out the value 7, rather than the value 5.

---

[1] But see Exercise 4.

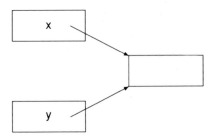

Figure 11.6 Two object variables pointing to the same value.

The reason for this surprising result is that x and y do not simply have the same value; they point to the same object. This situation is shown in Figure 11.6. The use of pointer semantics for objects in Object Pascal is particularly confusing since the alternative, *copy semantics*, is used for all other data types. If x and y were structures, for example, the assignment of y to x would result in the copying of information from y to x. Since two separate copies would thus be created, changes to y would not be reflected in changes in x.

11.2 ASSIGNMENT

Since both the memory-allocation strategies used in C++ and in Object Pascal have an effect on the meaning of assignment, we will summarize the exact meaning of assignment in the various languages we are considering.

As we noted in the last section, there are two different interpretations we can give to assignment:

Copy semantics. Assignment copies the entire value of the right side, assigning it to the left side. Thereafter, the two values are independent, and changes in one are not reflected in changes in the other.

Pointer semantics. Assignment changes the reference of the left side to be the right side. (This approach is sometimes referred to as *pointer assignment*). Thus, the two variables not only have the same value, but also refer to the same object. Changes in one will alter the value, which will be reflected in references obtained under either name.

Generally, if pointer semantics are used, languages provide some means for producing a true copy. It is also generally the case that pointer semantics are more often used when all objects are allocated on a heap (dynamically), rather than on the stack (automatically). When pointer semantics are used, it is common for a value to outlive the context in which it is created.

Object-oriented languages differ in which of the two semantics they use, providing one, the other, or combinations of both.

```
String& String::operator =(String& right)
{
  len = right.len; // copy the length
  s = right.s; // copy the pointer to values
  return (*this);
}
```

Figure 11.7 Overloading assignment for strings in C++.

Assignment in C++

The default algorithm used in C++ to assign a class value to a variable is to copy corresponding data fields recursively. It is, however, possible to overload the assignment operator (=) to produce any behavior desired. This technique, in fact, is so common that some C++ translators will issue a warning if the default assignment rule is used.

When assignment overloading is used, the interpretation is that the operator = is a method in the class of the left-hand side, with argument from the right-hand side. The result can be void if embedded assignments are not possible, although more typically the result is a reference to the left-hand side.[2] Figure 11.7 gives an example showing assignment of a string datatype, which redefines assignment so that two copies of the same string will share characters. (Note that assigning to a class object will *not* automatically invoke any constructors that may be defined for the class.)

A common source of confusion for new C++ programmers is the fact that the same symbol is used for assignment and for initialization. In conventional C, an assignment used in a declaration statement was simply a syntactic shorthand. That is, the effect of

```
int limit = 300;
```

was the same as:

```
int limit;

limit = 300;
```

In C++ an assignment used in a declaration may select the constructors invoked. That is, using the class declarations shown in Figure 4.3 (page 66), a statement such as:

```
Complex x = 4;
```

is interpreted to mean the same as the declaration:

```
Complex x(4);
```

---

[2]We can most easily permit multiple assignments by returning the value of the pointer this, as shown in Figure 11.7. We will return to a discussion of the variable this in Chapter 13.

Initialization is often used with reference variables, and yields a situation very similar to pointer semantics. If s is a valid String, for example, the following makes t an alias for the value of s, so that any change in one will be reflected in the other. As we have noted, declarations in C++ can be inserted into a program at any point.

```
... // use of variable s

String& t = s;

... // t and s now refer to the same value
```

As we will see in the case study to be presented in Chapter 17, reference variables are most often used to implement call-by-reference parameter passing. This use can be considered as a form of pointer assignment, where the parameter is being assigned the argument value. Of course pointer semantics in C++ can also be achieved through the use of pointer variables.

Parameter passing in general can be viewed in part as a form of assignment (the assignment of the parameter values to the arguments), and hence it is not surprising that the same issues occur as in assignment. For example, consider the definitions shown in Figure 11.8. Both the functions f and g take as argument a value declared as the base type, but g declares the value as a reference type. If f is called with a value of a derived type, the value is converted (*sliced*) to create a value of the base type as part of the assignment of the arguments. Thus if see is invoked from within f the virtual function from the base class will be used. On the other hand, this conversion, or slicing, does not occur as part of the parameter passing to g. Thus if see is invoked from within g the procedure from the derived class will be used. This difference in interpretation, which depends upon only the one character in the function header, is sometimes known as the *slicing problem*.

The overloading of the assignment symbol in C++, and the variety of parameter passing mechanisms provided by value and reference assignment, are powerful features, but they can also be quite subtle. For example, the assignment symbol used in initialization, although it is the same symbol as the assignment symbol used in statements, is not altered by a redefinition of the assignment operator. A good explanation of the uses and power of assignment in C++ is given by [Koenig 89b].

Assignment in Object Pascal

Object Pascal uses pointer semantics for assignment of objects. There is no system-supplied mechanism for producing a copy of an object. A common programming practice is to create a no-argument method copy, which yields a copy of the receiver, if this functionality is desired.

Notice that pointer semantics are used only for objects. All other types, such as arrays and records, use copy semantics for assignment. This is often confusing to the novice programmer.

```
class Base {
public:
  virtual void see();
};

class Derived {
public:
  virtual void see();
};

void f (Base);
void g (Base &);

Derived z;
f(z); g(z);
```

Figure 11.8   The slicing problem.

Assignment in Smalltalk

Smalltalk uses pointer semantics for assignment. The class Object, which is a superclass of all classes, implements two methods for copying objects; thus, copy assignment can be performed using a combination of assignment and message passing. The statement

```
X <- Y copy
```

creates a new instance just like y, in which the fields (instance variables) point to objects that are shared with the instance variables of the receiver. In contrast, the statement

```
x <- y deepCopy
```

creates a new instance just like y, in which the fields (instance variables) are initialized with copies of the fields of y.

That is, a copy (also called a shallowCopy) shares instance variables with the original, whereas a deepCopy also copies the instance variables. If y is an object that has three instance variables — named a, b, and c, for example — a copy (or shallowCopy) of y would look like this:

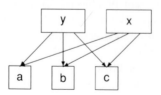

On the other hand, a deepCopy would create new copies of the instance variables, yielding a picture like this:

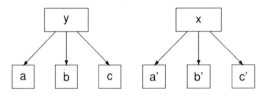

The instance variables are themselves created using the method copy. Classes are free to override any of the methods copy, shallowCopy, or deepCopy; so instances of some classes may exhibit different behavior.

Assignment in Objective-C

Objective-C uses pointer semantics for assignment of objects. A copy of an object can be obtained using any of the three methods copy, shallowCopy, or deepCopy, which are analogous to the methods used in Smalltalk.

```
id x, y, z;

\\ ... some definition of y

x = [ y copy ];

z = [ y deepCopy ];
```

11.3 EQUALITY

Like assignment, the process of deciding whether one object is equivalent to another is more subtle than might at first appear. In part, the difficulty in determining what exactly is meant by equality is a reflection of similar confusions in spoken English. If a speaker asks "Is the morning star the evening star?" for example, the answer can legitimately be given as either yes or no. If we take the view that the comparison being requested is between the actual objects denoted by the two terms (that is, the planet Venus in both cases), then the answer is clearly yes. On the other hand, we can imagine, for example, someone just learning the language who wishes to discover whether the term "the morning star" refers to the object that appears in the evening sky. The answer in this case is just as clearly no.

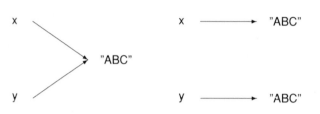

Figure 11.9   Identity and equality for character strings.

If the latter explanation seems too far-fetched, we might be tempted to assert that equality is always based on the objects being denoted. Consider, then, a speaker asking "Is the king of France a unicorn?" Are we to try to form the actual objects being denoted and then ask whether they are the same? Since neither object exists, are they both the same unknown? Is the answer to the question yes or no?

The study of reference, meaning, and equality in language is complex, and we will not here pursue it further. The interested reader might wish to explore the episode of the white knight in [Carroll 60], or some of the collected papers in [Rosenberg 71, Whorf 56]. Fortunately, equality in programming languages is usually a well-defined concept, if not a consistent concept among languages.

The most obvious dichotomy would mirror the distinction between the pointer semantics and copy semantics in assignment. Many languages use *pointer equivalence.* Two references to objects are considered pointer equivalent if they point to the same object. If we consider "the morning star" to be a pointer to Venus, then "the morning star" is equivalent to "the evening star" under this interpretation. This form of equivalence is also sometimes known as object *identity.*

Often, a programmer is interested not so much in whether two variables point to the identical object, as in whether the two objects possess the same value. This is the sense usually desired in comparing character strings, for example (Figure 11.9). But how is equality of value to be determined? For numbers or character strings, the mechanism is usually *bit-wise equality.* Two objects are equivalent in this interpretation if their bit representations in memory are the same.

For composite objects, such as records in Pascal, bit-wise equality may not be sufficient. Often, the memory layout for such values can possess empty space, or padding, which is not related to the values held by the object. Such padding should not be considered in determination of equality. Thus, a second mechanism, *member equality,* is used. In member equality, we test corresponding members for equality, recursively applying the rule until nonrecord members are found, where bit-wise equality is then applied. If all members agree, then two records are considered equal. If any disagree, then the two records are unequal. Such a relation is sometimes known as *structural equivalence.*

```
function Card.equal( aCard : Card ) : boolean;
begin
  if (suitValue = aCard.suit) and
     (rankValue = aCard.rank) then
    equal := true
  else
    equal := false
end;
```

Figure 11.10 A method testing equivalence of two cards.

Object-oriented programming techniques add their own twist to the struc-tural-equivalence test. As we have seen, instances of a subclass can possess fields not found in parent classes. If the interpretation of the test "x = y" is based on only the fields found in x, then it can happen (if x and y are instances of different classes), that "x = y" is true but "y = x" is false!

There is one sense in which the problem of equality is easier to solve than are the corresponding difficulties with assignment. Although assignment is usually considered part of the syntax and semantics of a language, and may not be changeable, the programmer is always free to provide her own methods (perhaps using slightly different syntax) for equality testing. Thus, there is no single consistent meaning for equality, and equality can mean something different for every class of objects.

Equality in Objective-C and Object Pascal

In both the languages Objective-C and Object Pascal, objects are always (or almost always, for Objective-C) represented internally by pointers. Thus, it is not surprising that the default meaning of the equality operator (= in Object Pascal, == in Objective-C) is identity, or pointer equality. Two object variables will test equal only if they point to exactly the same object.

Although it is not possible in either language to override the meaning of the built-in operator, it is common to define methods that provide alternative definitions of equality. Figure 11.10, for example, illustrates an equality test as a method in class Card (from Figure 3.7, page 44). Two cards are considered equal, in this case, if they have the same suit and rank, even if they are not the identical card.

Equality in Smalltalk

The Smalltalk programming language distinguishes between object identity and object equality. Object identity is tested using the operator formed as two equal signs (==). Object equality is tested using a single equal sign (=), and is considered to be a message passed to the left-side argument. The default

```
class A {
public:
  int i;
  A(int x) { i = x; }

  int operator== (A& x)
    { return i == x.i; }

};

class B : public A {
public:
  int j;
  B(int x, int y) : A(x) { j = y; }

  int operator== (B& x)
    { return (i == x.i) && (j == x.j); }
};
```

Figure 11.11   Overloading the equality operator in C++.

meaning of this message is the same as the identity operator; however, any class is free to redefine the symbol arbitrarily. The class Array, for example, defines equality to hold when the right-hand argument is an array of the same size, and corresponding elements are equal.

The fact that equality can be redefined arbitrarily means that there are no guarantees that equality will always be symmetric, or that the meaning of "x = y" will be related in any way to the meaning of "y = x."

Equality in C++

The language C++ provides no default meaning for equality. Classes can each provide their own meaning by overloading the == operator. The same rules are used to disambiguate overloaded operators as are used with other overloaded functions (see Section 5.3). For example, consider the class definitions shown in Figure 11.11. If a and b are instances of classes A and B, respectively, then both a == b and b == a will use the method found in class A, whereas b == b will use the method found in class B.

11.4   TYPE CONVERSION

In statically typed object-oriented languages, such as C++ and Object Pascal, it is not legal to assign a value from a class to a variable declared as an instance of a subclass. A value that is known (to the compiler) only as an instance of class Window cannot be assigned to a variable declared to be of class TextWindow.

```
class Link {
protected:
  Link *link;

  Link *  next ();
  void    setLink (Link *ele);
};

inline void Link::setLink(Link *ele) { link = ele; }

inline Link * Link::next() { return link; }
```

Figure 11.12 The class Link in C++.

The reasons for this restriction are perhaps already clear to you; we explore them in Exercises 1 and 2.

Nevertheless, there are rare occasions when it is desirable to break this rule. Most often, this situation occurs when the programmer knows, from further information, that a value, despite being maintained in a variable of some superclass, is in reality an instance of a more specific class. In these circumstances, it is possible (although not encouraged) to circumvent the type system.

In C++ and Objective-C, we accomplish this circumvention using the C construct called the *cast*. The cast directs the compiler to convert a value from one type to another. Most often, this technique is used with pointers, in which case no physical transformation takes place — only a logical one.

As an illustration, suppose that, instead of making each instance of Card maintain a linked-list pointer, we had instead written a generalized Link class, as in Figure 11.12. The class Card could then be made a subclass of Link. Since the method setLink is inherited from the superclass, it need not be repeated. There is a problem, however, with the inherited method next. The method next claims to return a pointer to an instance of Link, and not a Card. We know for a fact, however, that the object is actually a Card, since that is the only kind of object we are inserting into the list. We therefore rewrite the Card class to override the method next, and use a cast to change the return type (Figure 11.13). Notice that the method next is *not* declared to be virtual. It is not possible to alter the return type of a virtual procedure. It is important to remember that, in C++, this cast is legal only with pointers, and not with objects themselves (See Exercise 2). Also, C++ does not carry complete run-time information about the type of objects. Thus, an erroneous use of such forms may cause complete havoc.

In Object Pascal, the idea is similar. Since all objects in Object Pascal are treated internally as pointers, this conversion can be applied to any type of object, and not simply to pointers. Since Object Pascal permits a run-time test

```
class Card : public Link
{
  ...
  public:
  ...
  Card *  next ();
  ...
};

inline Card * Card::next ()
        { return (Card *) Link::next (); }
```

Figure 11.13   The class Card as a subclass of Link.

for the class of an object (Section 7.3), all such "questionable" coercions should
be screened by an explicit test prior to the assignment.

```
var
  x : TextWindow;
  y : Window;


begin
  ...
  if Member(y,TextWindow) then
    x := TextWindow(y)
  else
    writeln('illegal window assignment');
  ...
end;
```

Exercises

1. Explain why, in statically typed object-oriented languages (such as C++ and Object
   Pascal), it is not legal to assign a value from a class to a variable declared as an
   instance of a subclass. That is, something like the following will result in a compiler
   error message:

   ```
   TextWindow X;
   Window Y;
   
   ...
   
   X = Y;
   ```

2. Assume that the C++ memory-allocation technique operates in the manner described in Section 11.1. Explain what problems can arise if the user attempts to circumvent the problem of Exercise 1 using a cast. That is, writes the assignment as

   ```
   x = (TextWindow) Y;
   ```

3. Give an example, in either Object Pascal or C++, to illustrate why an entire program, and not simply a file, must be parsed before the size of any object can be determined using the approach of Section 11.1.

4. Show that it would be possible to define a language similar to Object Pascal that did not use pointer semantics for assignment. That is, give an algorithm for assignment for a language that uses the approach to memory management described in Section 11.1. but that does not result in two variables pointing to the same location when one is assigned to the other. Why do you think the designers of Object Pascal did not implement assignment using your approach?

12
Multiple Inheritance

In the discussion up to this point, we have assumed that a class will inherit from only one parent class. Although this situation is certainly common, there are nevertheless occasions where concepts are heir to two or more independent backgrounds. If you think of classes as corresponding to categories, as in Chapter 1, and you were to try to describe yourself in terms of the groups to which you belong, it is most likely you would encounter many nonoverlapping classifications. The author of this book is a parent, for example, as well as a professor, a male and a North American. Not one of these categories is a proper subset of any other.

Remember *Beth* the Potter from Figure 1.2 (page 7). Her neighbor, *Margaret*, is also an artist, a portrait painter. But the sort of painting Margaret does is different from that of *Paul*, who is a HousePainter (Figure 12.1). Although we normally view single inheritance as a form of specialization (a Potter is an Artist), it is more common to view multiple inheritance as a process of *combination* (a PortraitPainter is an Artist *as well as* a Painter).

12.1 INCOMPARABLE COMPLEX NUMBERS

A more concrete example will illustrate the difficulties resulting from having only a single inheritance hierarchy. In Smalltalk, the class Magnitude defines a protocol for objects that have measure — that is, that can be compared with one another. Individual characters (instances of class Char) can be compared if we use the underlying representation (for example, ASCII) as a basis for measure. A more common class of objects that can be compared is that of numbers, these objects are instances of the class Number in Smalltalk. In addition to being measurable, instances of class Number support arithmetic operations, such as addition and multiplication. These operations do not make sense for objects of class Char. There are various types of numbers supported by Smalltalk;

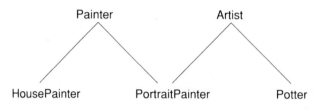

Figure 12.1   Inheritance as a form of combination.

examples include the classes Integer, Fraction, and Float. The class hierarchy was shown earlier in Figure 6.7 (page 97).

Now suppose we would like to add the class Complex, representing the complex-number abstraction. The arithmetic operations are certainly well defined for complex numbers, and it would be preferable to make the class Complex a subclass of Number; so that, for example, mixed-mode arithmetic would be provided automatically. The difficulty is that comparison between two complex numbers is at best an ambiguously defined concept. That is, complex numbers are simply not measurable.

Thus, we have the following constraints:

- The class Char should be a subclass of Magnitude, but not of Number.
- The class Integer should be a subclass of both Magnitude and Number.
- The class Complex should be a subclass of Number, but not of Magnitude.

It is not possible to satisfy all of these requirements in a single inheritance hierarchy. There are several alternative solutions to this problem:

1. Redefine the methods relating to measure in class Complex so as to produce error messages if they are invoked. This is subtyping for limitation, as described in Chapter 6. Although not elegant, this solution is sometimes the most expedient one if your programming language does not support multiple inheritance.

2. Avoid the use of inheritance altogether. Redefine every method in each of the classes Char, Integer, Complex, and so on. This solution is sometimes called *flattening the inheritance tree*. Of course, it eliminates all the benefits of inheritance described in Chapter 6 — for example, code reuse and guaranteed interfaces. In a statically typed language, such as C++ or Object Pascal, it also prevents the creation of polymorphic objects; for example, it is not possible to create a variable that can hold an arbitrary measurable object, or an arbitrary type of number.

3. Use part of the inheritance hierarchy, and simulate the rest. For example place all numbers under class Number, but have each measurable object (whether character or number) implement the comparison operations.

4. Make the two classes Magnitude and Number independent of each other, and thus require the class Integer to use inheritance to derive properties

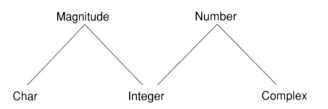

Figure 12.2   A multiple inheritance hierarchy for complex numbers.

from *both* of the parents. (See Figure 12.2. The class Float would similarly inherit from both Number and Magnitude.)

An important point to note about options 2 and 3 is that they are much more attractive in a dynamically typed programming language, such as Objective-C or Smalltalk. In a language such as C++ or Object Pascal, the definition of which types are "measurable" might be phrased in terms of classes; an object is "measurable" if it can be assigned to a variable declared to be of class Magnitude. In Smalltalk and Objective-C, on the other hand, an object is measurable if it understands the messages relating to measure, regardless of where in the class hierarchy it is defined. Thus techniques such as double-dispatching (Chapter 8) can be used to make complex numbers interact with other values even if they share no common ancestor classes.

A class that inherits from two or more parent classes is said to exhibit *multiple inheritance*. Multiple inheritance is a powerful and useful feature in a language, but also brings with it many subtle and difficult problems for the language implementor. Of the languages we are considering, only C++ supports multiple inheritance; although some research versions of Smalltalk also permit the feature. In this chapter, we will explore some of the advantages of, and some of the problems involved in, the use of this facility.

12.2   WALKING MENUS

A second example will illustrate many of the issues to keep in mind when you are considering the use of multiple inheritance. This example is inspired by the library for creating graphical user interfaces associated with an object-oriented language called Eiffel [Meyer 88a, Meyer 88b]. In this system, menus are described by a class Menu. Instances of Menu maintain features such as the number of menu entries, a list of menu items, and so on. The functionality associated with a menu includes the ability to be displayed on a graphical screen, and to select a menu item (Figure 12.3).

Each item in the menu is represented by an instance of class MenuItem. Instances of MenuItem maintain their text, their parent menu, and the command to be executed when the menu item is selected (Figure 12.4).

Menu
_____

display – *Draw entire menu.*
hilight – *Highlight current selection, un-
highlight previous selection.*
select – *Execute current menu item.*

Figure 12.3 A CRC card for class Menu.

A common facility in graphical user interfaces is what is known as a *walking menu*. A walking menu (sometimes called in other systems a *cascaded menu*) is needed when the menu item has several alternative parts. For example, a menu item in a terminal-emulator program might simply indicate "set options." When that item is selected, a second menu, the walking menu, is displayed and permits the user to select from a number of different available options (visual bell, audio bell, dark background, light background, and so on).

The walking menu is clearly a Menu. It maintains the same information as a Menu and it must perform as does a Menu. On the other hand, it is also clearly a MenuItem; it must maintain a name and the ability to execute (by displaying itself) when the associated entry is selected on the parent menu. Important behavior can be obtained with little effort by allowing the class WalkingMenu to inherit from both parents. For example, when the walking menu is asked to execute its associated action (inherited from class MenuItem), it will in turn display its entire menu (by executing the drawing method inherited from class Menu).

As with the use of single inheritance, the important property to remember when using multiple inheritance is the *is-a* relationship. In this case, multiple inheritance is appropriate because it is clearly the case that both the assertions "A walking menu *is-a* menu" and "A walking menu *is-a* menu item" make sense. When the *is-a* relationship is not satisfied, multiple inheritance can be misused. For example, it would not be appropriate to describe a class Automobile as a subclass of the two classes Motor and Body, or the class ApplePie as a subclass of the classes Pie and Apple. Clearly, an ApplePie *is-a* Pie, but it is not true that it is an Apple.

---

text – *Return title text.*
execute – *Execute   associated   action*
(overridden in subclasses).

Figure 12.4   A CRC card for class MenuItem.

When multiple inheritance is properly used, a subtle but nevertheless important change in the view of inheritance takes place. The *is-a* interpretation of inheritance, used in single inheritance, views a subclass as a more specialized form of another category, represented by the parent class. When multiple inheritance is used, a class is viewed as a *combination* or collection of several different components, each providing a different protocol and some basic behavior, which is then specialized to the case at hand.

A common example involves facilities for storing and retrieving objects from a permanent depository, such as a disk. Often, this facility is implemented as part of a behavior associated with a specific class, say Persistence or Storable. To add this ability to an arbitrary class, we can merely add the class Storable to the list of ancestors of the class.

Of course, it is important to distinguish being heir to independent backgrounds from being built out of independent components, as the example of an Automobile and a Motor illustrates.

12.3   NAME AMBIGUITY

A frequent difficulty cited in connection with multiple inheritance is that of names being used to mean multiple different operations. To illustrate this, we consider once more a programmer developing a card-game simulation. Suppose that there exists already a data abstraction CardDeck that provides the functionality associated with a deck of cards (such as shuffling, and being able to draw a single card from the deck), but has no graphical capabilities. Suppose further that another set of existing classes implements graphical objects. (We will develop such a class in Chapter 16.) Graphical objects maintain a location on a two-dimensional display surface. In addition, graphical objects must all know how to display themselves by means of the virtual method called draw.

The programmer decides that, to achieve maximum leverage from these two existing classes, he will have the class for the new abstraction, GraphicalDeck, inherit from both the classes CardDeck and GraphicalObject. It is clear that, conceptually, the class GraphicalDeck *is-a* CardDeck, and is thus logically descendant from that class, and also that a GraphicalDeck *is-a* GraphicalObject. The only trouble is the clash between the two meanings of the command draw.

As Meyer points out [Meyer 88b], the problem is clearly with the child, and not with the parent classes. The meaning of draw is unambiguous and meaningful in each of the parent classes when taken in isolation. The "problem" is with the combination. Since the problem arises only in the child class, the solution should also be found in that class. In this case, the child class must decide how to disambiguate the overloaded term.

The solution usually involves a combination of *renaming* and *redefinition*. By *redefinition* we mean a change in the operation of a command, as happens when a virtual method is overridden in a subclass. By *renaming* we simply mean changing the name by which a method is invoked, without altering the functionality of the command. In the case of our graphical deck of playing cards, the programmer might choose to have draw mean the process of drawing the graphical image, and to rename the process of removing a card from the deck drawCard.

Inheritance from Common Ancestors

A more difficult problem occurs if a programmer wishes to use two classes that both inherit from a common parent class. Suppose, for example, a programmer is developing a set of classes that implements the idea of *streams* for input and output. A stream is a generalization of a file, except that its elements can have more structure. We can have a stream of integers, for example, or a stream of reals. The class InStream provides a protocol for input streams. A user can open an input stream by attaching it to a file, retrieve the next element in the stream, and so on. The class OutStream provides similar functionality for output streams. Both classes inherit from a single parent class Stream. The information that points to the actual underlying file is maintained in the parent class.

Now suppose the user wants to create a combined input–output stream. It makes sense to claim that an input–output stream is a descendant of both an input stream and an output stream. Renaming, such as we described in the last section, can be used to resolve the meaning of any functions defined in both InStream and OutStream. But what about features inherited from the common grandparent? The difficulty is that the inheritance tree becomes a directed graph, rather than a

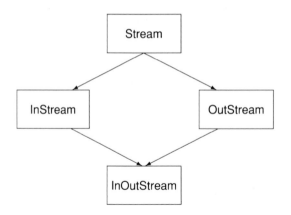

Figure 12.5 An inheritance graph.

simple tree (Figure 12.5). If all that is inherited from the common parent class is behavior (methods), then the resolution technique described previously can be used. If the parent class also defines data fields, such as a file pointer, then there are two choices. Do we want to have two copies of the data values, or only one copy? A similar problem occurs if the grandparent class uses constructors, or other initialization routines that should be invoked only once. In the next section, we will describe how this problem is handled in C++.

12.4 MULTIPLE INHERITANCE IN C++

We will illustrate the use of multiple inheritance in C++ by working through a small example. Suppose, in a previous project, a programmer has developed a set of classes for working with linked lists (Figure 12.6). The abstraction has been divided into two parts; the class Link represents the individual links in the list, and the class LinkedList stores the head of the list. The basic functionality associated with linked lists involves adding a new element. Borrowing a technique from functional programming, linked lists also provide the ability to execute a function on each element of the list, where the function is passed as an argument. Both of these activities are supported by associated routines in the class Link.

We form specialized types of links by subclassing class Link. For example, in Figure 12.7, the class IntegerLink is used to maintain integer values associated with each link. Figure 12.7 also gives a short program illustrating how this data abstraction is used.

Now suppose that, in the current project, this same programmer must develop a Tree datatype. After pondering this a while, our programmer discovers that a Tree can be thought of as a collection of linked lists. At each level of the tree, the link fields are used to point to siblings (trees that are all at the same level). However, each node also points to a linked list that represents its

```
class LinkedList {
public:
  Link *elements;

  LinkedList()
    { elements = (Link *) 0; }

  void add(Link *n)
    { if (elements) elements->add(n); else elements = n; }

  void onEachDo(void f(Link *))
    { if (elements) elements->onEachDo(f); }
};

class Link {
public:
  Link *next;

  Link()
    { next = (Link *) 0; }

  void setLink(Link *n)
    { next = n; }

  void add(Link *n)
    { if (next) next->add(n); else setLink(n); }

  void onEachDo(void f(Link *))
    { f(this); if (next) next->onEachDo(f); }
};
```

Figure 12.6   Classes to implement linked lists.

children. Figure 12.8 illustrates this design, where angled arrows are used to indicate child pointers, and horizontal arrows indicate sibling connections.

Thus, a node in the tree is both a LinkedList (because it maintains a pointer to its list of children) and a Link (because it maintains a pointer to its sibling). We indicate multiple inheritance, such as this, in C++ by simply listing the names of the superclasses, separated by commas, following the colon in the class description. As with single inheritance, each superclass must be preceded by a visibility keyword, either public or private. Figure 12.9 shows the class Tree inheriting in a public fashion from both Link and LinkedList. In addition to maintaining pointers to the children, nodes in a tree will also contain an integer value.

Now the problem of name ambiguity must be handled. The first problem involves the meaning of the function add. The ambiguity in the name is actually a reflection of the ambiguity in meaning. There are two senses to the add operation on tree; one is to add a child node; the other to add a sibling node.

```
class IntegerLink: public Link {
  int value;
public:
  IntegerLink(int i)  : Link()
    { value = i; }

  print()
    { printf("%d\n", value); }
};

void display(IntegerLink *x)
  { x->print(); }

main() {
  LinkedList list;

  list.add(new IntegerLink(3));
  list.add(new IntegerLink(17));
  list.add(new IntegerLink(32));

  list.onEachDo(display);
}
```

Figure 12.7   Specializing the Link class.

The first sense is that provided by the add operation in class LinkedList; the second is provided by the add function in class Link. After some reflection, our programmer decides to let add mean "add a child", but to provide two new functions as well that specifically name the intent.

Notice that all three of these functions are, in a sense, merely renamings. They provide no new functionality, but merely redirect the execution to a previously defined function. Some object-oriented languages (such as Eiffel) allow the user to specify such renamings without creating a new function.

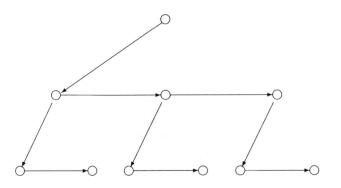

Figure 12.8   A tree viewed as linked lists.

```
class Tree: public Link, public LinkedList {
  int value;

public:
  Tree(int i)
    { value = i; }

  print()
    { printf("%d\n", value); }

  void add(Tree *n)
    { LinkedList::add(n); }

  void addChild(Tree *n)
    { LinkedList::add(n); }

  void addSibling(Tree *n)
    { Link::add(n); }

  void onEachDo(void f(Link *))
    { /* first process children */
      if (elements) elements->onEachDo(f);
      /* then operate on self */
      f(this);
      /* then do the siblings */
      if (next) next->onEachDo(f); }
};

main() {
  Tree *t = new Tree(17);
  t->add(new Tree(12));
  t->addSibling(new Tree(25));
  t->addChild(new Tree(15));

  t->onEachDo(display);
}
```

Figure 12.9   An example of multiple inheritance.

The ambiguity of the method onEachDo is more complex. Here, the appropriate action would be to execute a traversal of the tree, such as a preorder traversal. In a preorder traversal, the child nodes are visited first, followed by the current node, followed by the sibling nodes (which will, of course, recursively visit *their* children). Thus, execution is a *combination* of the actions provided by the underlying classes Link and LinkedList, as is shown in Figure 12.9.

Renaming is occasionally necessary due to a subtle interaction in C++ between the mechanisms of inheritance and parametric overloading. When an overloaded name is used in C++, the inheritance mechanism is first used to find

```
class A {
  public:

  void virtual display(int i)
    { printf("in A %d\n", i); }
};

class B {
public:
  void virtual display(double d)
    { printf("in B %g\n", d); }
};

class C: public B, public A
{
public:
  void virtual display(int i)
    { A::display(i); }

  void virtual display(double d)
    { B::display(d); }
};

main() {
  C c;
  c.display(13);
  c.display(3.14);
}
```

Figure 12.10   Inheritance and overloading interacting.

a name scope in which the function is defined. Parameter types are then used to disambiguate the function name *within that scope*. For example, suppose there are two classes A and B that both define a method display, but that take different arguments (Figure 12.10). The user might be tempted to believe that, because the two uses of display can be disambiguated by their parameter types, a child class can inherit from both parents and have access to both methods. Unfortunately, mere inheritance is not sufficient. When the user calls the method display with an integer argument, the compiler cannot decide whether to use the function in class A (which matches the argument more closely), or that in class B (which is the first method encountered in the method search, and which is applicable by performing an automatic conversion on the parameter value). Fortunately, the compiler *will* warn about this; however, the warning is produced at the point the ambiguous method is invoked, not at the point the class is declared.

The solution is to redefine both methods in the child class C, as shown in Figure 12.10. By doing so, we eliminate the contention between inheritance

```
class Stream {
  File *fid;
  ...
  };

class InStream : public virtual Stream {
  ...
  int open(File *);
  };

class OutStream : public virtual Stream {
  ...
  int open(File *);
  };

class InOutStream: public InStream, public OutStream {
  ...
  };
```

Figure 12.11   An example of virtual inheritance.

and overloading; both end up examining the class C, where it is clear to the compiler that the parametric overloading is indeed intentional.

In an earlier section we described a difficult problem that occurs when a class inherits from two parent classes both of which in turn inherit from a common grandparent class. This problem was illustrated with two classes InStream and OutStream, which both inherited from a common class Stream. If we want the derived class to inherit only one copy of the data fields defined in Stream, then the intermediate classes (InStream and OutStream) must declare that their inheritance from the common parent class is virtual. The virtual keyword indicates that the superclass may appear multiple times in descendant classes of the current class, but that only one copy of the superclass should be included. Figure 12.11 shows the declarations for the four classes.

An unfortunate consequence of the C++ approach is that, as Meyer points out, the name confusion is a problem only for the child class; nevertheless, the solution (making the common ancestor virtual) involves changes to the parent classes. It is the intermediate parent classes that give the virtual designation, rather than the final combined class.

Occasionally (but rarely), it *is* desirable to create two copies of the inherited data fields. For example, graphical objects and card decks might each be maintained on linked lists, by each being subclassed from the class Link. Since the two types of links are independent, they should both be maintained in the combined class GraphicalDeck. In this situation, the virtual keywords are omitted, and the desired outcome will be obtained. It is important to ensure, however, that the resulting name conflicts do not cause erroneous interpretations.

```
class D {
public:
  D() { ... }
  D(int i) { ... }
  D(double  d) { ... }
};

class A : virtual D {
public:

  A() : D(7)  { ... }
};

class B : virtual D {
public:
  B() : D(3.14) { ... }
};

class C: public A, public B
{
public:
  C() : B(),A() { ... }
};
```

Figure 12.12 Constructors in multiple inheritance.

The fact that visibility keywords can be attached to parent classes independently means that it is possible for a virtual ancestor class to be inherited
in different ways — for example, as both public and protected. In this case,
the lesser level of protection (for example, protected) is ignored, and the more
general category used.

When more than one parent class defines a constructor, the order of execution of the various constructors, and hence initialization of their data fields,
may be important. The user can control this by invoking the constructors for
the base classes directly in the constructor for the child class. For example,
in Figure 12.12, the user explicitly directs that, when an instance of class C is
initialized, the constructor for B is to be invoked first, before the constructor
for A. Reversing the order of the invocations of the constructor in the class C
would have the effect of reversing the order of initialization.

An exception to this rule occurs with virtual base classes. A virtual base
class is always initialized once, before any other initialization takes place, using
the constructor (provided by the system, if not by the user), which takes no
arguments. Thus, in Figure 12.12 the order of initialization when a new element
of type C is constructed will be first class D using the no-argument constructor,
then class B, then class A. The two seeming calls on the constructor for class D

that appear in the constructors for classes A and B in actual fact have no effect, since the parent class is marked as virtual.

If it is imperative that arguments for the virtual base class be provided with the constructor, it is legal for class C to provide these values, even though D is not an immediate ancestor for C (this is the only situation in which it is legal for a class to provide a constructor for another class that is not an immediate ancestor). That is, the constructor for class C could have been written as follows:

```
C() : D(12), B(), A() {...}
```

Constructors for virtual base classes must be invoked first, before the constructors for nonvirtual ancestors.

Virtual methods defined in virtual superclasses can also cause trouble. Suppose, for example, that each of the four classes shown in Figure 12.11 defines a method named initialize(). This method is defined as virtual in class Stream, and redefined in each of the other three. The initialize methods in InStream and OutStream each invoke Stream::initialize and in addition do some subclass-specific initialization.

Now consider the method InOutStream. It cannot call both the methods InStream::initialize and OutStream::initialize without invoking the method Stream::initialize twice. The repeated invocation of Stream::initialize may have unintended effects. The only ways to avoid this problem is to rewrite Stream::initialize such that it detects whether it has been initialized yet, or to redefine the methods in the subclasses InStream and OutStream such that they avoid the invocation of the method from class Stream. In the latter case, the class InOutStream must then invoke the initialization procedures explicitly for each of the three other classes.

Exercises

1. Cite two examples of multiple inheritance in real life (non–computer-associated) situations.

2. In [Wiener 89], a "practical example of multiple inheritance in C++" is described. The example defines a class IntegerArray, which inherits from the two classes Array and Integer. Do you think this example is a good use of multiple inheritance? Explain your answer.

3. Modify the Tree class definition such that it can be used as a binary tree. Provide facilities to retrieve or change the left or right child of any node. What assumptions do you need to make?

4. Extend your work in the previous question so as to implement a binary search tree. A binary search tree maintains a list of integers with the property that, at every node, the values in the left subtree are less than or equal to the value associated with the node, whereas the values stored in the right subtree are larger than the node value.

5. Discuss the concept of virtual inheritance in C++ from the point of view in Parnas' principles on information hiding (page 12).

6. Assume that Smalltalk allows multiple inheritance (some of the more recent systems do) and redesign the collection hierarchy examined in Chapter 14 to make use of this feature.

C H A P T E R

13
Polymorphism

The term *polymorphic* is from the Greek, and means roughly "many forms" (poly = many, morphos = form).[1] Thus, in biology, a polymorphic species is a species, such as Homo Sapiens, that is characterized by the occurrence of different forms or color types in individual organisms or among organisms. In chemistry, a polymorphic compound is one that can crystalize in at least two distinct forms (such as carbon, which can crystalize both as graphite and as diamonds).

In programming languages, a polymorphic object is any entity, such as a variable or function argument, that is permitted to hold values of differing types during the course of execution. Polymorphic functions are functions that have polymorphic arguments. Such functions are, of course, relatively easy to write in dynamically typed languages, such as Lisp or Scheme in the functional paradigm, or Smalltalk in the object-oriented paradigm. Figure 13.1 shows a Smalltalk method, called silly, which takes an argument x and returns the value x + 1 if x is an integer, the reciprocal of the value if x is a fraction, the reversal if x is a string, and the special value nil otherwise.

Polymorphism can also occur in more strongly typed languages. The most common form of polymorphism in conventional programming languages is *overloading*, such as the overloading of the + symbol to mean both integer and real addition. We will discuss this form of polymorphism in Section 13.2. Recent functional languages, such as ML [Milner 90], permit a style of strongly typed polymorphism called *parametric polymorphism*. In this style, a parameter can be characterized only partially, such as a "list of T," where T is left undefined. This permits list operations to be performed on the value, while permitting such functions to be applied to lists of different types.

One way to view polymorphism is in terms of high-level and low-level abstractions. A low-level abstraction is a basic operation, such as an operation

---

[1] You may recall the story of Morpheus, son of Sommus the god of sleep in Greek mythology. Morpheus could assume the form of any human being he wished.

```
silly: x
 " a silly polymorphic method "
 (x isKindOf: Integer) ifTrue: [ ↑ x + 1 ].
 (x isKindOf: Fraction) ifTrue: [ ↑ x reciprocal ].
 (x isKindOf: String) ifTrue: [ ↑ x reversed ].
 ↑ nil
```

Figure 13.1   A polymorphic function in Smalltalk.

on a data structure, that is built on top of only a few underlying mechanisms. A high-level abstraction is a more general plan, such as a sorting algorithm or the description of an operating system, that gives the general approach to be followed but does not specify the details.

Algorithms are usually described in a high-level fashion; whereas an actual implementation of a particular algorithm must be a high-level abstraction that is built on top of a specific low-level data structure. A simple example, a high-level recursive algorithm to compute the length of the list might be as follows:

```
function length(list) -> integer;

  if link is nil

    then return 1

  else

    return 1 + length(link)

end
```

An actual implementation in a conventional language, such as Pascal, would require exact type specifications not only for that portion of the data being manipulated here (the link fields) but also for everything else. Thus, the algorithm shown in Figure 13.2 could be used to compute the length of a linked list of integer values, but not to compute the length of a linked list of reals. The example provided on page 88 similarly made the distinction between a high-level abstraction, which provides the framework for an algorithm but no essential details, and a low-level abstraction, which provides the details needed for execution.

Most programs will consist of both high-level and low-level abstractions. A programmer familiar with the precepts of structured programming and data abstraction will more or less automatically recognize low-level abstractions and will design a software system, such as a new data structure, in a manner that is independent of a particular application. Thus, low-level abstractions become like tools, in that they can be carried from one project to another. In a conventional language, a high level abstraction, on the other hand, must be grounded in specific types of data structures. Therefore, it is difficult to carry a high-level abstraction from one project to another in anything more than an algorithmic sense. Thus, high-level abstractions, for even such simple tasks as computing the length of a list or searching a table for a specific value, therefore tend to be

```
type
  intlist : record
  value : integer;
  link :  ^ intlist;
  end;

function length(x :  ^ intlist) : integer;
begin
  if (x^.link = nil)
    then length := 1
  else
    length := 1 + length(link);
end;
```

Figure 13.2 A length function in Pascal.

written and rewritten for each new application.

The power of polymorphism is that it permits high-level algorithms to be written once, and reused repeatedly with *different* low-level abstractions. With this change high-level algorithms become tools as well, which a programmer can collect in libraries and use repeatedly without recoding. A programmer can write a single length function, and use it for many different types of lists. This ability greatly simplifies the programming process, by raising that process to a higher conceptual level.

In object-oriented languages, polymorphism occurs as a natural result of the *is-a* relationship and of the mechanisms of message passing and inheritance. One of the great strengths of the object-oriented approach is that these devices can be combined in a variety of ways, yielding a number of techniques for code sharing and code reuse.

Pure polymorphism occurs when a single function can be applied to arguments of a variety of types. We will discuss pure polymorphism in more detail in Section 13.5. In pure polymorphism, there is one function and a number of different interpretations. The other extreme occurs when we have a number of different functions all denoted by the same name. This situation is known as *overloading*, or sometimes *ad hoc polymorphism*; we will discuss it in Section 13.2. Between these two extremes are *overriding* and *deferred methods*, which we will discuss in Sections 13.3 and 13.4, respectively.[2]

---

[2]Once again we note that there is little agreement regarding terminology in the programming-languages community. In [Horowitz 84], [Marcotty 87], [MacLennan 87] and [Pinson 88], for example, *polymorphism* is defined in a manner roughly equivalent to what we are here calling *overloading*. In [Sethi 89] and [Meyer 88a] and in the functional programming languages community (such as [Wikström 87, Milner 90]) the term is reserved for what we are calling *pure polymorphism*. Other authors use the term for one, two, or all of the mechanisms described in this chapter. Two complete, but technically daunting, analyses are [Cardelli 85] and [Danforth 88].

13.1   POLYMORPHIC OBJECTS

With the exception of overloading, polymorphism in object-oriented languages is made possible only because of the existence of *polymorphic objects*. A polymorphic object is an object with many faces; that is, it is an object that can hold values of different types.

In dynamically bound languages (such as Smalltalk and Objective-C), all objects are potentially polymorphic. Any object can hold values of any type.

In statically typed languages (C++, Object Pascal, and Objective-C when used with static declarations), the situation is slightly more complex. Polymorphism occurs in these languages through the difference between the declared (static) class of a variable and the actual (dynamic) class of the value contained in the variable. As we noted in Chapter 7, this difference is maintained within the framework of the *is-a* relationship. A variable can hold a value of the same type as that of the declared class of the variable, or of any subclasses of the declared class.

In Object Pascal, this is true for all variables declared as object type. In C++, and in Objective-C when static declarations are used, polymorphic objects occur only through the use of pointers and references. As we noted in Section 11.1, when pointers are *not* used, the dynamic class of a value is always coerced into being the same as the static class of a variable.

When pointers (or references) are used, however, the value retains its dynamic type. To illustrate this, we consider the two classes One and Two shown in Figure 13.3. Class One defines a virtual method value that yields the value 1. This method is replaced in class Two by a method that yields the value 2. Next, three functions are defined. These functions take an argument of type One, passing it by value, by pointer, and by reference. When executed using an argument of type Two, as shown, the value parameter will be converted into a value of type One, and thus will produce the result 1. The other two functions, however, define arguments that are polymorphic. In both of these cases, the value passed will retain its dynamic type, and the value printed will be 2.

13.2   OVERLOADING

We say a function name is *overloaded* if there are two or more function bodies associated with the name. Note that overloading is a necessary part of overriding, which we discussed in Chapter 6 and will mention again in the next section, but the two terms are not identical and overloading can occur without overriding.

In overloading, it is the function *name* that is polymorphic — that is, has many forms. Another way to think of overloading and polymorphism is that there is a single abstract function that takes various different types of arguments. The actual code executed depends on the arguments given. The facts that the compiler can often determine the correct function at compile time (in a strongly typed language), and can generate only a single code sequence, are simply optimizations.

```
class One {
public:
  virtual int value()
    { return 1; }
};

class Two : public One {
public:
  virtual int value()
    { return 2; }
};

void directAssign(One x)
{  printf("by assignment value is %d\n", x.value()); }

void byPointer(One * x)
{  printf("by pointer value is %d\n", x->value()); }

void byReference(One & x)
{  printf("by reference value is %d\n", x.value()); }

main() {
  Two x;

  directAssign(x);
  byPointer(&x);
  byReference(x);
}
```

Figure 13.3 Polymorphic and non–polymorphic arguments in C++.

We have already seen an example in which overloading occurred without overriding. In Chapter 1, we examined the situation where I wanted to surprise my grandmother with flowers for her birthday. One possible solution is to send the message sendFlowersTo(...) to my local florist; another is to give the *same* message to my wife. Both my florist and my wife (an instance of class Spouse) will understand the message, and both will act on it to produce a similar result. In a certain sense, I could think of sendFlowersTo(...) as being one function, which is understood by both my wife and my florist. But each uses a different algorithm to respond to my request, and there is no inheritance involved (Figure 13.4). The first common superclass for my wife and Flo is the category Human (Figure 1.2, page 7), and it is certainly not the case that the behavior sendFlowersTo() is associated with all humans. For example, my dentist, who is also a human, would not understand the message at all.

To give an example more closely tied to programming languages, suppose a programmer is developing a library of classes representing common data

```
Procedure Spouse.sendFlowersTo(anAddress : address);
begin
  go to florist;
  give florist message sendFlowersTo(anAddress);
end;

Procedure Florist.sendFlowersTo(anAddress: address);
begin
  if address is nearby then
    make up flowers
    give message sendFlowersTo(anAddress)
                                          to delivery person
  else
    look up florist near anAddress;
    phone florist;
    give other florist message sendFlowersTo(anAddress);
end;
```

Figure 13.4   Methods for sending flowers.

structures. A number of different data structures can be used to maintain a collection of elements (sets, bags, dictionaries, arrays, and priority queues, for example), and these might all define a method **add** to insert a new element into the collection.

This situation — in which two totally separate functions are used to provide semantically similar actions for different datatypes — occurs frequently in all programming languages, and not simply in object-oriented languages. Perhaps the most common example is the overloading of the addition operator +. The code generated by a compiler for an integer addition is often radically different from the code generated for a floating-point addition, yet programmers tend to think of the operations as a single entity, the "addition" function.

In this example, it is important to point out that overloading may not be the only activity taking place. A semantically separate operation, *coercion*, is also usually associated with arithmetic operations. Coercion occurs when a value of one type is converted into one of a different type. If mixed-type arithmetic is permitted, then the addition of two values may be interpreted in a number of different ways:

- There may be four different functions, corresponding to integer + integer, integer + real, real + integer, and real + real. In this case, there is overloading but no coercion.

- There may be two different functions for integer + integer and real + real. In the other two cases, the integer value is coerced by being changed to a real value. Thus, mixed-type arithmetic is a combination of overloading and coercion.

- There may be only one function, for real + real addition. All arguments are coerced to being real. In this case, there is coercion only, with no overloading.

There is nothing intrinsic to the mechanism of overloading that requires that functions associated with an overloaded name have any semantic similarity. Consider a program that plays a card game, such as the solitaire game of Chapter 10. The method draw is used to draw the image of a card on the screen. Another likely class in such a program would be a class representing the deck of cards. A reasonable method in such a class would be the method draw, which would return the next card. This draw method is not even remotely similar in semantics to the draw method for class CardView, and yet they share the same name.

Note that this overloading of a single name with independent and unrelated meanings should *not* necessarily be considered bad style, and in general will not contribute to confusion. In fact, the selection of short, clear, and meaningful names such as add, draw, and so on contributes to ease of understanding and correct use of object-oriented components. It is far simpler for the programmer to remember that you can add an element to a set, than that to do so requires invoking the addNewElement method. (Or worse, that it requires calling the routine Set_Module_Adding_Method.)

All the object-oriented languages we are considering permit this style of overloading — that is, the occurrence of methods with similar names in unrelated classes. This does not mean that functions or methods can be written that take arguments of an arbitrary nature. The statically typed nature of C++ and Object-Pascal still requires specific declarations of all names, and thus polymorphism occurs more often as a result of overriding. The list of argument types, used to disambiguate overloaded function invocations, is called the *argument signature*.

There is another style of overloading in which procedures (or functions or methods) in the same context are allowed to share a name, and are disambiguated by the number and type of arguments supplied. This is called *parametric overloading*, and occurs in the object-oriented language C++, as well as in some imperative languages (such as Ada) and many functional languages. We have already seen examples of this in the overloading of the constructor function in the class Complex in Section 5.3. C++ permits any method, function, procedure, or operator to be overloaded in this fashion, as long as the arguments are such that the selection of which routine is intended by the user can be unambiguously determined at compile time. (When automatic coercions — for example, from character to integer, or from single-precision to double-precision floating-point — can occur, the algorithm used to resolve an overloaded function name becomes quite complex. More detailed information can be found in [Lippman 89, pages 151–165], or [Ellis 90]).

The mechanism of overloading is a necessary prerequisite to the other forms of polymorphism we will consider: overriding, deferred methods, and pure polymorphism. In addition, overloading is also often useful in reducing the "conceptual space"; that is, in reducing the amount of information that must be remembered by the programmer. Often, the reduction in programmer-memory space is just as significant as the reduction in computer-memory space permitted by code sharing.

13.3   OVERRIDING

We earlier described the mechanics of overriding (refinement and replacement) in the various object-oriented languages we are considering; we will not repeat that discussion here. Recall, however, the following essential elements of the technique. In one class (typically, an abstract superclass), there is a general method defined for a particular message. The majority of subclasses of the class in which this method is defined inherit and utilize this method. In at least one subclass, however, a method with the same name is defined. This method hides access to the general method for instances of this class (or, in the case of refinement, subsumes access to the general method). Thus, we say the second method *overrides* the first.

Overriding is often transparent to the user of a class, and, as with overloading, frequently the two functions are thought of as semantically a single entity.

An interesting example of overriding occurs in the class Magnitude in the Little Smalltalk system. Magnitude is an abstract superclass used for dealing with quantities that possess at least a partial, if not a total, ordering. Numbers are perhaps the most common example of objects that have magnitude, although concepts such as time and date can also be ordered, as can characters, points in a two-dimensional coordinate plane, and words in a dictionary. Recent versions of Little Smalltalk have defined the subclasses of class Magnitude roughly as shown in Figure 13.5.[3]

The six relational operators are defined in class Magnitude as shown in Figure 13.6.[4] Note that the definitions appear to be circular, each one depending on some number of the others. It is reasonable to wonder, therefore, how an infinite loop is ever avoided if any of them are invoked. The answer is that subclasses of class Magnitude must override and redefine at least one of the six relational messages. We leave it as an exercise for you to show that, if the message = and either < or <= are redefined, then all the remaining operators can be executed without a loop being entered.

The technique of overriding a method contributes to code sharing, insofar as instances of the classes that do *not* override the method can all share one

---

[3]This is a change from Smalltalk-80 and from the original version of Little Smalltalk, in which Collection was not considered a subclass of class Magnitude (see page 97).

[4]The following points should be noted: The operator ~= represents "is not equal to" in Smalltalk; the operator == is the test for object equality, as opposed to the test for numerical equality, which is a single equal sign.

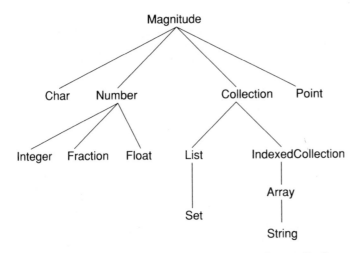

Figure 13.5 Subclasses of Magnitude in Little Smalltalk.

copy of the original. It is only in those situations where this method is not appropriate that an alternative code fragment is provided. Without the mechanism of overriding, it would be necessary for all subclasses to provide their own individual method to respond to the message, even though many of these methods were identical.

A potentially confusing aspect of overriding in C++ is the difference between overriding a virtual method and overriding a nonvirtual method. As we saw in Section 11.4, the virtual keyword is not necessary for overriding to take

```
<= arg
   ↑ self < arg or: [ self = arg ]

>= arg
   ↑ arg <= self

< arg
   ↑ self <= arg and: [ self ~= arg ]

> arg
   ↑ arg < self

= arg
   ↑ self == arg

~= arg
   ↑ (self = arg) not
```

Figure 13.6 The relational operators defined in class Magnitude.

place. However, the meaning in these two cases is very different. If the virtual keyword is removed from the methods value in Figure 13.3, the result 1 will be printed by all three functions. Without the virtual keyword, the dynamic type of a variable (even a pointer or reference variable) is ignored when a message is sent to the variable.

Even more subtle confusions may occur if a programmer tries to redefine a virtual function in a subclass, but declares (perhaps by mistake) a different argument signature. For example, the parent class might contain the declaration:

```
virtual void display (char *, int);
```

Whereas the subclass might define the method as:

```
virtual void display (char *, short);
```

This change causes the virtual overloading of the method display to become an "ordinary" (that is, a nonvirtual) redefinition of the function. When invoked as the parent type, for example, the first method would be selected, and not the second. Such errors are exceedingly subtle, since both forms are legal, and thus the compiler will never generate a warning message.

13.4   DEFERRED METHODS

A *deferred method* (sometimes called a *generic method*; in C++ called a *pure virtual method*) can be thought of as a generalization of overriding. In both cases, the behavior described in a superclass is modified by subclasses. In a deferred method, however, the behavior in the superclass is essentially null, a place holder, and *all* useful activity is defined as part of the overriding method.

One advantage of deferred methods is conceptual, in that their use allows the programmer to think of an activity as associated with an abstraction at a level higher than may actually be the case. For example, in a collection of classes representing geometric shapes, we could define a method to draw the shape in each of the subclasses Circle, Square, and Triangle. We could have defined a similar method in the superclass Shape. Such a method could not, in actuality, produce any useful behavior, since the superclass Shape does not have sufficient information to draw the shape in question. Nevertheless, the mere presence of this method would permit the user to associate the concept *draw* with the single class Shape, and not with the three separate concepts Square, Triangle and Circle.

There is a second, more practical reason for using deferred methods. In statically typed object-oriented languages, such as C++ and Object Pascal, a programmer is permitted to send a message to an object only if the compiler can determine that there is, in fact, a corresponding method that will match the message selector. Suppose the programmer wishes to define a variable of class Shape that will, at various times, contain instances of each of the different

```
class Shape {
  public:
    Point corner; // upper left corner;
    void setCorner(Point &p) { corner = p; }
    void virtual draw() = 0;
};

class Circle : public Shape {
  public:
    int radius;
    void setRadius(int i) { radius = i; }
    void draw() { drawCircle(corner + radius, radius); }
};
```

Figure 13.7   A deferred method (pure virtual method) in C++.

shapes. Such an assignment is possible, since a variable declared to be of a class can always contain instances of subclasses of that class. Nevertheless, the compiler would permit the message draw to be used with this variable only if it could ensure that the message will be understood by any value that may be associated with the variable. Assigning a method to the class Shape effectively provides this assurance, since this method cannot be invoked unless it is overridden by the subclass of the value in the variable. This is true even though the method in class Shape will never actually be executed.

Deferred Methods in C++

In C++, a deferred method (called a *pure virtual method*) must be declared explicitly, using the virtual keyword described in an earlier chapter. The body of a deferred method is not given; instead, the value 0 is assigned to the function, as shown in Figure 13.7. It is not possible to instantiate a class that contains a pure virtual method that has not been overridden without producing a compiler warning. The redefinition of pure virtual methods must be handled by an immediate subclass. Strictly speaking it is not legal, although some compilers will permit it, for a pure virtual method to be ignored by an immediate subclass and redefined further down in the class hierarchy.

Deferred Methods in Object Pascal

In Object Pascal, the indication that a method is overriding another method in an ancestor class is placed on the description of the method in the subclass — not, as in C++, in the superclass. This indication is performed by placing the keyword override after the description of the overriding method. The language does not distinguish a deferred method from any other overridden method, but

```
type
  Shape = object
    corner : Point;
    procedure setCorner(p : Point);
    procedure draw();
  end;

  Circle = object(Shape)
    radius : integer;
    procedure setRadius(i : integer);
    procedure draw(); override;
  end;

procedure Shape.draw();
begin
  writeln('descendant should define draw');
  halt();
end;
```

Figure 13.8   A deferred method in Object Pascal.

often a deferred method simply produces an error message. Figure 13.8 shows a
rewrite of the class description from Figure 13.7, illustrating the use of deferred
functions.

Deferred Methods in Objective-C

No special indication is needed to describe a deferred method in Objective-C.
Nevertheless, to aid in the creation of such methods, a message subclassRe-
sponsibility is defined in class Object (and therefore is accessible to all objects).
The method draw for class Shape can be written, for example, as shown in
Figure 13.9. When executed, the method subclassResponsibility places an error
notifier on the user's screen.

Deferred Methods in Smalltalk

The Smalltalk-80 language does not have any concept of a deferred method.
However, as in Objective-C, the method subclassResponsibility, defined in class
Object, can be used to simplify the task of writing methods that have the effect

```
@implementation Shape : Object
...
- draw { return [ self subclassResponsibility ]; }
...
@end
```

Figure 13.9   A deferred method in Objective-C.

```
draw

    " child classes should override this"
    ↑ self subclassResponsibility
```

Figure 13.10 A deferred method in Smalltalk.

of deferred methods. An example is shown in Figure 13.10, which illustrates the method for draw from the class Shape.

13.5 POLYMORPHISM

Many authors reserve the term *polymorphism* for situations where one function can be used with a variety of arguments, as opposed to overloading where there are multiple functions all defined with a single name.[5] Such facilities are not restricted to object-oriented languages. In Lisp or ML, for example, it is easy to write functions that manipulate lists of arbitrary elements; such functions are polymorphic, since the type of the argument is not known at the time the function is defined. The ability to form polymorphic functions is one of the most powerful techniques in object-oriented programming. It permits code to be written once, at a high level of abstraction, and to be tailored as necessary to fit a variety of situations. Usually, the programmer accomplishes this tailoring by sending further messages to the receiver for the method. Often, these subsequent messages are not associated with the class at the level of the polymorphic method, but rather are virtual methods defined in the lower classes.

An example will help us to illustrate this concept. As we noted in the section on overriding in this chapter, the class Magnitude in Smalltalk is an abstract superclass used for dealing with quantities that possess at least a partial, if not a total, ordering. Consider the method called between:and: shown in Figure 13.11. This method occurs in the class Magnitude, and presumably (according to the comment) tests whether the receiver is between two endpoints. It does this test by sending the message <= (remember, in Smalltalk all operators are treated as messages) to the lower bound with the receiver as argument, and to the receiver with the upper bound as argument. Only if both of these expressions yield true does the method determine that the receiver is between the two endpoints.

After this message has been sent to an object with a pair of arguments, what happens next depends on the particular meaning given to the message <=. This message, although defined in class Magnitude (see Figure 13.6),

---

[5] Although the extreme cases may be easy to recognize, discovering the line that separates overloading from polymorphism can be difficult. In both C++ and ML a programmer can define a number of functions, each having the same name, which take different arguments. Is it overloading in C++ because the various functions sharing the same name are not defined in one location, whereas in ML-style polymorphism they must all be bundled together under a single heading?

```
between: low   and: high
```

```
" test to see if the receiver is between two endpoints "
↑ (low <= self) and: [ self <= high ]
```

Figure 13.11   The method between:and: in class Magnitude.

is overridden in many of the subclasses. For integer values, the meaning is that of integer comparison; thus, between:and: can be used to test whether an integer value is between two other integer values. Floating-point values define $<$ similarly, with similar results. For mixed integer and floating-point values, the results depend on how conversions are performed, a topic we discussed in Chapter 8.

For characters, the relation $<=$ is defined in terms of the underlying ASCII collating sequence; and thus, between:and: tests whether a character is between two other characters. To see whether a variable x contains a lower-case letter, for example, we can used the following expression ($a is the token used to denote the literal character "a" in Smalltalk):

```
x between: $a and: $z
```

For Points, the relation $<=$ is defined as being true if the receiver is above and to the left of the argument. (That is, both the first and second components of the point are less than or equal to their corresponding part in the other point). Point objects are a basic datatype in Smalltalk; numbers respond to the @ operator by constructing a Point with their own value as the first coordinate and the argument as the second coordinate. Note that the definition of $<$ for points provides only a partial order, as not all points are thereby commensurate. Nevertheless, the expression

```
x between: 2@4 and: 12@14
```

is true if x is in the box defined by the points 2,4 in the upper-left and 12,14 in the lower-right corner.

For the class Set, the $<=$ relation is defined as subset.[6] A set is less than or equal to another set provided all elements of the first set appear in the second. So the set containing the three elements $\{1,2,4\}$ is between the sets $\{1,4\}$ and $\{1,2,4,7\}$.

For arrays, and in particular, for strings (a subclass of Array) — the relations are defined in terms of lexicographic (or dictionary) order. Two arrays are compared element-wise, with the first difference defining the relation; if no dif-

---

[6]The use of the operator $<=$ in sets is only found in versions 2 and 3 of Little Smalltalk.

ferences are found, the shorter array is smaller. Thus, the following expression would yield the value true:

```
'carbon' between: 'carbolic' and: 'carbonate'
```

The important point to realize is that, in all of these cases, there is only *one* method being used for between:and:. This method is polymorphic; it works with a number of different argument types. In each case, the redefinition of the messages involved in the polymorphic routine (in this case, the message <=) is used to tailor the code to specific circumstances.

13.6   EFFICIENCY AND POLYMORPHISM

An essential point to note is that programming always involves compromises. In particular, programming with polymorphism involves compromises between ease of development and use, readability, and efficiency. In large part, a concern for efficiency is an issue we have already considered and dismissed; however, it would be dishonest for us not to admit that there is an issue, however slight. A function, such as the between:and: method described in the last section, that does not know the type of its arguments can seldom be as efficient as a function that has more complete information. A relational test may correspond to only a few assembly-language instructions if the arguments are integer, whereas much more extensive operations are necessary if the arguments are points or sets.

Exercises

1. Do you think the value **nil** in Pascal, or the value NULL in C, should be considered polymorphic objects? Explain your answer.

2. Other than the arithmetic operations, what operations are typically overloaded in conventional languages such as Pascal or C?

3. By tracing the sequence of method invocations, show that overriding the = operator and either the < operator or the <= operator, causes all the six relational operations in Figure 13.6 to become defined. From the point of view of efficiency, is it better to override < or <=?

4. Suppose that in Smalltalk we have two classes Apple and Orange, subclasses of class Fruit. Show the minimal amount of code we would need to be able to compare apples to oranges.

5. Let One and Two be the classes defined in Figure 13.3. Describe what the output will be of the following sequence of statements, and explain why these results are produced. How will the results change if the virtual keyword is removed from the method value?

```
Two x;

One &a = x;

One *b;

One c;


b = &x;

c = x;


printf("values %d %d %d\n", a.value(),

                           b->value(), c.value());
```

14
Case Study:
Smalltalk Collections

The Collection hierarchy in Smalltalk defines the basic data structures used to maintain groups of objects. These correspond to the intrinsic data structures provided by more conventional languages, such as the **array** and **record** types in Pascal. The implementation of the collection classes in Smalltalk makes extensive use of polymorphism, and thus provides an excellent case study in that topic. In Chapter 17, we will describe similar data structures implemented in C++.

The basic data structures that can be manipulated by the user in Smalltalk programs include the following:

Array Similar to an array in a conventional language, an Array has a fixed size, and associates elements with integer keys in the range from 1 to the size of the array. An Array is ordered by the ascending key values. Although the keys in an array must be integer, the element values can be arbitrary objects, and need not all be the same type.

Bag A Bag is an unordered collection of values. The collection is accessed by value. There are no keys associated with values in a Bag. The values can be arbitrary objects, and can be repeated multiple times.

ByteArray A ByteArray is an array in which the element values are restricted to being integers in the range 0 to 255. Since the value can therefore be represented in a machine byte, there is an efficient memory layout for instances of this class. This datatype is used extensively by the system internally; it is used less frequently by users.

Dictionary A Dictionary is a generalization of the concept of an array. Like an Array, a Dictionary is a collection of key–value pairs. However, unlike an Array, the collection is unordered, and the key values can be arbitrary objects.

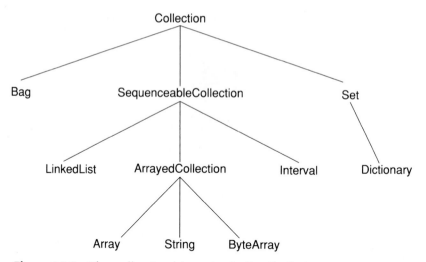

Figure 14.1   The collection hierarchy in Smalltalk-80.

Interval An Interval is an ordered collection of values representing an arithmetic
    sequence. Such an object can be characterized by the starting and ending
    values and the step size between elements of the interval. The step size can
    be positive or negative.

List A List is an ordered, nonindexed collection of arbitrary values. Elements
    can be added to either end of a list.

Set A Set is an unordered collection of values, similar to a Bag. Unlike a Bag,
    a value cannot appear twice in a Set.

String A String represents an ordered collection of characters. It is considered
    an indexed collection, where the index value is the position of the character
    in the string.

Given only this basic description of the classes we would like to implement, there is still a wide range of possible ways to structure an inheritance
hierarchy in an actual implementation. To illustrate this range, we show the
inheritance hierarchy used by the collection classes in the Smalltalk-80 system
(Figure 14.1), in the first version of the Little Smalltalk system, the version
described in [Budd 87] (Figure 14.2), and in the latest release (version 3) of the
system (Figure 14.3). The latter system will be the version we explore in this
chapter.[1]

---

[1]The later versions of Little Smalltalk have eliminated the Bag datatype, using in its place the
datatype List. The only distinction between a Bag and a List is that the former is unordered,
whereas the latter is not. Note also that, in line with its name, there has been a trend toward
simplification in the Little Smalltalk system.

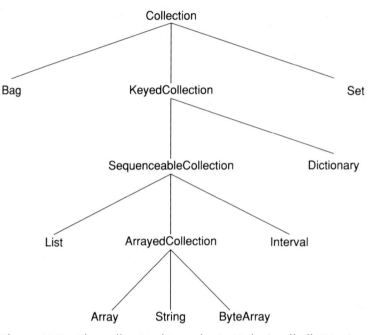

Figure 14.2   The collection hierarchy in Little Smalltalk (Version 1).

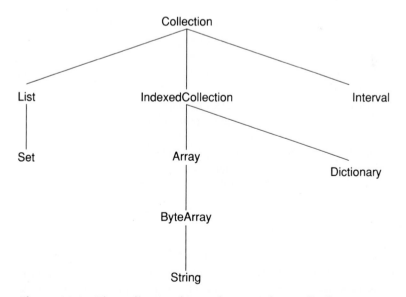

Figure 14.3   The collection hierarchy in Little Smalltalk (Version 3).

14.1 IMPLEMENTATION APPROACHES

In part, the diversity of the implementation techniques that have been used in defining the collection classes derives from the wide variety of uses of inheritance we outlined in Chapter 6. An emphasis on efficiency for a particular data structure will lead to one style of organization, an emphasis on clear conceptual design will lead to another, and a concern for code size or ease of implementation yet a third.

In particular, the various ways of structuring the collection classes contrast graphically the process of subclassing for the purposes of construction and subclassing for the purposes of specification or specialization. In Smalltalk-80, for example, a dictionary is implemented as a set of association (key–value) pairs, and is therefore made a subclass of class Set. From the point of view of specification or specialization, however, there is no relationship between the two *concepts* of set and dictionary. A similar relationship exists between the classes Set and List in the Little Smalltalk system. In the exercises we will explore the advantages and disadvantages of some of the alternative ways in which the collection hierarchy can be structured. We here provide only a short general idea of the approach used in defining the collection classes that we will describe.

The classes Array, ByteArray, and String are primitive classes. Most of the operations in these classes depend on underlying system support, in the form of calls on primitive operations. These primitive operations are in essence the building blocks on which all other structures are built.

An Interval needs internally to maintain only the information necessary to generate the elements on demand. These are represented by the instance variables lower, upper, and step. Values are generated as required.

A Dictionary is implemented using a hash table with chaining. All objects in the Smalltalk system respond to the message hash with an integer hash value. An instance variable in the class Dictionary holds the array that maintains the actual table. Entries in the table are divided into triples. The first triple contains a key, the second contains a value, and the third contains the bucket for overflow entries. The bucket consists of a series of objects from class Link. Each Link object maintains a key–value pair, and a pointer to the next Link.

A List is similarly implemented as a collection of Link values. Only the value fields are used when links appear in a List.

A Set is implemented as a special type of List, which checks to ensure that an element is not already present in the collection before inserting a new value.

14.2 OPERATIONS

The basic operations that are performed by the collection data structures include adding and removing elements, determining the size of the collection, querying about the presence or absence of elements, and iterating over the elements. These are provided by a common set of messages, as shown in Table 14.1. As

	Col	Index	Array	Str	Dict	Intv	List	Set
at:		•						
add:							•	•
at:		•						
at:ifAbsent:		•			•		•	
at:put:			•		•			
binaryDo:			•		•			
do:	•		•			•	•	
includes:	•							
includesKey:		•	•					
isEmpty	•							
occurrencesOf:	•							
printString	•			•				
reject:	•							
select:	•	•						
size	•		•	•				
sort	•							

Table 14.1   Classes implementing methods in the collection hierarchy.

we noted at the beginning of this chapter, extensive use of polymorphism permits a considerable reduction in the amount of actual code that must be provided. Table 14.1 shows which methods are implemented by every class; other classes obtain their functionality by inheriting the methods from superclasses. The sparsity of this table indicates graphically the reduction in code size permitted through the use of polymorphic methods.

Loops and Iteration

We start our exploration of the collection classes with the method used to iterate over the elements of a collection. We do this because, paradoxically, almost all the other operations are ultimately defined in terms of this activity. The basic method used for this purpose is do:. The method do: takes a one-parameter block as an argument, and executes this block for each element of the collection, passing the element as an argument to the block. The method is not implemented in class Collection, but must be implemented by every subclass of class Collection.

The class Interval is perhaps the easiest example to understand. As we have noted already, an interval is characterized by a lower and an upper bound and a step size, maintained internally by the instance variables lower, upper and step. The method do: is therefore defined as follows:

```
do: aBlock      | current |

  current <- lower.
```

```
(step > 0)

  ifTrue: [ [ current <= upper ] whileTrue:

    [ aBlock value: current.

      current ← current + step ] ]

  ifFalse: [ [ current >= upper ] whileTrue:

    [ aBlock value: current.

      current ← current + step ] ]
```

The method uses a while loop, generating each value from the arithmetic progression in turn. Given that numbers will respond to the message to:by: by constructing an interval, the equivalent of a Pascal **for** loop is therefore written in Smalltalk as follows:

```
(1 to: 20 by: 2) do: [:x | (x + y ) print ]
```

In class Array, the method do: is implemented in terms of intervals and the ability to determine the size of the array (which we will discuss shortly):

```
do: aBlock

  (1 to: self size) do:

    [:i | aBlock value: (self at: i) ]
```

A List implements the method do: by passing on the message to the links. As the class Link implements only the more general message binaryDo:, which takes a two-parameter block, a new block is constructed which ignores the first parameter:

```
do: aBlock

  (links notNil)

    ifTrue: [ links binaryDo: [:x :y | aBlock value: y]]
```

Finally, the abstract superclass IndexedCollection similarly implements the message do: in terms of binaryDo:

```
do: aBlock

  self binaryDo: [:i :x | aBlock value: x ]
```

The method binaryDo: makes sense only for indexed classes, subclasses of IndexedCollection. It is implemented in class Array as follows:

```
binaryDo: aBlock

  (1 to: self size) do:

    [:i | aBlock value: i value: (self at: i) ]
```

it is implemented in class Dictionary as follows:

```
binaryDo: aBlock
    (1 to: hashTable size by: 3) do:
      [:i | (hashTable at: i) notNil
        ifTrue: [ aBlock value: (hashTable at: i)
            value: (hashTable at: i+1) ].
          (hashTable at: i+2) notNil
      ifTrue: [ (hashTable at: i+2)
            binaryDo: aBlock ] ]
```

Injection

A common operation on collections is to reduce the collection to a single value. Taking the sum of an array of integer values is an example, as is concatenating a sequence of strings. In Smalltalk, this reduction is generalized by the method inject:into:. This method takes an initial scalar value and a two-argument block. It performs the block on each element of the collection, passing as arguments to the block the current running value (the first argument initially) and the current element. The result of the block is used for the next evaluation of the block, or is returned as the result when the elements are exhausted. For example, the sum of an array called weights might be computed using the expression

```
weights inject: 0 into: [:x :y | x + y]
```

The method inject:into: is implemented only once, in the class Collection. It is thereby, however, available by inheritance in all subclasses.

```
inject: thisValue  into: binaryBlock      | last |
    last <- thisValue.
    self do: [:x | last ← binaryBlock
    value: last value: x].
    ↑ last
```

Notice that this one method will work regardless of which of the many versions of the do: method is invoked.

Computing the Number of Elements

The computation of the size of (number of elements in) a collection is a good illustration of the use of the method inject:into:. The method size is implemented in the class Collection as follows:

```
size
    ↑ self inject: 0 into: [:x :y | x + 1]
```

Although, in theory, this method will work for all subclasses of collection, for reasons of efficiency, the classes Array and String redefine the method size to use a primitive operation (see Exercise 2).

The method isEmpty can be used to determine whether a collection has any elements. It is defined in class Collection:

```
isEmpty
```

```
↑ self size == 0
```

Printing

Another use of inject:into: is to produce a printable representation of a collection. All objects in Smalltalk respond to the method printString with a string that represents their value. This method is implemented in class Collection as a loop that iterates over the elements, concatenating their printed values. Note that classes respond to printString with the class name.

```
printString
```

```
↑ ( self inject: self class printString , ' ('
      into: [:x :y | x , ' ' , y printString]), ' )'
```

The method is overridden in class String so that the string value surrounded by quote marks is returned.

Selection

All the elements that satisfy some criterion can be generated using the method select:, which takes as an argument a one-parameter block that should yield either a true or a false value, which indicates whether the element should be included or not. The method is defined in class Collection so as to return a list:

```
select: aBlock
```

```
↑ self inject: List new
        into: [:x :y | (aBlock value: y)
                            ifTrue: [x add: y]. x]
```

In class IndexedCollection, the select method is overridden so as to return a Dictionary which will include both the key and value elements:

```
select: aBlock
```

```
↑ self binaryInject: Dictionary new
      into: [:s :i :x | (aBlock value: x)
                            ifTrue: [ s at: i put: x ]. s ]
```

A symmetric method, reject:, yields all the elements that do not satisfy a criterion. In class Collection, this method is implemented in terms of select:, by inversion of the condition. Notice that, by doing so, only one version of reject: need be defined.

```
reject: aBlock
    ↑ self select: [:x | (aBlock value: x) not ]
```

Testing Elements

We can use the method includes: to determine whether an element is present in a collection. This method is implemented in the class Collection as follows:

```
includes: value
    self do: [:x | (x = value) ifTrue: [ ↑ true ] ].
    ↑ false
```

The number of times an element occurs in a collection can be determined by the method occurrencesOf:, defined in class Collection:

```
occurrencesOf: anObject
    ↑ self inject: 0
           into: [:x :y | (y = anObject)
               ifTrue: [x + 1]
               ifFalse: [x] ]
```

For indexed collections, it is reasonable to ask not only whether the collection includes a specific value, but also whether it includes a given key. We make this determination with the method includesKey:, which must be implemented by all subclasses of IndexedCollection. The general method implemented in class IndexedCollection produces the result by attempting to index using the value, returning false if the task is unsuccessful. This latter process is accomplished by the method at:ifAbsent:, which we will describe shortly.

```
includesKey: aKey
    " look up, but throw away result "
    self at: aKey ifAbsent: [ ↑ false ].
    ↑ true
```

In class Array, a slightly more efficient overriding asks whether the key is in the range from 1 to the size of the array:

```
includesKey: index
    ↑ index between: 1 and: self size
```

Retrieving Elements

For indexed collections, it is possible to ask for the value associated with a specific key. This query is implemented by the method at:, which is immediately redefined in class IndexedCollection in terms of a more general message we have just seen, which gives the action to perform if the key is invalid.

> **at:** aKey
>
> ↑ self at: aKey ifAbsent: [smalltalk error:
>
> 'index to at: illegal']

The method at:ifAbsent: is defined in the classes List, Dictionary, and In-dexedCollection in a general way in terms of includesKey:, which we have already seen:

> **at:** index ifAbsent: exceptionBlock
>
> ↑ (self includesKey: index)
>
> ifTrue: [self basicAt: index]
>
> ifFalse: exceptionBlock

The message basicAt: is the low-level retrieval method, used to generate a value once all the error checking has been performed. It is implemented by primitive methods.

Inserting Elements

For indexed collections, the proper way to insert elements into the collection is to use the method at:put:, which takes both a key and an element value. The method is implemented in class Dictionary to perform a hash-table insertion (overriding any previous value that may have existed under the given key), and in class Array (which checks that the key is in the range appropriate for the collection).

It is not possible to add elements to an interval. For a list, the method simply inserts the new element in the beginning, which in turn merely creates a new link node:

> **add:** aValue
>
> ↑ self addFirst: aValue

> **addFirst:** aValue
>
> links ← Link new; value: aValue; link: links

Elements can be added to either the front or the back of a list (using the methods addFirst: and addLast:), or elements can be added in an arbitrary fashion using the method add:ordered:, which takes as an argument a one-parameter block, inserting the indicated element at either the end of the list or when the preceding element in the list returns false according to the block. Using this latter method, any collection can be sorted. The result is always a list in which the elements have been ordered. The method sort (defined in class Collection) uses the standard less-than comparison for sorting, whereas the method sort: permits the user to provide an arbitrary block for comparisons.

sort

```
↑ self sort: [:x :y | x < y ]
```

sort: aBlock

```
↑ self inject: List new

   into: [:x :y | x add: y ordered: aBlock. x]
```

In class Set, the add: method is redefined so that it first checks to see whether the element is present in the set. This is the *only* method actually defined in class Set; all other behavior is inherited from superclasses!

add: value

```
(self includes: value)

   ifFalse: [ self add: value ]
```

14.3 THE YO-YO PROBLEM

The philosophy underlying object-oriented programming holds that objects should be characterized in terms of their behavior, rather than of their implementation. Ideally, then, a programmer attempting to understand a section of code written in an object-oriented style should require only descriptions of the meaning to be associated with each operation an object performs, and should not need to read the actual code that is used to implement the behavior of the object.

When a programmer is not able to understand a code unit from the description, and the programmer is forced to read the actual code for an object to understand what the object is doing, then the mechanisms of overriding and inheritance, which we have seen provide a great benefit in program *development*, suddenly become a great hindrance in program *intelligibility*.

To illustrate this problem, suppose that a team of programmers did not understand how an object of class Array in Smalltalk produces a printable representation. To find out, they start to simulate the action of message passing using the class hierarchy that includes the subclass Array. The programmers fail to find a method in that class, so they search the next class up in the class hierarchy — namely, IndexedCollection. Again, no method is found, so they

printString inject:into: do: size at: at:ifAbsent: includesKey: basicAt:

Collection

IndexedCollection

Array

Figure 14.4   The yo-yo problem illustrated.

search one level higher, looking in class Collection. Finally, a method is found — namely, the method we described in Section 14.2.

They discover that printString is implemented by the message inject:into: being passed to the pseudo-variable self. Knowing that a message sent to self will start the search with the class of the receiver, the programmers again start a search for a corresponding method in the class Array, followed by a search of IndexedCollection, and finally Collection, where a method is finally discovered.

Once more, inject:into: is defined in terms of do:, but fortunately they quickly discover the method do: in the class Array. The method do: requires the message size, and there are at least two of these, but the one in class Array seems to be the correct selection. Then, there is the message at:, which is not defined in class Array.

Again, a search of the class hierarchy is performed, which yields the fact that at: is defined in class IndexedCollection in terms of at:ifAbsent:. The latter is still not found in class Array, but a method is found in the superclass. This method uses includesKey:. So they search for this method, finding it in the base class Array, defined once more in terms of the method size. Finally, they reach a call on the method basicAt:, which is defined by a primitive operation in class Array, and their search is over.

The constant movement up and down the class hierarchy provides the name for this difficulty; the *yo-yo problem* [Taenzer 89]. Figure 14.4 graphically illustrates the movement up and down the class hierarchy as our programmers attempt to discover exactly what is happening at each step of the process.

The yo-yo problem will often occur when a programmer creating a subclass replaces an existing method (perhaps inadvertently), instead of refining the method. The method in the parent class will then not be executed, and subsequent methods may fail because of actions that were not performed.

The yo-yo problem should not be construed to mean that object-oriented programs are more difficult to understand than are programs written in a non–object-oriented fashion. Indeed, quite the opposite is usually true. Object-oriented programs can be very easy to understand, but only if the behavior of every class, and the meaning of every method, is clearly specified to the reader in a manner that is independent of the actual code. It is only when the reader is reduced to examining the code to determine what is going on that the yo-yo problem arises and programs may become difficult to understand.

Another way to think about the yo-yo problem is that the necessity to document clearly the behavior of any class increases dramatically as the depth of the class hierarchy increases. It may not be too much to expect a programmer to study carefully a single class definition in order to understand a new data structure, but to require the programmer to read and understand a complex class hierarchy is requiring her to perform a task that is considerably more difficult than we would expect from the mere increase in code size.

In short, object-oriented programming techniques not only *permit* the programmer to think in higher-level abstractions, but they should *force* the code reader to do so as well.

Exercises

1. Show that it is not necessary for the class Array to implement the method do:. (Hint: Consider how do: is implemented in class IndexedCollection.) What would be the difference in performance if the method were eliminated? Is the increase in code size worth the improved performance?

2. Show that, for the message do: to work in class Array, the method size that is inherited from class Collection must be overridden.

3. Show that, if the class Array did not override the method includesKey:, then attempts to use the method at:ifAbsent: would result in infinite loops.

4. Consider the *is-a* relationship. From a purely conceptual point of view, argue whether it makes more sense to say that a Bag *is-a* Set (it is a set that allows elements to be repeated) or that a Set *is-a* Bag (it is a bag in which each element is permitted to appear only once). Next, consider the two implementations that would result from these two views. Which view makes more sense in terms of the implementation?

5. Develop code for a class representing a binary tree. Implement methods to insert a node into the tree, and to delete a node from the tree, as well as the message do: which iterates over all other elements of the tree. Where in the Collection hierarchy have you placed your class? What inherited methods can you then use with your class?

6. The following are various ways in which the basic data structures could have been implemented. For each, discuss whether the change makes sense from a conceptual point of view and from an implementation point of view.

   a) A Dictionary can be considered a subclass of class Set, where the elements are key–value pairs. (This is how a dictionary is implemented in Smalltalk-80).

   b) An Array can be considered a subclass of Dictionary, in which the key values are restricted to being integers.

   c) A Dictionary can remain where it is in the class hierarchy, but maintain an instance variable that is a Set of key–value pairs.

   d) A Bag can be implemented as a subclass of Dictionary, where the key is the element in the set and the value is the number of times that the element occurs.

15
Visibility and
Dependency

In Chapter 1, we identified the interconnected nature of software created in a conventional fashion as a major obstacle in the realization of the goal of developing reusable software components. This fact has long been recognized in the software engineering community, where there is a large body of literature that deals with various ways of characterizing the nature of connections, and with rules for avoiding harmful connections [Gillett 82, Fairley 85]. In this chapter, we will explore some of these issues in the context of object-oriented programming.

We can express interconnections in terms of visibility and dependency. The term *visibility* is used to describe a characterization of *names* — the handles by which objects are accessed. An object is visible in a certain context if the name of the object is legal and denotes the object. A related term frequently used to describe visibility is the *scope* of an identifier.

Visibility is related to connectedness in the sense that, if it is possible to control and reduce the visibility of names for an identifier, then we can more easily characterize how the identifier is being used. In Smalltalk, for example, instance variables have their visibility restricted to methods; they cannot be accessed directly except within a method. This does not mean that such values cannot be accessed or modified outside of the class; all such uses, however, must be mediated by at least one method. In Object Pascal, on the other hand, instance variables are visible wherever a class name is known. Thus, the language provides no mechanisms to ensure that instance variables are modified only by methods; instead, we must rely on the appropriate conduct of users.

The concept of *dependency* is used to relate one portion of a software system to another. If a software system (such as a class, or a module) cannot exist in any meaningful way without another system, then the first system is said to be dependent on the second. A child class is almost always dependent on its parent, for example. Dependencies can also be much more subtle, as we will discover in the next section.

15.1   COUPLING AND COHESION

The concepts of *coupling* and *cohesion* were introduced by Stevens, Constantine, and Myers [Stevens 81] as a framework for evaluating effective use of modules. We will discuss the idea with regards to a language supporting modules, and then will describe the counterparts of these ideas in an object-oriented language.

Coupling describes the relationships between modules, and *cohesion* describes the relationships within a module. A reduction in interconnectedness between modules (or classes) is therefore achieved via a reduction in coupling. On the other hand, modules (or classes) that are well designed should have some purpose; all the elements should be associated with a single task. Therefore, in a good design, the elements within a module (or class) should have internal cohesion.

Varieties of Coupling

Coupling between modules can arise for different reasons, some of which are more acceptable, or desirable, than are others. A ranked list might look something like the following:[1]

- Internal data coupling

- Global data coupling

- Control (or sequence) coupling

- Parameter coupling

- Subclass coupling

Internal data coupling occurs when one module (or class) is allowed to modify the local data values (instance variables) in another module (class). This sort of activity makes understanding and reasoning about programs difficult, and should be avoided whenever possible. In Section 15.2, we will explore one heuristic used to reduce internal data coupling in object-oriented systems.

Global data coupling occurs when two or more modules (classes) are bound together by their reliance on common global data structures. Again, this situation frequently complicates the understanding of modules taken in isolation, but is sometimes unavoidable.

---

[1]This list is adapted from the presentation by Fairley [Fairley 85], although he does not discuss subclass coupling, and other terms have been changed slightly to make them more language independent.

In an object-oriented framework, an alternative to global data coupling that is frequently possible is to make a new class that is charged with "managing" the data values, and to route all access to the global values through this manager. (This approach is similar to our use of access functions to shield direct access to local data within an object.) The technique reduces global data coupling to parameter coupling, which is easier to understand and control.

Control or sequence coupling occurs when one module must perform operations in a certain fixed order, but the order is controlled by another module. A database system might go through the stages, in order, of performing initialization, reading current records, updating records, deleting records, and generating reports; however, each stage would be invoked by a different routine, and the sequencing of the calls could be dependent upon code in a different module. The presence of control coupling indicates that the designer of a module was following a lower level of abstraction than was necessary (each of the various steps versus a single directive "process a database".) Even when control coupling is unavoidable, prudent policy usually dictates that the module being sequenced assure itself that it is being processed in the correct order, rather than relying on the proper handling of the callers.

Parameter coupling occurs when one module must invoke services and routines from another, and the only relationships are the number and type of parameters supplied and the type of value returned. This form of coupling is common, easy to see, and easy to verify statically (with tools that check parameter calls against definition, for example); therefore, it is the most benign option.

Subclass coupling is particular to object-oriented programming. It describes the relationship a class has with its parent class (or classes, in the case of multiple inheritance). Through the action of inheritance, an instance of a child class can be treated as though it were an instance of the parent class. We will see, in the case study in Chapter 16, that the use of this feature permits the development of significant software components (such as windowing systems) that are only loosely related, via subclass coupling, to other portions of an application.

Varieties of Cohesion

The internal cohesion of a module is a measure of the degree of binding of the various elements within the module. As with coupling, cohesion can be ranked on a scale of the weakest (least desirable) to the strongest (most desirable) as follows:

- Coincidental cohesion
- Logical cohesion
- Temporal cohesion
- Communication cohesion
- Sequential cohesion

- Functional cohesion

- Data cohesion

Coincidental cohesion occurs when elements of a module are grouped for no apparent reason. This grouping often is the result when someone "modularizes" a large monolithic program by arbitrarily segmenting the program into several small modules. It is usually a sign of poor design. In an object-oriented framework, we would say that coincidental cohesion occurs when a class consists of methods that are not related.

Logical cohesion occurs when there is a logical connection among the elements of the module (or methods in a class), but no actual connection in terms of either data or control. A library of mathematical functions (sine, cosine, and so on) might exhibit logical cohesion if each of the functions was implemented separately without reference to any of the others.

Temporal cohesion occurs when elements are bound together because they must all be used at approximately the same time. A module that performs program initialization is a typical example of temporal cohesion. Here, a better design probably would distribute the various initialization activities over the modules more closely charged with subsequent behavior.

Communication cohesion occurs when elements of a module, or methods in a class, are grouped because they all access the same input–output data or devices. The module or class is acting as a "manager" for the data or the device.

Sequential cohesion occurs when elements in a module are linked by the necessity to be activated in a particular sequential order. Sequential cohesion often occurs as a result of an attempt to avoid sequential coupling. Again, a better design usually can be found if the level of abstraction is raised. (Of course, if it is necessary for actions to be performed in a certain order, then this sequentiality must be expressed at some level of abstraction; but the important principle is to hide this necessity as much as possible from all other levels of abstraction.)

Function cohesion is a desirable type of binding in which the elements of a module or the methods in a class are all related to the performance of a single function.

Finally, data cohesion in a module occurs when the module defines internally a set of data values, and exports routines that manipulate the data structure. Data cohesion occurs when a module is used to implement a data abstraction.

You often can estimate the degree of cohesion within a module by writing a brief statement of the purpose for the module and examining the statement (similar to the CRC card description we used in Chapter 2). The following tests are suggested by Constantine:

1. If the sentence that describes the purpose of a module is a compound sentence containing a comma or containing more than one verb, the module is probably performing more than one function; therefore, it probably has sequential or communicational binding.

2. If the sentence contains words relating to time, such as "first," "next," "then," "after," "when," or "start," then the module probably has sequential or temporal binding. An example would be "wait for the instant teller customer to insert a card, then prompt for the personal identification number."

3. If the predicate of the sentence does not contain a single, specific object following the verb, the module is probably logically bound. For example, "Edit all data" has logical binding; "Edit source data" may have functional binding.

4. If the sentence contains words such as "Initialize" or "Clean up," the module probably has temporal binding.

Coupling and Cohesion in Object Oriented Systems

In Chapter 1, we noted that, in many ways, a class can be viewed as a logical extension of a module — as a "module in the small," as it were. Thus, design rules for modules carry over easily to design rules for objects. Objects from distinct classes should have as little coupling as possible, not only to make them more understandable, but also so that they may easily be extracted from a particular application and reused in new situations. On the other hand, each object should have some definite purpose, and each method should further that purpose in some manner. That is to say, the object must form a cohesive unit.

In the next section, we will examine a rule, specific to object-oriented systems, that, if followed, serves to reduce the degree of coupling between objects.

15.2   THE LAW OF DEMETER

Style guidelines for program coding range from the abstract, such as the directive "modules should exhibit internal cohesion and minimize external coupling", to the concrete, such as "no procedure should contain more than 60 lines of code." Concrete guidelines are easy to understand, and are easy to apply, but often lull programmers (and managers) into a false sense of security and may in fact direct attention away from the real problem. As an aid in reducing complexity, the rule banning all procedures of more than 60 lines is an approximation at best; a short procedure with complicated control flow may be much more difficult to understand and code correctly than is a far longer sequence of straight-line assignment statements.

Similarly, the fanatical attempt some people made a few years back to ban goto statements from programming languages was often misunderstood. The goto itself was merely a symptom of a disease, not the disease itself. The assertion was not that goto statements are intrinsically bad and programs that avoid them are uniformly improved, but rather was that it is more difficult to produce an easily understood program using goto statements than to do so without using them. It is the understandability of programs that is important, and not the use or nonuse of goto statements. Nevertheless, we cannot overlook the utility of a simple rule that is easy to apply and that is effective *most* of the time in achieving some desirable end, and we could ask whether any such guidelines might be developed specifically for object-oriented programs.

One such guideline has been proposed by Karl Lieberherr as part of his work on an object-oriented programming tool called Demeter; thus, the guideline is called the Law of Demeter [Lieberherr 89a, Lieberherr 89b]. There are two forms of the law, a strong form and a weak form. Both forms strive to reduce the degree of coupling between objects by limiting their interconnections.

Law of Demeter. In any method M attached to a class C, only methods defined by the following classes may be used:

1. The instance variable classes of C.
2. The argument classes of method M (including C); note that global objects or objects created inside the method M are considered arguments to M.

We can rephrase the law in terms of instances (or objects) instead of methods; we arrive at the following:

Law of Demeter (weak form). Inside a method, data can be accessed in and messages can be sent to only the following objects:

1. The arguments associated with the method being executed (including the self object),
2. Instance variables for the receiver of the method,
3. Global variables,
4. Temporary variables created inside the method.

The strong form of the law restricts access to instance variables to only those variables defined in the class in which the method appears. Access to instance variables from superclasses must be mediated through the use of accessor functions.

Law of Demeter (strong form). Inside a method it is only permitted to access or send messages to the following objects:

1. The arguments associated with the method being executed (including the self object),
2. Instance variables defined in the class containing the method being executed,
3. Global variables,
4. Temporary variables created inside the method.

It is instructive to consider what forms of access are ruled out by the law of Demeter, and to relate the law back to the concepts of coupling and cohesion described in the last section. The major style of access eliminated by programs that satisfy the rule is the direct manipulation of instance variables in another class. Permitting access in this form creates a situation where one object is dependent on the internal representation of another, a form of internal data coupling. On the other hand, satisfaction of this rule means that classes generally can be studied and understood in isolation from one another, since they interact only in simple, well-defined ways.

Allen Wirfs-Brock and Brian Wilkerson go even further than the Law of Demeter [Wirfs-Brock 89a], and argue that even references to instance variables from within a method always should be mediated by accessor functions. Their argument is that direct references to variables severely limit the ability of programmers to refine existing classes.

15.3 ACTIVE VALUES

An active value [Stefik 86], is a variable for which we want to perform some action each time the value of the variable changes. The construction of an active-value system illustrates why parameter coupling is preferable to other forms of coupling, particularly in object-oriented languages.

Suppose there exists a simulation of a nuclear power plant, which includes a class Reactor that maintains various pieces of information about the state of the reactor. Among these values is the temperature of the heat mediator — the water that surrounds the cooling rods. Further, suppose that the modification of this value has been designed so that it is performed, in good object-oriented fashion, by invoking a method setHeat. This class is pictured in Figure 15.1.

Imagine the program has been developed and is working, when the programmer decides it would be nice to have a visual display that shows the current temperature of the moderator continuously as the simulation progresses. It is desirable to do this as noninvasively as possible; in particular, the programmer does not want to change the Reactor class. (This class may have been written by another programmer, for example, or it may be used in other applications where this new behavior is not desired.)

A simple solution is to make a new subclass of Reactor — say, Graphical-Reactor, which does nothing more than override the setHeat method, updating

```
@ interface Reactor : Object
{
    ...
    double heat;
    ...
}
- (void) setHeat: (double) newValue;
@end
```

Figure 15.1 A class maintaining an inactive value.

```
@implementation GraphicalReactor : Reactor
- (void) setHeat: (double) newValue
  {
    /* code necessary to */
    /* update gauge   */

    [ super setHeat: newValue ];
  }
@end
```

Figure 15.2   A class implementing an active value.

the graphical output before invoking the superclass methods (Figure 15.2). The programmer thus needs only to replace the creation of new Reactor objects with GraphicalReactor objects. This creation probably takes place once during initialization. As long as all changes to the Reactor value are mediated through the method setHeat, the gauge will reflect the value accurately.

Smalltalk and Objective-C both support a more generalized concept called *dependency*. Any object can be marked as being dependent on some other object. The run-time system maintains a list of all known dependents. Any object, when it modifies itself, can tell the system to notify all of its dependents. The dependents will then receive a message indicating that the object has been modified, and can take appropriate action. Unlike the scheme described previously, however, the dependency system works only when dependents know that someone may be waiting on their change. This scheme will not work when, as in the Reactor example, it is necessary to be as noninvasive of the original code as possible.

15.4   SUBCLASS CLIENTS AND USER CLIENTS

We have several times noted that an object, like a module, has a public face and a private face. The public side encompasses all features, such as methods and instance variables, that can be accessed or manipulated by code outside the module. The private face includes the public face, as well as methods and instance variables accessible only within the object. The user of a service provided by a module (the client) needs to know the details of only the public side of a module. Details of implementation, and other internal features not important for the utilization of the module, can be hidden from view.

Alan Snyder [Snyder 86] and other researchers have noted that the addition of the mechanism of inheritance means that classes in an object-oriented language have yet a third face — namely, those features accessible to subclasses but not necessarily to other users. The designer of a subclass for a given class will probably need to know more internal implementation details of the original class than will an instance-level user, but may not need as much information as the designer of the original class.

```
class CardPile
{
public:
  CardPile();
  CardPile(int, int);

  void virtual   addCard (CardLink *);
  int   virtual   canTake(Card *);
  int        contains (int, int);
  void virtual   display();
  void virtual   initialize();
  CardLink *  removeCard ();
  void virtual   select(int, int);

private:
  int  x;     // x location of pile
  int  y;     // y location of pile

protected:
  CardLink *top;  // first card in pile
};
```

Figure 15.3 Private, protected and public members.

We can think of both the designer of a subclass and a user of a class as "clients" of the original class, since they make use of the facilities provided by the class. Since these two groups have different requirements, however, it is useful to distinguish them by different terms; *subclass clients* and *user clients*. User clients create instances of the class, and pass messages to these objects. Subclass clients create new classes based on the class.

In the classes we developed as part of our solitaire game in Chapter 10, the class Card declares to be private the variables r and s, which maintain the rank and suit of the card. Only methods associated with class Card could access or modify these values. The data associated with class CardPile, on the other hand, are divided into the three categories private, protected, and public (Figure 15.3). The variables x and y can be accessed or modified only by methods associated with the class CardPile. The variable top, on the other hand, can be accessed and modified by methods associated with the class or subclasses, such as methods associated with the class TablePile. The only public interface is through methods; there are no publicly accessible instance variables. By eliminating publicly accessible instance variables, the language provides mechanisms that can be used to help ensure that no data coupling is permitted between this class and other software components. (However, the language only provides the mechanism. It is still the responsibility of the programmer to use the features properly — for example, by declaring all data members as private or protected.)

We can think of software evolution and modification in terms of user and subclass clients. When a class designer announces the public features of a class, he is making a contract to provide the services thus described. He can consider and implement changes in the internal design freely, as long as the public interface remains unchanged (or perhaps only grows). In a similar fashion, although perhaps less common and less obvious, the designer of a class is also specifying an interface to subclasses. A common and subtle source of software errors occurs when the internal details of a class are changed and subclasses cease to operate. By dividing, if only by convention, the private internal details of a class from the various levels of public interface, the programmer sets the boundaries for acceptable change and modification. The ability to make changes to existing code safely is critical in the maintenance of large and long-lived software systems.

The notion of a subclass client may strike some readers as odd, since, when an instance of the subclass is created, the class and the subclass are melded into one object. Nevertheless, the notion makes good sense when we consider the creators or designers of the class. Often, the designer of a subclass and the designer of the original class are two different individuals. It is good object-oriented programming practice for the designer of any class to consider the possibility that, at some future point, her class may be subclassed, and to provide adequate documentation and software connections to facilitate this process.

15.5 CONSTRUCTION AND INHERITANCE

One of the great strengths of object-oriented programming is that the mechanism of inheritance can be used for a variety of different purposes. We saw this in Chapter 6, where we described how inheritance could be used for specialization, specification, variance, generalization, and construction. It is on the latter that we wish to concentrate in this section.

When a class is subclassed for the purposes of construction, some or all of the behavior of the superclass is conceptually hidden from clients. Nevertheless, the bare mechanism of inheritance does not hide the visibility of methods inherited from the superclass. In the example in Chapter 6, the class Dictionary was used to provide a basis for building the class SymbolTable. Although the functionality associated with dictionaries was used in implementing symbol tables, the user did not need to know that, in fact, a symbol table was a kind of dictionary, and did not need to (probably should not) have direct access to the methods from the superclass. Inheritance by itself cannot hide this information, because the *is-a* relationship, which we are using as our central metaphor for inheritance, explicitly demands that any subclass must be able to represent an instance of the superclass. That is, if we have a variable declared to be a Dictionary, we should be able to assign a value of type SymbolTable to it.

The various object-oriented languages we are considering differ in the degree to which they can be used to enforce the hiding of the superclass. The language C++ is the most complete in this regard. In C++, a class can inherit

```
class SymbolTable : private Dictionary
{
public:
  void add(char * key, char* value)
    { atput(key, value); }
  char *lookup(char * key)
    { at(key); }
};
```

Figure 15.4 A private inheritance.

in a private or public fashion from another class. Consider the class definitions shown in Figure 15.4. Here, the class SymbolTable is being built on top of an existing class Dictionary, which implements the methods atput and at for string-valued arguments. The class SymbolTable renames these methods as add and lookup. Furthermore, since the inheritance is performed in a private fashion (as indicated by the keyword private in the heading), a variable of type SymbolTable cannot be legally assigned to a variable of type Dictionary, nor can the user of the SymbolTable class access any fields or methods inherited from the parent class.

In the case study to be presented in Chapter 17, we will see that private inheritance can sometimes greatly reduce the amount of code required for the development of a new class.

15.6 CONTROL OF ACCESS AND VISIBILITY

In this section, we will briefly outline the various information hiding features of the object-oriented languages we are considering, and will note how each of the languages support the concepts we have discussed in earlier sections of this chapter.

Visibility in Smalltalk

The Smalltalk system provides few facilities for the protection and hiding of either data or methods. Instance variables are always considered private and are accessible only within the methods associated with the class in which the variables are defined or in subclasses. Access to instance variables from outside the object must be accomplished indirectly through access functions.

Methods, on the other hand, are always considered public: They can be accessed by anybody. Just as there are no facilities for making instance variables public, there are no facilities for enforcing the hiding of methods. It is common, however, for certain methods to be labeled "private," meaning that they should be used by only the class itself and should not be invoked by user clients. It is good practice to respect these suggestions, and to avoid using private methods.

Visibility in Object Pascal

The Object Pascal language provides weak facilities for managing the visibility of object fields. All fields — both data and methods — are public, and are accessible to both user clients and subclass clients. It is only by convention or agreement that data fields are restricted to subclass clients and that methods are open to user clients. Even though style guidelines such as the law of Demeter cannot be strictly enforced by the system, they are still valuable notions and should be respected by programmers. In addition, it is helpful for programmers to use comments to indicate those methods in a class that they expect to be overridden in subclasses.

Visibility in C++

Of the languages we are considering, C++ provides by far the most complete range of facilities for controlling access to information. As we have noted in earlier chapters, these facilities are provided through the introduction of three new keywords; public, protected and private.

When these keywords are used in the field-definition part of class descriptions, their effect can be described almost directly in terms of the concepts from Section 15.4. Figure 15.3 provided an example of private, protected, and public fields. The data that follow the public: access specifier are available to everybody — to both subclass and user clients alike. The data that follow the protected: access specifier, on the other hand, are accessible only within the class and subclasses. Thus, these fields are intended for subclass clients, but not for user clients. Finally, the private: designator precedes fields that are accessible only to instances of the class itself, and not to either subclass or user clients. In the absence of any initial designation, fields are by default considered private.

Philosophically, the C++ access control mechanisms are intended to provide protection against accident, not guarantee security from malicious users. There are several ways to defeat the protection system. Probably the most direct technique involves the use of functions that return pointer or reference values. Consider the class shown in Figure 15.5. Although the field safe is declared private, a reference to the value is returned by the the method sorry. Thus, in an expression such as

```
Sneaky x;

x.sorry() = 17;
```

the value of the data member safe will be changed from 10 to 17, even if the call to sorry takes place in user (client) code.

A more subtle point is that access specifiers in C++ control the access of members, not visibility. To illustrate this, consider the classes shown in Figure 15.6. An error occurs because the function f attempts to modify the variable i, which is inherited from class X, although it is inaccessible (because it is declared private:). If the access modifiers controlled visibility, rather than

```
class Sneaky
{
  private:
    int safe;
  public:
    Sneaky() { safe = 10; }   // initialize safe to 10
    int &sorry() { return safe; }
}
```

Figure 15.5 A sneaky circumvention of protection.

accessibility, the variable i would be invisible and the global i would have been updated.

Access modifiers define properties of a class, not of instances. Thus, the notion of private fields in C++ does not correspond exactly to the concept developed in Section 15.4. There, private data were accessible to only an object itself, whereas, in C++, the private fields are accessible to any object of the same class. That is, in C++, an object is permitted to manipulate the private members of another instance of the same class.

For example, consider the class declaration shown in Figure 15.7. Here the rp and ip fields, representing the real and imaginary parts of a complex number, are marked as private. The binary operation + is overridden to provide a new meaning for the addition of two complex numbers. Despite the private nature of the rp and ip fields, the operator function is permitted to access these fields in the argument x, because the argument is of the same class as the receiver.

Constructor and destructor functions, such as the constructor function Complex in Figure 15.7, are usually declared public. Declaring a constructor as protected implies that only subclasses or *friends* (see subsequent discussion of friends) can create instances of the class, while declaring it as private restricts creation only to friends or other instances of the class.

```
int i;

class A {
private:
  int i;
};

class B : public A {
  void f();
};

B::f()
{ i++; }   // error - A::i is private
```

Figure 15.6 Modifiers control access, not visibility.

```
class Complex {
private:
  double rp;
  double ip;
public:
  Complex(double a, double b) { rp = a; ip = b; }
  Complex operator + ( Complex & x)
    { return Complex(rp + x.rp, ip + x.ip); }
};
```

Figure 15.7   Accessing private members in another instance.

The weak form of the law of Demeter can be enforced in part by declaration of all data fields as protected. The strong form corresponds to declaring such fields as private. A more detailed analysis of the law of Demeter for C++ can be found in [Sakkinen 88].

While the access modifiers in C++ provide power and flexibility far in excess of the other languages we are considering, making effective use of these features requires foresight and experience. As with the question of whether to make a method virtual or not, one serious problem with degree of control provided by the C++ language is that the ease with which a subclass can be formed is often dependent upon how much thought the designer of the original class gave to the possibility of subclassing. Being overly protective (declaring information private that should be protected) can make subclassing difficult. Problems arise if the subclass designer cannot modify the source form of the original class — for example, if the original is distributed as part of a library.

Private Inheritance.   The keywords public and private are also used to preface the name of a superclass in a class definition. When used in this fashion, the visibility of information from the superclass is altered by the modifier. A subclass that inherits in a public fashion from another class corresponds to the notion of inheritance we have been using in the book up to this point. If a subclass inherits in a private fashion, the public features of the superclass are reduced to the level of the modifier.

This feature is useful when subclassing is used for the purposes of construction, in the sense of Section 15.5. As we noted in Section 15.5, if the subclass SymbolTable inherits from the class Dictionary in a protected or private fashion, instead of in a public fashion, then user clients will be prevented from accessing directly the functionality associated with the superclass.

When a class inherits in a non public fashion from another class, instances of the subclass cannot be assigned to identifiers of the superclass type, as is possible with public inheritance. An easy way to remember this limitation is in terms of the *is-a* relationship. Public inheritance is an overt assertion that the *is-a* relationship holds, and thus that an instance of the subclass can be used when the superclass is called for. A Dog *is-a* Mammal, for example, and thus a Dog can be used in any situation in which a Mammal is called for. Private

```
class Complex {
private:
  double rp;
  double ip;
public:
  Complex(double, double);
  friend double abs(Complex&);
};

Complex::Complex(double a, double b)
{
  rp = a;
  ip = b;
}

double abs(Complex& x)
{
  return sqrt(x.rp * x.rp + x.ip * x.ip);
}
```

Figure 15.8   A C++ friend function.

inheritance, on the other hand, does not maintain the *is-a* relationship, since instances of a class that inherits in such a manner from a parent class cannot always be used in place of the parent class. Thus, it would not make sense to use a SymbolTable where an arbitrary type of Dictionary was required, for example. If a variable is declared to be a type of Dictionary, we cannot assign a value of type SymbolTable to it (whereas we could if the inheritance were public).

Friend Functions.   Another aspect of visibility in C++ is the concept of a *friend function*. A friend function is simply a function (not a method) that is declared using the friend modifier in the declaration of a class. Friend functions are permitted to read and write the private and protected fields within an object.

Consider the class declaration shown in Figure 15.8, which extends the class shown earlier in Figure 15.7. The fields rp and ip of the data structure representing complex numbers are declared to be private, and thus are generally not accessible outside of methods associated with the class. The function abs, which incidentally overloads a function of the same name defined for double-precision values, is not a method; it is simply a function. However, since the function has been declared to be a friend of the complex class, it is permitted to access all fields of the class, even private fields.

It is also possible to declare classes, and even individual methods in other classes, as friends. We will see an example of friend classes in Chapter 17. The most common reasons for using friend functions are that the friend function requires access to the internal structure of two or more classes, or that it is necessary for the friend function to be invoked in a functional style, rather than in a message passing style (that is, as abs(x) instead of as x.abs().)

```
class Complex {
public:
  const double rp;
  const double ip;
  Complex(double, double);
};

Complex::Complex(double a, double b)  :  rp(a), ip(b)
{
  /* empty statement */
}
```

Figure 15.9   A C++ constant data member.

Friend functions are a powerful tool, but they are easy to abuse. In particular, friend functions introduce exactly the sort of data couplings that we identified in the beginning of this chapter as being detrimental to the development
of reusable software. Whenever possible, more object-oriented encapsulation
techniques (such as methods) should be preferred over friend functions. Nevertheless, there are times when no other tool can be used, such as when a function
needs access to the internal structure of two or more class definitions. In these
cases, friend functions are a useful abstraction [Koenig 89c].

Constant Members.   In C++, the keyword const is used to indicate a
quantity that is unchanging during the lifetime of the object. Global variables
that are so declared become global constants. Constant variables that are declared local to a procedure are accessible only within the procedure, and cannot
be modified except in the initialization statement which creates them.

Often data members act as constants, but their initial value cannot be determined until the object is created. For example the data members representing
the real and imaginary fields in the Complex number class shown in Figure 15.8
should never be altered once the complex number is created. In Chapter 3 we
called such fields *immutable*. The const keyword provides yet another way to
create immutable fields.

Although it is not permitted to assign to constant data members, they can be
initialized in C++ using the same syntax used to invoke parent class constructors
as part of the constructor process (see Section 9.3 for a discussion of invoking
parent class constructors). Consider the class definition shown in Figure 15.9.
Here the fields rp and ip have been declared constant, so there is no danger in
making them public, as they cannot be modified. To provide an initial value the
constructor seems to invoke rp and ip as if they were superclasses. This is the
only way (other than initialization at compile time) that constant data members
can be assigned. Once the body of the constructor starts executing the value of
the constant data member cannot be altered.

```
@interface Ball : Object
{
  double direction;
  double energy;
@public
  double x;
  double y;
}
  ...
@end
```

Figure 15.10 An Objective-C class illustrating the @public keyword.

Data members declared as reference variables can be initialized in the same manner. The constant keyword can be applied to function or procedure members as well, however a discussion of that topic is beyond the scope of this book.

Visibility in Objective-C

In Objective-C, instance variable declarations must appear in the interface description of a class. It is not possible to define new fields in the implementation section, even though such values are not part of the interface, since they are accessible only within methods (they are protected, to use the C++ terminology). The visibility of instance variable fields can be modified using the @public keyword, which makes all fields following the keyword publicly accessible to users. For example, Figure 15.10 shows an interface definition for a class Ball, representing a graphical ball object. The location of the ball, represented by the coordinates in the x and y fields, are publicly accessible, whereas the direction and energy of the ball are protected.

Unlike in instance variable fields, it is possible to define methods in the implementation section of a class that are not declared in the interface portion. Such methods are visible, and can be invoked, only within that portion of the program that follows the definition of the new method.

There is no way to create a method that can be invoked by subclass clients but not by user clients, and there is no way to create truly private instance variable values.

Exercises

1. Design a tool that could examine programs written in your favorite object-oriented language and report violations of the law of Demeter.

2. The strong form of the law of Demeter prevents access to inherited instance variables. Describe the advantages and disadvantages of this restriction. Consider issues such as the coupling between classes and the effect on the understandability of code. You might want to examine some of the arguments presented in [Snyder 86], [Lieberherr 89b].

3. Do you think the strong form of the law of Demeter also should have restricted access to global variables? Support your opinion by well-reasoned arguments. You might want to look at the article by Wulf and Shaw [Wulf 73] in preparing your answer.

4. What other concrete rules, similar to the law of Demeter, can you think of that have the properties that (1) the satisfaction of the law usually leads to systems with fewer interconnections and more cohesion and (2) exceptions in which the rule must be violated are rare. In particular, the law of Demeter addresses the coupling between different objects. Can you think of a guideline that encourages greater cohesion within an object?

5. There is an alternative level of visibility that, like protected (subclass client) data, is also more restrictive than public information and less restrictive than information to which access is permitted only inside an object. Under this alternative, instances of the same class have access to the internal state of an object, even when such access is denied to all others. In C++, for example, an object can access any field in another instance of the class, even if those fields are private or protected. In other languages, such as Smalltalk, this style of access is not permitted. Discuss the advantages and disadvantages of each approach.

6. Another possible variation on visibility rules for subclass clients would be to permit access to an immediate ancestor class but not to more distant ancestors. Discuss the advantages and disadvantages of this rule. (This issue is presented in [Snyder 86].)

7. Of the languages we are considering, only C++ has explicit facilities for distinguishing those features accessible to subclass clients from those accessible to user clients. Nevertheless, all languages have some mechanism for describing the programmer's intent through the use of comments. Often, structured comments, such as compiler directives, are used to provide optional information to a language system. Describe a commenting convention that could be used to denote levels of visibility. Then, outline an algorithm that could be used by a software tool to enforce the visibility rules.

16
Case Study: A Billiards Game

In this chapter, we develop a simple simulation of a billiard table. The program is written in Object Pascal, and is designed to be executed on an Apple Macintosh. The complete source for the billiards program is given in Appendix C.

The billiard table as the user sees it will consist of a window containing a rectangle with holes (pockets) in the corners and 16 balls (Figure 16.1). By clicking the mouse the user can strike the cue ball, which in turn can strike and hit other balls.

The emphasis in our development will be on the construction of reusable components that have minimal interconnections with other portions of the simulation. Subclass coupling will be used extensively to join together portions of the application. Subclass coupling permits major portions of the application to be developed with little or no knowledge of how they will be utilized, so these sections of code can be used in many different applications. In the exercises, we will explore other programs that could make use of these components.

16.1   A SIMPLE WINDOW INTERFACE

The first task in our application is to create two classes and routines that, taken together, will handle almost all the repetitive tedium involved in creating Macintosh applications. This system is similar to, although vastly simpler than, several commercial systems, such as the MacApp classes distributed by Apple [Schmucker 86, Wilson 90].

There is a certain amount of initialization code that is part of almost every Macintosh application. We will put this code in a routine called globalInitializations, which should be the first statement executed by any application. The

233

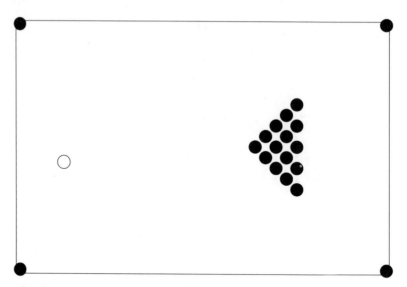

Figure 16.1   A billiard table.

design of this routine is admittedly an example of temporal cohesion (which we castigated in Chapter 15), but it appears to be preferable to other techniques given the design of the Macintosh toolbox.

The basic idea in developing object-oriented reusable user-interface code (or reusable controlling code for almost any application) is to make use of subclass coupling to specialize the code. General-purpose abstract superclasses will be defined that implement the broad framework for all applications. This general framework will make frequent use of certain methods. By overriding these methods, we can specialize the application in many different ways. The superclasses, being "abstract," are totally unaware of these specializations, and thus are independent of each application.

The first class created by our application is called SimpleWindow (Figure 16.2). An instance of SimpleWindow provides the "bare bones" functionality for a Macintosh window. The class takes care of processing events, handling activations and deactivations, determining window motion, and so on. To specialize the behavior of a window in any particular application, the user overrides certain methods. The most important of these methods is the method update, which is called when the window needs to be redrawn.

Macintosh applications are typically event-driven. This means that programs are written to be largely reactive, rather than proactive. The main program, after it has performed initializations, enters a loop waiting for the user or the system to perform some action. In our case, the loop is found in the method eventLoop. When the user performs an action — such as moving the mouse, entering a character with the keyboard, or selecting a menu item — the appropriate reaction is performed for that event.

```
SimpleWindow = object
    { data fields }
  theWindowPtr: windowPtr;
  name: STR255;
  windowRect: Rect;
  winType: integer;
  done: boolean;
  event: eventRecord;
    { creation methods }
  procedure setAttributes;
  procedure establish;
    { event handling }
  procedure eventLoop;
  procedure eventLoopTask;
  procedure endEventLoop;
    { window events - seldom overridden }
  procedure activate;
  procedure deactivate;
  procedure menu (which: LongInt);
  procedure menuChoice (theMenu, theItem: integer);
  procedure buttonDownEvent;
  procedure keyEvent;
  procedure handleDrag;
  procedure handleGrow;
  procedure doGoAway;
    { window events - often overridden }
  procedure buttonDown (x, y: integer);
  procedure keyPressed (c: char);
  procedure update;
end;
```

Figure 16.2   The class SimpleWindow.

Each event has an associated method. By overriding these methods, the user supplies specialized behavior for the given application. The most common form of specialized behavior involves reacting to button presses and key presses. These behaviors are invoked by the methods buttonDown and keyPressed, respectively.

The second class provided by the SimpleWindow unit is used to create new menus. The class SimpleMenu (Figure 16.3) can read menu items from resource files or create them directly from information supplied by the user. In our application, we will take the latter approach. There is a special creation method used to generate the "Apple" menu category that is characteristic of Macintosh applications. Simple menus are all maintained on a single global linked list. To create a new type of menu, the user must subclass and override the method selectItem, which is invoked when a menu item is chosen.

```
SimpleMenu = object
      { data fields }
   theMenuID: Integer;
   theMenuPtr: MenuHandle;
   link: SimpleMenu;
      { creation methods }
   procedure readFromResource (id: integer);
   procedure createNewMenu (title: Str255);
   procedure createAppleMenu (aboutTitle: Str255);
      { adding elements to menu }
   procedure addItem (title: Str255);
   procedure addSeparator;
      { action to take when selected }
      { must be overridden by user }
   procedure selectItem (itemNumber: integer);
end;
```

Figure 16.3   The class SimpleMenu.

The most important points to note about these two classes are that they are
independent of any particular application, and can be reused directly in multiple
applications. Specialized behavior in any particular application is achieved by
subclassing from these general classes. In terms of coupling and cohesion, the
only coupling between the windowing classes and the classes that compose the
application is simple subclass coupling.

16.2   A GRAPHICAL UNIVERSE

Our next component of the simulation will be a tool that manages a graphical
universe. A graphical universe is simply a collection of graphical objects. Each
graphical object (Figure 16.4) possesses a location and size (represented by a
rectangular region), as well as the ability to draw itself. Graphical objects can
move, and, in the process, can strike each other. To determine when a graphical
object has hit another graphical object, we use a method intersectsWith, which
tests to see whether the two regions overlap.[1]

Once more, subclass coupling is used to isolate one component of the
application, the graphical universe manager, from more specialized aspects of
the application — namely, the balls and walls (cushions) themselves. The
methods to update and draw a graphical object are deferred methods; that is,

---

[1]Of course, a great simplification is the assumption that the borders of all graphical objects are
defined by rectangular regions. Although this assumption may make the programming easier, it
may not correspond to reality if the two objects represent, for example, balls. One way to to solve
this problem, which we have not done in this simple simulation, would be to override the method
intersectsWith.

```
GraphicalObject = object
    link: GraphicalObject;
    region: Rect;
    procedure moveTo (x, y: integer);
    function intersectsWith
            (anObject: GraphicalObject): boolean;
    procedure erase;
      { the following overridden in subclasses }
    procedure update;
    procedure draw;
    procedure hitBy (anObject: GraphicalObject);
  end;
```

Figure 16.4   The class GraphicalObject.

although they are part of the specification for every graphical object, they are not implemented in that class. Instead, they must be implemented in every subclass of class GraphicalObject.

The class ObjectUniverse (Figure 16.5) provides behavior for a universe of graphical objects. An object universe maintains two collections of graphical objects: a list of fixed objects (such as walls and holes) that do not move during the course of the simulation, and a list of movable objects. Objects are inserted into the universe with either the method installFixedObject or the method installMovableObject. The method draw simply loops over all the graphical objects, instructing them to draw themselves.

The object universe is the main controller for the simulation. When the method updateMoveableObjects is called, every movable object is passed the message update. If any of those objects, during the course of updating themselves, invokes the method continueSimulation, then the list of movable objects

```
ObjectUniverse = object
    moveableObjects: GraphicalObject;
    fixedObjects: GraphicalObject;
    continueUpdate: boolean;
    procedure initialize;
    procedure installFixedObject (newObj: GraphicalObject);
    procedure installMovableObject
            (newObj: GraphicalObject);
    procedure draw;
    procedure updateMoveableObjects;
    procedure continueSimulation;
    function hitObject
            (anObject: GraphicalObject): GraphicalObject;
  end;
```

Figure 16.5   The class ObjectUniverse.

```
Wall = object (GraphicalObject)
    convertFactor: real;
    procedure setBounds
                (left, top, right, bottom:
                    integer; cf: real);
    procedure draw; override;
    procedure hitBy (anObject: GraphicalObject); override;
    end;

Hole = object (GraphicalObject)
    procedure setCenter (x, y: integer);
    procedure draw; override;
    procedure hitBy (anObject: GraphicalObject); override;
    end;

Ball = object (Hole)
    direction: real;
    energy: real;
    procedure draw; override;
    procedure update; override;
    procedure hitBy (anObject: GraphicalObject); override;
    function x: real;
    function y: real;
    end;
```

Figure 16.6   The graphical objects in the billiard simulation.

is scanned a second time. This process continues until the list has been scanned
with no object asking that the simulation be continued.

   Notice that all this activity — such as maintaining the list of objects, updating objects, and managing the simulation — is performed without any specific
knowledge of the particulars of any simulation. Once more, the only coupling
used between the graphical universe and the particular objects in the universe is
subclass coupling. We have yet to define any code that is specific to our billiard
simulation; we will do that in the next section.

16.3   GRAPHICAL COMPONENTS OF THE BILLIARDS GAME

The graphical components of our billiard simulation consist of two fixed graphical objects (walls and holes or cushions and pockets), and one movable class
of objects (the balls). These objects are represented by the classes Wall, Hole
and Ball, respectively (Figure 16.6).

   There are specialized initialization methods for walls and holes that provide
information particular to those classes. For Balls the only particular information
needed for initialization is the location, which is provided by the inherited

method moveTo. Wall objects maintain a constant that is used to determine the angle of reflection when an object strikes the wall; Ball objects maintain an energy level and direction as part of their instance information.

All three classes must implement the virtual method draw, if they are to have any graphical display. In addition, they all provide behavior to be performed when they are struck, by redefining the virtual method hitBy. When a Wall is struck by a Ball, it absorbs a certain amount of energy and then reflects the Ball. The reflection is accomplished by a change in the direction of the Ball. When a Hole is struck, it absorbs all the energy of the Ball and removes the Ball from the playing area, unless the Ball is the cue ball in which case it is placed back at the starting location for the game. When a Ball is struck by another Ball, the energy of the first Ball is split between the two balls and they move apart from each other in different directions.

The only object to override the method update is the class Ball. If a Ball has any energy associated with it, the update process will move the Ball a small amount along its current direction, in the process using a certain amount of energy and possibly striking another object. The simulation is continued as long as any Ball possesses a nonzero amount of energy.

The module that implements the graphical components of the game also defines several global variables. The variable theUniverse is our universe of objects (an instance of ObjectUniverse). The variable cueBall represents a cue ball, which is the only ball the user can actually hit.

16.4   THE MAIN PROGRAM

Once we have defined the basic data structures for our application, writing the main program is relatively easy. There are two new classes defined in the final module (Figure 16.7). The class BilliardMenu provides the mechanism to create the single menu and menu item used by our application. It defines a new method initialize to localize the creation information, and overrides the method selectItem to perform the appropriate action when the menu item is selected. In our application, there is only a single menu item, "quit," which simply halts the event loop and thereby terminates the application.

The class BilliardSimulation inherits behavior from the class SimpleWindow. The class provides an initialization method that not only initializes the window, but also creates the various walls, holes, and balls that compose the graphical universe. Once the universe is initialized, the user interacts with the game by means of key and button presses. When a button press occurs, the angle between the current cursor location and the cue ball is determined and a certain amount of energy is imparted to the cue ball in the opposite direction. The graphical universe is then started, and the simulation continues as long as the cue ball, and any ball it may strike, possess energy.

```
BilliardMenu = object (SimpleMenu)
   procedure initialize (title: STR255);
   procedure selectItem (itemNumber: Integer); override;
end;

{ the main simulation window }
BilliardSimulation = object (SimpleWindow)
   procedure initialize;
   procedure buttonDown (x, y: integer); override;
   procedure update; override;
   procedure keyPressed (c: char); override;
   procedure createWalls;
   procedure createHoles;
   procedure rackBalls;
end;
```

Figure 16.7 Classes defined in the main unit.

Exercises

1. Suppose you want to perform a certain action every time the billiards program executed the event loop task. What is the easiest way to implement this feature?

2. Suppose you want to make the balls colored. What portions of the program would you need to change?

3. Add a new menu item called "restart." When restart is selected, it should rack the balls to restart the simulation.

4. Add a visual display for the number of balls that have been sunk in holes. What portions of the program did you need to change?

5. Write an application that uses the SimpleWindow and GraphicalUniverse classes in a different way. A good choice is an ecological simulation, such as the following:

   • A fish world, which contains three types of fishes. Big fish eat middle-sized fish, which eat little fish. Each fish maintains as instance information an age, sex, and a hunger factor. The behavior of a fish at any instance will depend on the fish's state; hungry fish go in the direction of food (perhaps eating the food if it is near enough), mature female fish lay eggs, old fish die and are removed, little fish go in a direction opposite of larger fish, and so on.

   • A rabbit-wolf simulation. This is similar to the fish world, except that the inhabitants are rabbits and wolves. Add warrens where rabbits can hide from wolves, but where no food is available. Rabbits must come out of their hiding places to eat, but are then prey for the wolves. Wolves roam in packs, searching for rabbits.

6. The type of interface described here is "modeless". This means the programmer is free to perform any action, such as hitting a keypress or moving or depressing the mouse, at any time. Oftentimes a "modal" interface, where the user is restricted to

only a few actions, is desired. For example an error may result in an alert window being displayed. Further activity is delayed until the user presses a button indicating they are aware of the error.

Explain how modal interfaces can be implemented. (Hint: each class has the ability to execute a separate event loop).

17

Case Study: Container Classes in C++

In this chapter, we will develop a collection of data-structure classes in C++. Because these data structures are all used to maintain collections of elements, they are often known as *container classes*. Although these classes do have a utility all of their own, our major goal in the exposition will be to illustrate how subclass coupling can be used to create general-purpose classes even in the presence of strong typing, to illustrate the differences between overridding and overloading, between public and private inheritance, and between pointers and references. The complete source for the classes described in this chapter is given in Appendix D.

Container classes are the prototypical examples of objects that would benefit from the availability of *parameterized classes*, which we will discuss in the next chapter. While currently considered an experimental feature, parameterized classes have been proposed for C++, and several different versions currently exist. It is likely that at some time in the near future a standard format for parameterized classes will be adopted for C++, at which point container classes such as we present here could be rewritten to use this feature.

17.1 THE BASIC ELEMENTS

In the absence of parameterized classes, the static typing of C++ implies that our container classes cannot hold arbitrary objects, since the type of the values held in the class must be known at compile time. To overcome this difficulty, we define a basic Element class, which will be a parent class for any value held in a container. The class description of Element is shown in Figure 17.1.

The public face of an element provides almost no functionality. Elements can be compared to other elements, and can compute an unsigned hash value.

```
typedef int Boolean;

class Element
{
  friend class List;

public:
  Element ();

  virtual Boolean    operator == (Element& x) ;
  virtual Boolean    operator != (Element& x) ;
  virtual unsigned  hash() ;

private:
  Element *    lnk;
  Element *  link ();
  void      setLink (Element* n);
  void      insert (Element& n);
  void      removeNext ();
};

inline void Element::setLink(Element* n)
{  lnk = n;  }

inline Element::Element ()
{  setLink(0);  }

inline Element* Element::link ()
{  return lnk;  }
```

Figure 17.1 The definition of class Element.

All of these functions are declared as virtual, and generally are overridden in subclasses. The default definition of the equality operator is to test for identity (equality is true if the two arguments are identically the same object). While the language C does not have an explicit boolean datatype, making the type Boolean an alias for type integer will aid in distinguishing those methods which yield a boolean value from those which yield other integer results. For the inequality operator, the default is simply to negate the equality test; for the hash function, the default value is the constant 0. These definitions are shown in Figure 17.2.

The class List is declared as a friend of the class Element. Methods in that class will be permitted to invoke otherwise private members in elements. These private fields are involved in the use of elements as part of a linked list. The link field, and the routines used to set the link, are all declared private and thus can be invoked only by the class Element itself and by the friend class List.

```
//
//   virtual methods and non-inline methods
//   from class Element
//

Boolean Element::operator == (Element& x)
{   return this == &x;  }

Boolean Element::operator != (Element& x)
{   return ! ( *this == x);  }

unsigned Element::hash()
{   return 0;  }

void Element::insert (Element& n)
{
  // insert new element, updating links
  n.setLink(link());
  setLink(&n);
}

void Element::removeNext ()
{
  // remove next element, if there is one
  if (link())
    setLink(link()->link());
}
```

Figure 17.2 Implementation of class Element.

The contrast between the two methods setLink and insert illustrates the difference in the use of pointers and references. The setLink method is used merely to set the value of the link field. The insert method, on the other hand, is used to insert another element immediately after the current value, updating the link fields of both the current and inserted elements appropriately. References should be used when it can be guaranteed that the corresponding argument will be non-empty. In the setLink method, there are no such guarantees; indeed, a null pointer often will be passed as argument to this method. (Null pointers are used to indicate the end of the linked list). The method insert will be invoked only when there is an actual value for the argument.

Although elements are basic to the design of the container classes, they are hardly useful by themselves. In practice, for containers to carry useful information, the user must define subclasses of class Element. Through the mechanism of subclass coupling and the *is-a* relation, instances of these classes can then be used as elements in our containers. One such class is shown in Figure 17.3. An IntElement maintains a constant integer value, established using the constructor.

```
//
//  IntElement - integer elements
//     elements which maintain integer values
//
class IntElement : public OrderedElement {
public:
  const int value;
  IntElement (int i);

  unsigned virtual hash();

  Boolean virtual operator== (Element&);
  Boolean virtual operator< (OrderedElement&);

  int &  intReference();
  void display();
};

IntElement::IntElement (int i) :
                     OrderedElement(), value(i) {}

unsigned IntElement::hash()
{ return (unsigned) value; }

int &  IntElement::intReference()
{ return value; }

void IntElement::display()
{ printf(" %d ", value); }

// define equality and relations in terms of
//      underlying integers
Boolean IntElement::operator == (Element& x)
{  return value == ((IntElement &) x).value; }

Boolean IntElement::operator < (OrderedElement& x)
{  return value < ((IntElement &) x).value; }
```

Figure 17.3 An integer element class.

for the class. The equality test is redefined to test for equality of the integer values; the hash function is redefined to return this value as an unsigned integer. The class definition, inline functions, and function bodies are all shown together in Figure 17.3; in practice, of course, they would be split between an implementation and an interface file.

17.2   LINKED LISTS

The first collection class we will define will maintain a linked list of element values. This linked list can be used as a stack or a queue, as we will permit adding or removing elements from either end of the list. In addition, arbitrary elements can be removed from the list, and we can determine the number of elements contained in the list.

One data item maintained by each instance of the class List is a pointer to the first element of the list. For this reason, the class List looks functionally, as far as implementation is concerned, like a list element. We can make good use of this fact by subclassing in a private fashion the class List from the class Element. Doing so permits almost one-half of the methods for class List to be implemented as simple renamings of methods inherited from class Element (Figure 17.4). Private inheritance is used, since a List cannot be used itself as though it were an Element. The subclassing is performed merely for implementation, and does not preserve the specification of the parent class Element.

The second data value maintained by each list is a pointer to one of the list elements. This value is manipulated by the method reset and the operators ++ and (), which together provide a way of iterating over the elements of the list, without breaking the encapsulation of the links. The procedure print, shown in Figure 17.5, illustrates this use.

Although the class List can be used directly as it is defined, subclassing the class can often almost eliminate any appearance that the elements of the list must be subclasses of class Element. As an illustration, Figure 17.6 gives the definition of the class IntList, used to maintain lists of integers. The methods relating to addition, accessing, and removal are modified so as to take integer, rather than IntElement, arguments. The IntElement constructor is used to turn these integer elements into the appropriate class for use by the List methods. Notice that the redefinition of methods such as addList hides the definition in the earlier scope. Figure 17.7 illustrates the use of the class IntList.

The method add adds a new dynamically created instance of IntElement to the data structure. The method remove also requires an IntElement, however it is not needed following the operation. Thus the remove method declares the IntElement as a local variable, which will be automatically deleted following the call on the method List::removeEqual.

17.3   SETS

The next data structure we will consider corresponds to the abstract concept of a set. Like a list, a set can contain an arbitrary number of elements. Unlike a list, no element may appear in the set more than one time. Sets are by definition unordered, although, of course, any specific implementation will impose some implementation-dependent ordering. But the lack of ordering permits a great simplification in the interface.

```
//
//------------------------------------------- List
//

class List : private Element  {
public:
    // addition
  void       addFirst (Element& x);
  void       addLast (Element& x);
    // removal
  void       removeEqual (Element& x);
  void       removeFirst ();
  void       removeLast ();
    // testing
  Boolean    includes (Element& x);
  Boolean    isEmpty ();
  int     size ();
    // access
  Element *  first ();
  Element *  last ();
  Element *  next();
  void    reset();
  Boolean    operator++();
  Element *  operator()();
protected:
  void       addAfterCurrent(Element& y);

private:
  Element *  current;
};

inline void List::reset() { current = 0; }

inline Element* List::operator()() { return current; }

inline void List::addFirst(Element& x)
                                  { Element::insert(x); }

inline Element* List::first() { return Ele-
ment::link(); }

inline int List::isEmpty() { return first() == 0; }

inline void List::addAfterCurrent(Element& y)
                                  { current->insert(y);}

inline void List::removeFirst() { List::removeNext(); }
```

Figure 17.4 The linked List class List.

```
void print(IntList& x)
{
  x.reset();
  while (x++)
    x()->display();
  printf("\n");
}
```

Figure 17.5 Iterating over elements of a list.

```
class IntList : public List {
public:
  IntElement *   first ();
  IntElement *   last ();
  void    add (int);
  void    addFirst (int);
  void    addLast (int);
  void    remove (int);
  IntElement *  operator()();
};

IntElement * IntList::operator()()
{   return (IntElement *) List::operator()(); }

IntElement * IntList::first()
{ return (IntElement *) List::first(); }

IntElement * IntList::last()
{ return (IntElement *) List::last(); }

void IntList::add(int i)
{ List::addFirst(* new IntElement(i)); }

void IntList::addFirst(int i)
{ List::addFirst(* new IntElement(i)); }

void IntList::addLast(int i)
{ List::addLast(* new IntElement(i)); }

void IntList::remove(int i)
{ IntElement p(i);
  List::removeEqual(p); }
```

Figure 17.6 The integer list class IntList.

```
main() {
  IntList A;

  printf("List tests\n");

  // first add a few elements
  A.addFirst(5);
  A.add(23);
  A.addFirst(4);
  A.addLast(6);
  print(A);
  printf("size is %d\n", A.size());

  // display the first and last elements
  printf("first last ");
  A.first()->display();
  A.last()->display();
  printf("\n");

  // try removing a few
  printf("remove element ");
  A.remove(23);
  print(A);
  printf("remove first ");
  A.removeFirst();
  print(A);
  printf("remove last ");
  A.removeLast();
  print(A);
}
```

Figure 17.7   Using the class IntList.

By inheriting in a private fashion from class List, almost all of the implementation of sets can be achieved by renaming. In fact, of the seven methods defined for class Set (Figure 17.8), six can be written as inline methods, and five of these defined simply by altering the visibility of the methods from class List. The one remaining method is the function to add an element to the set. Since adding an element to a set requires a test to determine whether the value is in the set, it is implemented as a conventional (that is, not an inline) function. As with the inheritance of List from Element, the inheritance of Set from List is private because the *is-a* relationship is not preserved. From the abstract point of view, a Set is not a form of List, although we are implementing it as such.

As was the case with integer lists, a great deal of the appearance of sets can be improved by subclassing from the class Set. Figure 17.9 shows the definition of the class IntSet, which maintains sets of integer values. As before, the methods add and remove are redefined so as to take integer arguments, rather than el-

```
//
//----------------------------------------- Set
//

class Set : private List {
public:
  void      add (Element& x);
  void      remove (Element& x);
    // alter accessibility on the following
  List::includes;
  List::size;
  List::reset;
  List::operator ++;
  List::operator ();
};

inline void Set::remove(Element& x)
{  List::removeEqual(x);  }
```

Figure 17.8   Definition of the class Set.

```
class IntSet : public Set {
public:
  void      add (int);
  void      remove (int);
  IntSet&     operator += (int);
  IntElement *  operator()();
};

void     IntSet::add(int i)
{  Set::add(* new IntElement(i));  }

void     IntSet::remove(int i)
{  IntElement p(i);
    Set::remove(p);  }

IntSet&     IntSet::operator += (int x)
{  add(x); return *this;  }

IntElement * IntSet::operator()()
{  return (IntElement *) List::operator()();  }
```

Figure 17.9   The integer set class IntSet.

```
printf("Set test\n");
IntSet S;

// add a few elements to the set
S.add(12);
(S += 14) += 23;
S.add(12);
print(S);
// remove the element that was added twice
S.remove(12);
print(S);
printf("size is %d\n", S.size());
```

Figure 17.10   Using the class IntSet.

ements. To make sets even easier to use, we define the operator += to add a new element to a set and to return the set, so that strings of additions can be run together. This is illustrated in Figure 17.10, which shows a use of the class IntSet.

17.4   ORDERED COLLECTIONS

Unlike sets and lists, which are by definition unordered, the next data structure that we will discuss always maintains its elements in an ordered form. So that it can do so, however, it requires some definition of ordering. Elements, you will remember, know only how to compare for equality. So that the programmer may define what it means to be ordered, we create a new form of element, called an OrderedElement (Figure 17.11). An OrderedElement is publically an element, and thus can be used wherever elements are required. In addition, the class OrderedElement defines the relational operators; and thus, two instances of OrderedElements can be compared against each other.

The relational operators are defined, as in Smalltalk (see Figure 13.6, page 193) in a circular fashion. Thus, the redefinition of a single relational operator in conjunction with the equality operator is sufficient to give meaning to all six relational operations.

As is the class Set, the class Ordered is built on top of the class List, inheriting from that class in a private manner. Also like the class Set, almost all the functionality involved in ordered collections is implemented as simple renaming of similar functions in class List, or as casts of results from functions in that class (Figure 17.12). In this case, the casting of the pointers returned from the list functions is justified, since we know that the only way an element can be added to an ordered collection is through the method Ordered::add. Since the argument to this method was an OrderedElement, it must still be so when it is taken out.

```
class OrderedElement : public Element {
public:
  Boolean virtual    operator <  (OrderedElement& x) ;
  Boolean virtual    operator <= (OrderedElement& x) ;
  Boolean virtual    operator >  (OrderedElement& x) ;
  Boolean virtual    operator >= (OrderedElement& x) ;
};

Boolean OrderedElement::operator < (OrderedElement& x)
{    return x > *this; }

Boolean OrderedElement::operator <= (OrderedElement& x)
{    return (*this < x) || (*this == x); }

Boolean OrderedElement::operator > (OrderedElement& x)
{    return x < *this; }

Boolean OrderedElement::operator >= (OrderedElement& x)
{  return x <= *this; }
```

Figure 17.11   The class OrderedElement.

The one method that cannot be provided directly by the functionality inherited from class List is the routine to add a new element to the ordered list. This method must iterate over the elements in the list to discover the appropriate position, then must add the new member. The function to do this is shown in Figure 17.13.

As with sets and lists, subclassing of the class Ordered can largely hide the manipulation of elements from the user. This hiding is illustrated in the code in Appendix D, and is not reproduced here.

17.5   TABLES

The final data structure we will define is the *table*. A table is a collection of key–value pairs, where the key and value items can be arbitrary elements. In actual fact, the table is built on top of two other classes, Association and AssociationList. Since these classes appear only in the implementation, they are defined in the implementation file, and not in the interface file for the collection data structures.

The class Association is shown in Figure 17.14. The class is made a subclass of Element, so associations can be entered into the list data structures we have defined. In addition, each instance of the class maintains a pointer to a key and a value element. The key element is set as part of the construction of a new association, and cannot change. The functions key and value return references to the key and value fields. The latter returns a reference to the pointer for the value field, which permits values to be null. We will discuss the reason

```
//
//-------------------------------------------- Ordered
//

class Ordered : private List {
public:
  void          add (OrderedElement& x);
  OrderedElement *  max();
  OrderedElement *  min();
  void          remove (OrderedElement& x);
  OrderedElement *  operator()();
  OrderedElement *  next();

  List::includes;
  List::size;
  List::reset;
  List::operator++;
};

inline void Ordered::remove(OrderedElement& x)
{   List::removeEqual(x);  }

inline OrderedElement *  Ordered::min()
{   return (OrderedElement *) List::first();  }

inline OrderedElement *  Ordered::max()
{   return (OrderedElement *) List::last();  }

inline OrderedElement * Ordered::operator()()
{   return (OrderedElement *) List::operator()();  }

inline OrderedElement * Ordered::next()
{   return (OrderedElement *) List::next();  }
```

Figure 17.12 Definition of class Ordered.

for overloading the equality operator when we see how the latter is used in the class AssociationList.

The class AssociationList (Figure 17.15) is a subclass of class List, used to maintain lists of associations. As with the class IntList, the class AssociationList redefines the method used in iteration so that it explicitly returns an Association, rather than simply an Element. The other iteration methods need not be altered.

The heart of the Table data structure is an array of association lists. This table is used as a hash table, with the association list serving as a chained list of values that have all hashed to the same location. To determine whether a certain key appears already in the table, for example, we compute the hash value for the key, then normalize it according to the size of the table. Indexing into the

```
void Ordered::add(OrderedElement& x)
{   OrderedElement *p;

    p = (OrderedElement *) List::first();
    // base cases - empty list or first element
    if ((!p) || (x < *p)) {
      List::addFirst(x);
      return;
      }

    // looping case, loop until we find right location
    reset();
    while ((*this)++)
      if (next() && (x < *next())) {
        List::addAfterCurrent(x);
        return;
        }
    List::addLast(x);
}
```

Figure 17.13   The method Ordered::add.

table yields an instance of AssociationList. The includes method (inherited from class List) can then be used to see whether the key appears.

The includes method uses the equality operator (==) to test whether the element appears in the list. The elements of the list are instances of Association, whereas the argument passed to includesKey is a key value. The desired effect is therefore produced by the overriding of the equality operator in the class Association as follows:

```
int Association::operator == (Element& x)

{

   return key() == x;

}
```

The equality operator invoked within this function will be determined by the value of the key.

The class Table (Figure 17.16) provides methods to determine whether a key appears in the table, to return the list of keys or values from the table, to remove an element with a given key, and to compute the size of the table; the primary interface to the data structure, however, is the subscripting operator. Subscripting is used both to insert an element into the collection and to retrieve elements from the collection.

```
//
//---------------------------------------- Association
//

class Association : public Element
{
  friend class Table;

public:
  Association (Element&);  // constructor - arg is key

  Boolean virtual   operator == (Element&) ;

private:
  const Element&  associationKey;
  Element*  associationValue;
  Element&  key() ;
  Element*&  value();
};

inline Element&  Association::key()
{    return associationKey; }

inline Element*& Association::value()
{    return associationValue; }

inline Association::Association(Element& x)  :
                    associationKey(x)
{    associationValue = (Element *) 0; }
```

Figure 17.14 The class Association.

So that it may be used on either the right or left side of an assignment arrow, the subscript expression must return a *reference* to a *pointer* to an element. The subscript method is shown in Figure 17.17. It computes the hash value of the index, as was done in the includes method, then iterates down the association list to see whether the element appears already. If it does appear, the value reference from the association is returned. If the element does not appear, a new association is created using the index as a key. The value field for this new association is then returned.

Appendix D shows how a subclass can be defined in which the key and value fields are arbitrary structures, hiding the use of the subclass Element.

```
//
//-------------------------------- AssociationList
//

class AssociationList : public List
{
public:
  void      add(Association& x);
  Association *  operator()();
};

inline void AssociationList::add(Association& x)
{  List::addFirst(x);  }

inline Association * AssociationList::operator()()
{  return (Association *) List::operator()();  }
```

Figure 17.15   The class AssociationList.

```
//
//----------------------------------------- Table
//

class Table
{
public:
  Table (int sz = 17);     // constructor - size of table

  Boolean    includesKey (Element& x);
  List&      keys ();
  void       removeKey (Element& x);
  int        size ();
  List&      values ();
  Element*&   operator [] (Element& x);

protected:
  const int tablesize;     // size of the table
  AssociationList *elements;   // table values

};
```

Figure 17.16   The class Table.

```
Element*& Table::operator [] (Element& x)
{    AssociationList& list = elements[x.hash() % tablesize];

  // see if already there
  list.reset();
  while (list++)
    if (*list() == x)
      return list()->value();

  // not there, make new association
  Association *p = new Association(x);
   list.add(*p);
  return p->value();
}
```

Figure 17.17   The subscripting operator in class Table.

Exercises

1. By building on the existing classes described in this chapter, implement the class Bag. Like a Set, a Bag contains unordered elements. Unlike in a Set, however, elements can be repeated in a Bag. Include a method that will determine the number of times an element appears in the Bag.

2. Explain why subclassing of class Element, as was done for integer lists and integer sets, cannot be used to form heterogeneous collections (collections in which not all elements are of the same type).

3. Trace the sequence of function calls involved in a subscript operation on a table.

4. The insertion or removal time for our ordered list is basically linear (that is, the time is proportional to the number of elements in the list.) How might this time be reduced? Describe a data structure that has the same interface as the class Ordered, but execution time logarithmic in the number of elements.

18
A Second Look at Classes

We have relied largely on an intuitive sense of what constitutes a *class*. Unfortunately, intuition differs from person to person. Some people think of a class as a template, a cookie-cutter with which multiple different instances can be created, a factory assembly line spewing out objects; other people think of a class as a generalized form of record; and so on. In this chapter, we investigate some of the more subtle issues involved with classes.

18.1 THE NATURE OF CLASSES

What exactly is a class? The answer to this question depends on what language you are considering. Broadly speaking, there are two general schools of thought on the issue. Some languages, such as C++ and Object Pascal, consider a class to be a *type*, similar to an integer or a record type. Other languages, such as Smalltalk and Objective-C, consider a class to be an *object*. In the next two sections we will consider some of the implications of these two different points of view.

Classes as Types

To understand the implications of the notion that a class is simply a type, we must first try to understand the meaning of the term *type* in programming languages. Unfortunately, the concept of type is used for a great many purposes. The following list, taken from [Wegner 86], illustrates a few of the many answers that could be given to the question "What is a type?"

- Application programmer's view: Types partition values into equivalence classes with common attributes and operations.

- System evolution (object-oriented) view: Types are behavior specifications (predicates) that may be composed and incrementally modified to form

259

new behavior specifications. Inheritance is an important mechanism for incrementally modifying behavior that supports system evolution.

- Type-checking view: Types impose syntactic constraints on expressions so that operators and operands of composite expressions are compatible. A type system is a set of rules for associating a type with every semantically meaningful subexpression of a programming language.

- Verification view: Types determine behavioral invariants that instances of the type are required to satisfy.

- System programming and security view: Types are a suit of clothes (armor) that protects raw information (bit strings) from unintended interpretations.

- Implementation view: Types specify a storage mapping for values.

The list is not intended to be complete; many aspects of the notion of type are not covered. For example, a type (array or record, for example) also conveys information about permissible syntax. Nevertheless, the list is sufficient for our purposes as a starting point for a discussion of classes as types.

Programming languages such as C++ and Object Pascal treat classes as an extension of the idea of the structure (or record). Like a record, a class defines fields; and each instance of the class maintains its own values for these fields. Unlike a record, a class can also have fields that represent functions or procedures (and, unlike the data fields, there is only one copy of each such function, shared by all instances of the class).

This view of classes fits nicely with most of the views we listed. From the points of view of the application programmer and of system evolution, all instances of a type will have common fields, and they will at least respond to the same set of commands. Certainly object-oriented techniques are even better than conventional methods for protecting raw bits from direct manipulation by the programmer. As soon as we add the mechanism of inheritance to classes, however, the view of types becomes somewhat more complex. In one sense, we can think of inheritance as simply a means of extending an existing record type. But this view is not entirely accurate, and we will consider two ways in which inheritance complicates the view of types.

An overridden method is not simply replacing a field in a record, but rather is altering the behavior of the object in a potentially arbitrary fashion. Consider the effect of this change on the process of verification. A programmer may develop a set of classes, and, by associating input and output conditions with each method, prove the correctness of a particular program. Next, a second programmer creates subclasses of the original classes, overriding some of the methods. If our view of subclasses corresponds to the *is-a* relation (Section 2.4), then, since an instance of the subclass *is-a* instance of the superclass, we should be able to substitute instances of the subclass for instances of the superclass in the program and still hope that the resulting program will remain correct.

While common programming practice (and common sense) dictate that an overridden method should not deviate too radically from the parent method, there

```
class ParallelCard : public CardView
{
  // inherit everything, but change drawing
public:
  void draw()
    { if (! fork()) { CardView::draw(); exit(0); }
};
```

Figure 18.1 A card with parallel drawing capabilities.

is generally no guarantee that the behavior or effect of an overridden method will have any relationship to the behavior of the method in the superclass. (Indeed, it usually will not have the same behavior or there would be no need for overriding.) Thus we are *not* in general assured that the the same input–output conditions will hold for the two methods. If one of these conditions is violated, the basis for our belief in the correctness of the program is invalidated, and the program probably will fail. A common source of the yo-yo problem (Section 14.3) is a programmer replacing, perhaps unintentionally, a method with a different method that does not preserve some important behavior.

For example, suppose we had argued for the correctness of the solitaire program presented in Chapter 10. Part of that argument would have involved an explanation of the routine draw in class TablePile, which displays one row on the tableau. To create this drawing, this routine simply loops over the cards from bottom to top, erasing the board under each card and redrawing the card image. Thus, the underlying cards are drawn, and then are partially erased in the process of the stack being drawn.

Suppose that the application has been developed, and that we have argued, either formally or informally, for its correctness. A new programmer now decides that she can improve the efficiency of the drawing routines using parallelism. Since drawing operations are somewhat time consuming, when a card is asked to draw itself, it will simply fork off a process to perform the drawing operation, and will continue execution in parallel. Techniques such as we described in Section 15.3 make this change easy to program. All that is necessary is to make a new class — for example, ParallelCard, that inherits from class CardView and overrides the single method draw. A class description for this class is shown in Figure 18.1. The programmer can then change the references to class CardView in the initialization portion of the program to use ParallelCard instead.

Unfortunately, the result of this change is to remove the certainty that, by the time we are drawing a card, all the cards in the pile below will have been drawn. Thus, it is possible — indeed, it is likely — that a random order of drawing will be produced, leading to a mangled display, such as that shown in Figure 18.2.

The important point is that the interface to the method has not changed, and in large part the effect of the method has not changed (both the original and

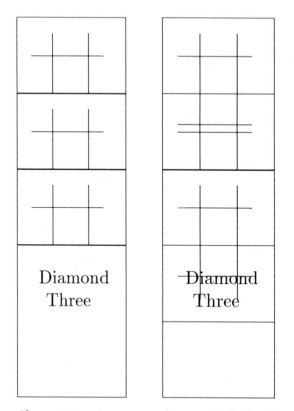

Figure 18.2   A proper and a mangled pile of cards.

the revised methods still draw the card), but some small portion of the behavior we associated with the method draw has changed. Since our arguments for the correctness of the program depended on the assumption there there would be no change, the altered program fails.

This example also illustrates that even the testing of programs can be altered by inheritance. The original program could be developed and throughly tested. A later programmer might be tempted to think that as long as the *is-a* relationship is maintained, an alteration will not invalidate the earlier testing. Unfortunately, this assumption is, in general, not valid, and any change should be verified through regression testing [Perry 90].

The object-oriented language Eiffel [Meyer 88a] overcomes at least some aspects of this problem in an interesting way. Assertions can be attached to methods, and are inherited by and cannot be overridden in subclasses (although they can be extended). The compiler will generate code to check, at run time, the veracity of the assertions. Thus, a minimum degree of functionality can be ensured for a method, irrespective of any overriding that may take place. Of course, some assertions may be difficult to phrase in terms of executable code, such as the assertion that the card is completely drawn before the program returns from the method.

Next, consider the relationship between types and storage mappings. Here, too, inheritance results in subtle problems that are not present in more conventional types, such as records or arrays. Since, in the "classes as records" view, an instance of a subtype for a class is an extension of an instance of the original class, it can, of course, take up more space. As we saw in Chapter 11, however, this change in size complicates such seemingly trivial issues as assignment.

In summary, the conception of class as a type fits nicely with much of our intuitive understanding of the idea of "typeness," but the fit is not exact. The second view — that of classes as objects — eliminates some of these problems by avoiding a discussion of type altogether.

Classes as Objects

We have emphasized from the beginning of this book that the basic philosophy in object-oriented programming is the delegation of responsibility for activity. Every object is responsible for its own internal state, and makes changes to that state according to a few fixed rules of behavior. Alternatively, every activity must be the responsibility of some object, or it will not be performed. Certainly, the creation of new instances of a given class is an activity. The question is, who (that is, which object) should have the responsibility for this behavior?

One model is to have a centralized "object-creation" object. A request for the dynamic creation of a new object is translated into a call to this object, passing to it as arguments the size of the requested object and the list of methods to which the new object will respond. Although this model is workable, it places the responsibility for remembering this information (size and methods) on the caller.

A better solution encapsulates this information, placing a layer of management between the user who desires the creation of a new object and the code that performs the allocation of the memory. Responsibility for knowing the size of objects and the methods to which they will respond is placed in the intermediate management level, and thus need not be known by either the user or the allocation code. Working in this manner, we arrive at a scheme where we have one new object for each class in the system. The major responsibility of this object is simply to create new instances of the class. To do this, it must maintain information about the size of the class it represents and the methods to which instances of this class will respond. In a practical sense, this object *is* the class.

Every object must be an instance of some class, however, and this object is no exception. Of what class is this object an instance? The answer, in Smalltalk and similar systems, is that it is an instance of a class called Class. Figure 18.3 shows a CRC card (both front side and back) for the class Class in the Little Smalltalk system. By convention, the value of this object is maintained in a variable that has the same name as the class itself. That is, the variable Set

Class – *class of all classes*

---

new – *Make new instance of class.*
addSubclass:super:instanceVariables:–
  Add a new subclass.
method: – *Return method by given name.*

Class – *data values maintained*

---

name – *Name of class as string.*
instanceSize – *Number of instance variables.*
methods – *Dictionary containing all the methods.*
superClass – *Superclass object.*
variables – *Array of names of variables.*

Figure 18.3   CRC card for class Class (both sides).

contains as a value the object, with a structure similar to that shown in Figure 18.3, that is responsible for creating new instances of the class.

Creation is accomplished by means of the message new, which is defined as a method in class Class. Every created object is an instance of some class, and maintains a pointer back to the object representing that class. During the process of message passing, this pointer is used to find a method that matches the selector for the message being evaluated.

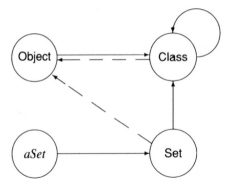

Figure 18.4   Instance and subclass relationships.

To understand this structure, you must differentiate between the *subclass* relationship and the *instance* relationship. The class Class is a subclass of the class Object; and thus, the object Class points to the object Object as its superclass. On the other hand, the object Object is an instance of the class Class; and thus, Object points back to Class. Class Class is itself a class, and thus an instance of itself. If we examine a typical class, say class Set, then the object Set is an instance of class Class but a subclass (indirectly) of class Object. A particular set is an instance of the class Set. These relationships are illustrated in Figure 18.4, where solid lines are used to represent the *instance* relationship and dashed lines the *subclass* relationship.

Metaclasses and Class Methods.   We have already noted that initialization is often an important part of object creation (Chapter 4). Since objects are responsible for maintaining their own state, it would be useful if the object in charge of creating new instances of a class could also ensure that the object was properly initialized. The meaning of "initialize," however, is different from class to class. If all class objects are instances of the same class, we cannot specialize their behavior; that is, they must all execute the same method and thus perform in the same manner.

A related problem is that often creation and initialization require more information than simply the values shown in Figure 18.3. To create an array, for example, we need to know the number of positions to allocate to the array. Other classes may require even further information.

Both of these problems require that we specialize the behavior of the class object, so it is not surprising that the same mechanism is used in the solution. We have always insisted that behavior be associated with classes, not with individual objects (all instances of a class will share the same behavior). If we want the class variables to have their own individual behavior, the only solution is to make them instances of their own classes.

Object – *The superclass of all objects*
  Collection – *The abstract superclass of all collections*
    Bag – *A class for multi-set data objects*

Figure 18.5   A portion of the class hierarchy from Smalltalk-80.

Object – *The superclass of all objects*
  Class – *Behavior common to all classes*
    Metaclass-Object – *initialization of all Objects*
      Metaclass-Collection – *initialization of Collections*
        Metaclass-Bag – *initialization of Bags*

Figure 18.6   A portion of the corresponding metaclass hierarchy.

A *metaclass* is a class of a class. In Smalltalk-80 a metaclass is implicitly and automatically constructed for each class defined by the user. Each metaclass has only one instance, which is the class object itself. Metaclasses are organized into a class–subclass hierarchy that mirrors the class–subclass hierarchy of the original class, but has metaclasses and has class Class at the root, instead of class Object. Figure 18.5 shows a portion of the class hierarchy in Smalltalk-80; Figure 18.6 shows the corresponding metaclass hierarchy.[1]

Code that is specific to a single class can be associated with the metaclass for that class. For example, instances of the class Bag maintain a dictionary that is used to hold the actual values. The metaclass for Bag overrides the method new to perform default initialization of this dictionary when new instances are created. This behavior is accomplished by a method new being defined in class Metaclass-Bag that overrides the method from class Class. That method is shown in Figure 18.7.

Since class Bag is an instance of class Metaclass-Bag, the method shown in Figure 18.7 will be the method selected to respond to the message new. The method first passes the message on to the superclass, which performs an action similar to that shown in Figure 18.3. The superclass thus creates the new object. Once the new object is returned, the message setDictionary is sent to this object. This method, shown in Figure 18.8, merely sets the instance field contents to a newly created dictionary.

If you find this discussion confusing, you are not alone. The concept of metaclasses has a reputation for being one of the more exotic and arcane aspects of Smalltalk-80. Nevertheless, it serves a useful purpose; namely it

---

[1] The picture has been slightly simplified for ease of discussion. In the actual Smalltalk-80 system, the class Class is a subclass of class ClassDescription, which is in turn a subclass of class Behavior. The method corresponding to the description of the method new in Figure 18.3 is in fact found in class Behavior, and not in class Class. These distinctions are unimportant for our discussion here.

```
new
    " create and initialize a new instance"
    ↑ super new setDictionary
```

Figure 18.7   The class method new in class Bag.

permits us to specialize behavior for the initialization of individual classes without leaving the pure object-oriented framework. Given the confusing nature of metaclasses, however, most programmers are grateful that the systems in which metaclasses are used largely isolate the programmers from being aware of them. In Smalltalk-80, for example, class methods are created as part of browsing the base class, and not the metaclass. Clicking the "class" or "instance" box in the second pane indicates whether the metaclass or the actual class is being described. Similarly, in Objective-C, methods that are preceded by a plus sign in the first column (so-called factory methods) are associated with the metaclass, whereas those that begin with a minus sign are class methods.

We have shown how class methods, which are defined by means of metaclasses, can be used to solve one of the problems outlined at the beginning of this section: specializing initialization. We now return to the second problem: the initialization of objects when more information than simply the size of the object is required. We will show how class methods can be used to solve this problem, and more.

We will use as our examples the Smalltalk-80 class Date, instances of which represent a given date in a given year. Each instance of Date does its task by maintaining two values: the year number, and a number between 1 and 366 representing the day number. A new instance of Date can be created in a variety of ways. The message "Date today," for example, yields an instance of Date representing the current date. Dates can also be defined by the user explicitly giving a year and day value. The code shown in Figure 18.9 is then invoked. This code performs a small amount of error checking, making certain the day number is positive and is not larger than the number of actual days in the year, modifying both the day number and year number accordingly. When it is certain that legal values are known, it uses the new method to create a new object, and initializes the object with the given values.

The message daysInYear:, invoked in the method shown in Figure 18.9, illustrates another use for class methods; namely, they are a way to provide functionality associated with the general idea of the class, but not necessarily

```
setDictionary
    " set a new dictionary in the contents variable"
    contents <- Dictionary new
```

Figure 18.8   The method setDictionary in class Bag.

```
newDay: dayCount  year: referenceYear
  " Answer with a Date which is dayCount days after "
  " the beginning of the year referenceYear."
  | day year daysInYear |
  day <- dayCount.
  year <- referenceYear.
  [day > (daysInYear <- self daysInYear: year)]
    whileTrue:
      [year <- year + 1.
       day <- day - daysInYear].
  [day <= 0]
    whileTrue:
      [year <- year - 1.
       day <- day + (self daysInYear: year)].
  ↑ self new day: day year: year
```

Figure 18.9   The class method newDay:year: in class Date.

with any specific instance. The object Date can be asked for the number of days in any specific year, and will return an integer without actually building a new instance of class. It does this using the same mechanism of defining a class method, except that, in this case, the class method returns an integer rather than a new value. The method **daysInYear**, and the method **leapYear:**, which it calls, are shown in Figure 18.10.

Posing in Objective-C.   An interesting artifact of the "classes as objects" view is the concept of *posing* in Objective-C. We have several times seen situations where the programmer wished to substitute one class with another in an existing application. Usually, the new class inherited from the original class, and modified only a small portion of the behavior. Examples are the GraphicalReactor class of Section 15.3, and the ParallelCard class described in

```
daysInYear: yearInteger
  " Answer the number of days in the year, yearInteger"
  ↑ 365 + (self leapYear: yearInteger)

leapYear: yearInteger
  " Answer 1 if the year yearInteger is a leap year; "
  " answer 0 if it is not."
  (yearInteger \\ 4 ~= 0 or:
    [yearInteger \\ 100 = 0 and:
    [yearInteger \\ 400 ~= 0]])
      ifTrue: [ ↑ 0]
      ifFalse: [ ↑ 1]
```

Figure 18.10   The class method daysInYear: in class Date.

Section 18.1. In both of those cases, we indicated that it would be necessary to change the creation messages to use the new class in place of the original.

Objective-C provides a unique alternative to this technique that is much less invasive of the original code. Any class can be instructed to pose as another class. In effect, the *poser object* takes the place of the original class object. For example, the user could write the following statement:

```
[ GraphicalReactor poseAs: [ Reactor class ]];
```

All subsequent references to the class Reactor, including messages to create new instances of the class, would in fact be sent to the class GraphicalReactor. Most often, the object doing the posing is a class object that represents a subclass of the class being replaced; thus, the majority of messages will be passed back to the original class (now the superclass).

18.2   CLASS DATA

Regardless of which view of the nature of classes we take, it is frequently desirable to have a data area that is shared by all instances of a class. All Windows might be maintained on a common linked list, for example, or all Cards in a single deck.

The conventional solution would make use of a global variable. Such a variable would certainly be accessible to and shared by all instances of the class, since it is accessible to and shared by all objects. Such broad accessibility, however, flies in the face of the object-oriented philosophy, which is one of limiting access, and of centralizing responsibility for activities in specific individuals. Thus, the object-oriented view requires us to seek another alternative. That alternative is to create values that are accessible to instances of a class, but to no others. Such values are know as *class variables*.

A subtle problem concerns how the initialization of class variables can be accomplished. In a certain sense, all instances of a class are equal: They all share the same behavior. Yet there is only one copy of any class variable. The difficult aspect of class variables involves avoiding the dual problems of (1) not initializing the class data at all and (2) initializing them more than once. One solution, in both Smalltalk and Objective-C, is that the system will ensure that the class method initialize is sent to each class before any other message. The response to the initialize method can then be used to set the values of any class variables. This message is taken care of implicitly, and there should be no reason for the user ever to invoke the initialize method directly.

The implementation of the concept of class variables is not possible in all the languages we are considering, and, in any case, the mechanisms are quite different in the various languages. In the following sections, we will describe the mechanics of creating class variables in those languages that support the concept.

```
Magnitude subclass: #Date
  instanceVariableNames: 'day year'
  classVariableNames: 'DaysInMonth FirstDayOfMonth
    MonthNames SecondsInDay WeekDayNames'
  poolDictionaries: ''
  category: 'Numeric-Magnitudes'
```

Figure 18.11   The class creation message for class Date.

Class Variables in Smalltalk

From the user's point of view, we create class variables by simply listing them by name when we create a new class. Figure 18.11, for example, shows the declaration of the class Date. As we noted in the last section, instances of Date are used to represent calendar days. The class variables are used to maintain several arrays of information that are useful when manipulating dates. These include the number of days in non leap-year months, the names of the months, the days of the week, and so on. Internally, such variables are treated as instance variables of the metaclass associated with the class. Initialization of class variables can be accomplished as part of the class method initialize.

Class Variables in C++

The language C++ redefines the keyword static when the latter is used in the context of a class description.[2] In this context, the word implies that one copy of the value is created, and that this value is shared by all instances of the class. Such values, which we are calling class variables, are called *static members* in C++. The normal visibility rules (indicated by the keywords private, protected, or public) can be used with static members to limit accessibility outside the methods associated with the class.

By declaring the fields CardWidth and CardHeight in the class CardView described in Chapter 10 (Figure 18.12), we avoid the creation of separate constants in each instance of the class.

A static member is initialized outside the class definition in a manner similar to global variables, the class name disambiguation serving to tie the declaration to the proper class. As with global variables, only one initialization of a static data member can occur within a program.

---

[2]The keyword static must be one of the most overloaded keywords in the C/C++ language. In addition to the meaning given here, when applied to a global variable or a function, it indicates a reduction of scope, and when applied to a local variable, it means an extension of lifetime.

```
//
//   --------------------------   class Card
//
class CardView
{
  public:
    // constructor
  CardView(Card *);
  CardView(int s, int c);

    // constants
  static const int CardWidth = 68;
  static const int CardHeight = 75;

  ...
};

const int CardView::CardWidth = 68;
const int CardView::CardHeight = 75;
```

Figure 18.12 A class description showing a static field.

Because there is only one copy of a static member in a class, a publicly accessible static member can be accessed directly. For example, the class CardPile can display a pile of cards using the code shown in Figure 18.13.

Note that static members need not be public, and, if they are not, the accessibility of the data follows the normal visibility rules. C++ also permits methods to be declared static. Static methods can access only static data, and are in many ways similar to class methods described earlier for Smalltalk and Objective-C.

Class Variables in Objective-C

There is no explicit support for class variables in Objective-C. We can create something similar by declaring simple C static variables in the implementation portion of a class. Such values are accessible only within the file containing

```
void CardPile::display()
{
  if (top == nilLink)
    game->clearArea(x, y, x+CardView::CardWidth,
                          y+CardView::CardHeight);
  else
    top->draw();
}
```

Figure 18.13 Use of static members from outside a class.

```
# import "Date.h"

static char *dayNames[ ] = {"Sunday", "Monday", "Tuesday",
    "Wednesday", "Thursday", "Friday", "Saturday"};

@implementation Date
  ...
@end
```

Figure 18.14   Static variables in implementation files in Objective-C.

the implementation; they cannot be accessed in subclasses or by users. For example, methods in the class Date in Figure 18.14 can reference the static array dayNames. (This trick also works in C++, as long as all functions accessing the data reside in the same file.)

18.3   ARE CLASSES NECESSARY?

Given the subtle issues involved in objects, instances, classes, metaclasses, and the like, we might wonder whether an object-oriented language could be constructed without the mechanism of classes. The surprising answer is yes, although it is not yet clear whether programming in such classless object-oriented languages is any easier or faster than is programming in class based languages, or whether the resulting programs are any more efficient.

The object-oriented approach is related to a view of understanding that asserts that people categorize information by appealing to an abstract idealization of a concept. The Greek philosopher Plato claimed, for example, that our understanding of the concept of "chair" was not grounded in any specific chair, but was instead derived from an idealized abstraction of the notion of "chairness." All physical objects are only approximations to this more perfect abstraction — they are mere shadows of the ideal.

A less prosaic view of understanding asserts that people acquire information by learning from specific instances, and then slowly discarding incidental specifics to build a more general abstraction. A person's understanding of the concept "elephant," for example, may be grounded in a specific elephant he encountered at a particular zoo when he was young. He then understands a second Elephant by relating it to the earlier example — the new elephant may have smaller ears, for example, so the learner decides that the size of the ear is not an essential characteristic of elephantness. By repeating this relating process a number of times, the person develops a general characterization of a concept. Each characterization is simply a thread that leads back to specific instances on which the characterization is based. (The description given here is, of course, greatly simplified; the version studied by linguists and philosophers is considerably more complex. We must account for exceptions, for example. The observation of an albino elephant does not suddenly make our learner change his association of the color gray with elephants.)

In programming languages, this concept of relating specific instances is known as *delegation* [Lieberman 86]. In delegation, there are no classes; instead, a programmer creates specific instances of objects, and behavior is associated with individual objects. Whenever an object is similar to an existing object, the program can delegate a portion of its behavior to the original object. Any message not understood by the new object will be passed on to the delegated object. This object in turn may have delegated its behavior to another object, and so on.

Thus, we can build a language out of *objects*, which possess variables and methods, and *delegation*, by which an object can defer responsibility for any unrecognized methods to another object. Sharing takes place in such languages by the use of common delegates.

As an illustration, let us build a simple graphics system. Suppose we are provided with a line-drawing object, which can respond to only one message — namely, drawFromTo(a, b, c, d). In response to this message, the object will draw a solid line from the coordinates (a,b) to (c,d).

We first build a *pen*, which is a drawing instrument that remembers its coordinates. The pen object encapsulates two variables, x and y, and defines a suite of methods for setting and retrieving these values: getX(), getY(), setX(a), setY(b). Next, the pen object defines two methods for drawing with the pen nib — namely, moveTo(a,b), which merely moves the pen without drawing, and drawTo(a,b), which draws a line. These methods could be defined by the following pseudo-code:

```
method moveTo(a, b)

   self setX(a)

   self setY(b)

end
```

```
method drawTo(a, b)

   self drawFromTo(self getX(), self getY(), a, b)

   self moveTo(a, b)

end
```

The pen object delegates responsibility for the drawFromTo method to the line object (Figure 18.15).

Suppose the programmer wants to create a second pen. Using the delegation technique, the programmer first provides a description of the object, relating the object (if possible) to existing objects. One description might be "the second pen should behave exactly like the first pen, only it should maintain its

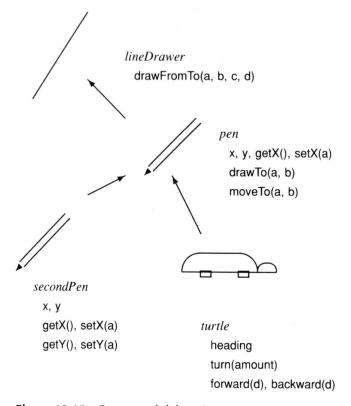

lineDrawer
drawFromTo(a, b, c, d)

pen
  x, y, getX(), setX(a)
  drawTo(a, b)
  moveTo(a, b)

secondPen
  x, y
  getX(), setX(a)
  getY(), setY(a)

turtle
  heading
  turn(amount)
  forward(d), backward(d)

Figure 18.15   Patterns of delegation.

own coordinates." From this description, it is clear that the second pen should maintain its own variables, and should define methods for setX and the rest. Because it delegates to the first pen, however, these are the *only* methods that need to be defined; all other behavior can be inherited from the first pen. When a message is sent to the second pen, the receiver (the second pen) is sent as part of the message along the delegation path. When subsequent messages are sent to the "self" object (called the *client* in Lieberman's terminology), the search commences once more with the original receiver. Thus, the messages setX and getX — used, for example, in the drawTo method — will be matched to those in the second pen and not to those in the first pen. This process of matching is similar to the way in which method binding always begins with the base class of the receiver; it results in the delegation equivalent of the yo-yo problem.

It is not necessary for delegating objects to redefine their variables. Suppose we wanted to create a kaleidoscopePen, which reflected every line around both the x and y axis, drawing four lines for each single line of the original pen (Figure 18.16). We could create an object that redefined only the single method drawTo. All other behavior could be delegated to the original pen. Since the x

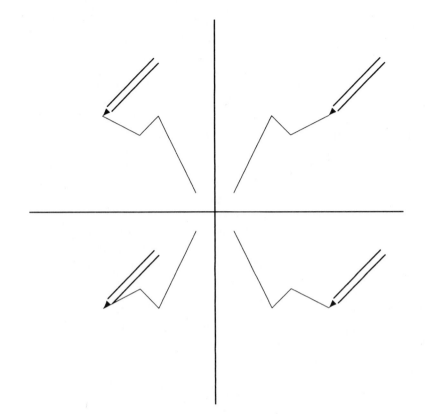

Figure 18.16   Output of a kaleidoscopePen.

and y variables are those of the original pen, changes to the kaleidoscopePen would result in changes to the original pen. The new drawTo method is as follows:

```
method drawTo(a, b)
  self drawFromTo(self getX(), self getY(), a, b)
  self drawFromTo(- self getX(), self getY(), - a, b)
  self drawFromTo(self getX(), - self getY(), a, - b)
  self drawFromTo(- self getX(), - self getY(), - a, - b)
  self moveTo(a, b)
end
```

Now, suppose the programmer wants to define a *turtle*. A turtle [Abelson 81] is a pen that maintains not only a location, but also an orientation. In addition to drawing, a turtle can be instructed to turn, and to move forward or backward in the direction of its current orientation. If we use an existing pen to hold the turtle coordinates, the turtle needs to define only the single variable heading, as well as the methods turn(amount), forward(amount), and backward(amount).

An interesting feature of delegation-based systems is the ability to change delegates dynamically. Once the turtle facility has been constructed, if the user changes the delegate from a pen to a dashedPen, the turtle suddenly develops the ability to draw not only straight, but also dashed, lines. (Of course, changing to a delegate who does not understand all the messages required by an object can cause formerly operational code to break down).

In a certain sense, the object–delegate relationship is similar to the instance–class relationship; with the exception that there are no longer two types of entities. The delegate is simply another object. Nevertheless, it is common to create classlike factory objects, which do nothing more than create copies of an existing object. For example, it is possible to generate a turtle factory that will, when requested, return a new turtle that is independent of all other turtles.

The primary reference for delegation is Lieberman [Lieberman 86]. His paper showed that, using delegation, we can simulate inheritance. The reverse — that, using inheritance, one could simulate delegation — was shown by Stein [Stein 87]. A delegation-based language called Self has been described by Ungar [Ungar 87]. Tomlinson provides a good analysis of the time and space requirements of delegation and inheritance [Tomlinson 90], concluding that inheritance is generally faster and, surprisingly, requires less space.

18.4   PARAMETERIZED CLASSES

In the object-oriented model, when a programmer wants to create a special-ized version of an existing class, the mechanism of inheritance is used most frequently. Inheritance has its limitations, however. Consider the creation of generalized data structure classes, such as linked lists. A node in such a list might have a structure such as shown in Figure 18.17. There are two data fields maintained by the object: a link to the next node and the actual data object. The link field clearly can be defined as a pointer to another linked list node, but what type should be used for the data field? One choice is to create a new class — for example, Element — and force the user to declare all val-ues that might appear on a linked list as subclasses of this base class. (This is the approach we used in Section 11.4, and in Chapter 17.) Although this is possible, it is a less than satisfactory solution. For one thing, it forces the programmer to anticipate the use of a data item in a linked list, and to struc-ture her class hierarchy accordingly. The programmer could not make a linked list of instances of Shapes, for example, or of Window, unless the designer of the original class foresaw this use and declared his class to be a subclass of Element.

Alternatively, a programmer can create her own subclass of Element and then point to the actual data. The class ShapeElement in Figure 18.18 for example, illustrates a link that simply maintains a pointer to an instance of

```
class LinkedList {
  public:
    Element *data;
    LinkedList *link;
  ...
  };
```

Figure 18.17   A linked list node in C++.

Shape. This technique forces the creation of an extra class description and the overhead of an extra level of indirection on the user. (This approach is also used in Chapter 17.)

There is yet a more serious problem: there is a fundamental conflict between the dynamic polymorphic behavior of inheritance and the goals of static compile-time type checking. Consider the situation where linked lists have been defined as in Figures 18.17 and 18.18, along with several other types of link nodes similar to Figure 18.18. When the user assigns a value to the data field of the linked-list node (Figure 18.17), the compiler treats the data as though they were an instance of Element. The fact that they may, in fact, be a ShapeElement, for example, is "forgotten." Now consider what happens when the user tries to access or extract the data as though they were an instance of ShapeElement. Even if the actual value is indeed an instance of ShapeElement, there is no way for the compiler to verify this fact. The compiler will complain that an instance of a superclass is being assigned to a value declared to be from the subclass. As we saw in Chapter 11, there is often good reason why this situation is not permitted in object-oriented programming languages.

A better solution to this problem is to add the ability to *parameterize* class descriptions. Using parameterized classes, the user declares a class template in which the types of various fields are left unfilled. A parameterized class can be thought of as a family of classes, where the parameter value is used to generate specific qualified versions of the class. Specific instances can then be created from these qualified classes. Thus instead of the two level class–instance distinction, there are three levels: parameterized class, qualified class, and instance.

Parameterized classes are not currently part of any of the languages we are considering; however, they have been proposed as an extension to C++ (see [Ellis 90, pages 341–351], where the feature is marked "experimental"). It is


```
class ShapeElement : public Element {
  public:
    Shape *data;
  ...
  };
```

Figure 18.18   Definition of a class specific data node.

```
template<class T> class vector {
  T* v;
  int sz;
public:
  vector(int);
  T& operator[ ] (int);
};
```

Figure 18.19   A parameterized vector in C++.

likely, therefore, that future versions of the C++ language will support them. The following example is taken from Ellis, [Ellis 90].

Parameterized classes are defined in C++ by use of the template keyword. This keyword is followed by what amounts to an argument list, with the exception that the list is surrounded by angle brackets, and, in addition to ordinary arguments, class types can be indicated. The latter must be preceded by the keyword class. An example is shown in Figure 18.19, which describes a template for generalized vector structures.

The user creates specific classes by filling in the parameterized type values with specific types. For example, the following creates a vector of length 10 containing integers, and a second vector of length 30 containing complex numbers. These vectors can then be manipulated using the operations provided in the class template:

```
vector<int> v1(10);

vector<complex> v2(30):


v1[3] = 17;

v2[22] = complex(7, 10);
```

The template keyword must also be used in method definitions. Here is the method body for the subscripting operator described in Figure 18.19:

```
template<class T> T& vector<T>::operator[ ] (int i)

{

  if (i < 0 || i >= sz) error("vector: range error");

  return v[i];

}
```

In addition to being used in C++, parameterized classes are found in the object-oriented languages Eiffel [Meyer 88a], and CLOS [Bobrow 88], and in a few others.

Exercises

1. What aspects of the notion of *type* are not covered by Wegner's categories (Section 18.1.). Define new views to reflect these aspects.

2. Study the techniques of verification in conventional programming languages (good explanations are given in [Gries 81, Dijkstra 76]). What problems do you run into when you attempt to apply these techniques to object-oriented languages?

3. The message new passed to the object Dictionary in the method shown in Figure 18.8 will actually be interpreted in the class MetaclassDictionary, which may override it to provide default initialization for dictionaries. Draw the metaclass hierarchy Dictionary, similar to the hierarchy for class Bag shown in Figure 18.6. Then, trace the actual method invoked by the new message shown in Figure 18.8.

4. Discuss some of the advantages and disadvantages of class methods. Is the increased flexibility provided by class methods offset by the complexity incurred by the introduction of metaclasses?

5. Give a pseudo-code description of a second turtle, which shares behavior but no data with the first turtle created in Section 18.3.

6. Using delegation, create an object called twoPen that draws parallel lines with two pens that are held a fixed distance from each other.

7. By making use of class objects, sketch the proof that delegation can be used to simulate inheritance.

8. Explain why parameterized classes will help in the creation of homogeneous collections (collections in which all elements are of the same type), but not heterogeneous collections (collections containing a variety of types of elements).

19
Implementation

It is not the intent of this book to provide a detailed description of the implementation of the various programming languages we have been considering. Nevertheless, a general understanding of the several approaches that can be employed to produce the effect of an object-oriented style of execution is useful to the reader attempting to understand how object-oriented languages differ from more conventional systems. In this chapter, we provide a general overview of some of the more important implementation techniques, as well as pointers to the relevant literature for the reader who desires more complete information.

Broadly speaking, there are two major approaches to programming language implementation: compilers and interpreters. A *compiler* translates the user's program into native machine code for the target machine, and is invoked as a separate process, independent of program execution. An *interpreter*, on the other hand, is present during execution, and is the system that runs the user program.[1] Generally, a program that is translated by a compiler will execute faster than will a program that is run under an interpreter. On the other hand the time between conception, entering text, and execution in a compiled system may be longer than the corresponding time in an interpreter. Furthermore, when errors occur at run time, the compiler often has little more than the generated assembly language to offer as markers pointing to the probable location of the error. An interpreter, on the other hand, will usually relate back the error to the original text the user entered. Thus, there are advantages and disadvantages to both techniques.

---

[1] As is true of most distinctions, while the endpoints are clear, there are large gray areas in the middle. There are compilers — Lightspeed C for the Macintosh, for example — that compile interactively as the programmer enters portions of the program. Thus, the compiler is present in memory even during execution (at least during the debugging stages). These compilers gain some of the advantages of the interpreter world while giving the execution-time advantage of the compiler technique. Similarly, some interpreters can translate either into an intermediate representation or into native code.

Although some languages are usually compiled and others are usually interpreted, there is nothing intrinsic in a language that forces the implementor always to select one technique over the other. The language C++ is usually compiled, but there are C++ interpreters. On the other hand, Smalltalk is almost always interpreted, but experimental Smalltalk compilers have been produced.

19.1   COMPILERS

A typical characteristic of compilers is that a certain amount of information is lost during the translation from source program to machine code. Most notable of these changes is the translation from symbolic names to numerical addresses. Variables that are local to a procedure, for example, are addressed in the compiled code not by their name, but rather by a fixed offset relative to the activation record created at procedure entry.[2] Similarly, fields in a record are described by their offset from the start of the record, not by their name.

As we have noted in earlier chapters, an object has certain similarities to a record or structure in a more conventional language. Like those in a record, the data fields (instance variables) in an object can be allocated fixed locations relative to the beginning of the object. Subclasses can only extend this memory area — they cannot reduce it. Thus, the memory layout of a descendent class is strictly larger than that of the ancestor class, and the offsets of the data items from the superclass must match the locations of the corresponding fields in the subclass.

Consider the classes GraphicalObject and Ball from the billiards simulation described in Chapter 16 (pages 237 and 238). A GraphicalObject maintains the instance variable fields link and region. A Ball adds to this the fields direction and energy, but maintains the fields of the earlier class in exactly the same offsets (Figure 19.1). That the offsets of the fields from the parent class are preserved in the child class is important; it permits methods defined in the parent class to manipulate the instance data using fixed offsets, and thus such routines will execute correctly regardless of the classes of the arguments. For example, the moveTo method defined in class GraphicalObject will perform as intended regardless of the class of the receiver, since it manipulates only the region portion of the object.

The most novel feature of object-oriented programming, from the implementation point of view, is that the interpretation of a message can depend on the type (class) of the receiver. Thus, somehow, each object must maintain a means to determine which procedure is to be invoked for each possible message that it understands. Furthermore, we would like the mechanism that is used to bind a method to a procedure to execute as fast as possible.

---

[2]The activation record is a portion of the run-time stack set aside at procedure entry to hold parameters, local variables, and other information. Further details on the run-time environment of programs can be found in a compiler-construction textbook, such as [Aho 85, Fischer 88].

An instance of Wall

link
region
convertFactor

An instance of Ball

link
region
direction
energy

Figure 19.1 Fields in subclasses matched to those in superclasses.

Virtual Method Tables

One possible approach would be to allocate fields in an object for methods, exactly the way space is allocated for data fields. The values in these fields would be pointers to the appropriate method (Figure 19.2). For a method to be invoked, it would suffice to take the value found at the correct offset in an object, dereference it to yield a procedure, then call the procedure.

This approach, although efficient in terms of execution speed, is wasteful of another important resource — namely, space. Each object would need to maintain space (one pointer) for each method. Furthermore, the creation of such an object would involve initializing all the method fields, which is unnecessarily costly. A compromise between speed and space is possible, based on the observation that all instances of the same class will share the same methods. Thus, a *single* table can be created for each class. All instances of the class will contain *one* pointer to this table (Figure 19.3). Initialization of a new instance includes the setting of this *virtual method table pointer*.

This table is called a *virtual method table*. The values in the table are pointers to procedures. If we assume that these procedures are known to the compiler and do not change during execution, the table can be created statically at compile time. To execute a method, we need to know only the offset of the method in the virtual method table.

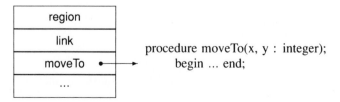

Figure 19.2 Methods that are simply data fields.

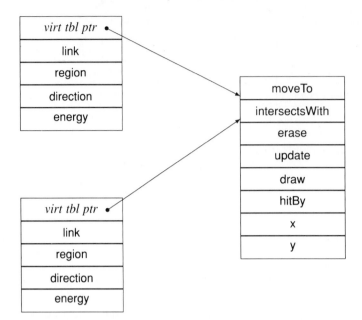

Figure 19.3   Two balls sharing a virtual method table.

As with the data areas, the virtual method table of an ancestor class will
be a subset of the virtual method table of a descendant class, and offsets in the
former will be equally appropriate for the latter. A class that inherits methods
from a superclass merely copies the common portion of the virtual method table
into the table for the subclass. When a method is overridden in a subclass, it
is necessary to alter only the entry for the method that is changed. Figure 19.4
shows the virtual method tables for the two classes Ball and Wall, which are
both descendents of the class GraphicalObject. Notice that they share pointers
to those methods inherited from the parent class, and that the order of the entries
is that given in the parent class, not the order given in the child class (refer back
to Figure 16.4, page 237, and Figure 16.6, page 238, to see this).

Once a compiler knows how to access the pointer to a method, the method
can be invoked in the same manner as a conventional procedure. The receiver
is treated as though it were the first parameter in the argument list, so that it is
available as the value of the variable self (this, in C++). Assume, for example,
that vtab is the internal field name used to represent the virtual method table in
the class of an object x, and that the offset of the method hitBy in that table is
location 12. Then, a method invocation, such as

```
x.hitBy(y)
```

if the target language happened to be C, would be translated internally into
something similar to the following:

```
(*(*(x.vtab))[12])(x, y)
```

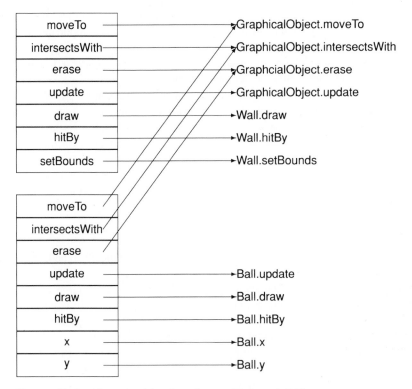

Figure 19.4 Virtual tables for classes Wall and Ball.

Notice that the method name does not appear in the final generated code, and that this code will select the appropriate method whether x is a Ball, a Wall, or any other graphical object. The overhead, in terms of execution time, for a message send is simply two levels of pointer indirection and one subscript operation.

Name Encoding

We have noted already that, since methods are all known at compile time and cannot change at run time, the virtual tables are simply static data areas established by the compiler. These data areas consist of pointers to the appropriate methods. Because linkers and loaders resolve references based on symbols, some mechanism must be provided to avoid name collisions when two or more methods have the same name. The typical scheme combines the names of the class and of the method. Thus the draw method in class Ball might become Ball::draw internally. Usually, the user need never see this name, unless he is forced to examine the assembly-language output of the compiler.

In languages such as C++ that allow methods to be further overloaded with disambiguation based on parameter type, even more complicated Gödel-like encodings of the class name, method name, and argument types are required. For example, the three constructors shown in Figure 4.3 (page 66) might be known internally as Complex::Complex, Complex::Complex_float, and Complex::Complex_float_float, respectively. Such internal names, called *mangled* names, can become very long. As we have seen, this internal name is not used during the process of message passing, but rather is used merely in the construction of the virtual tables, and to make unique procedure names for the linker.

The introduction of multiple inheritance somewhat complicates the technique of using virtual method tables, however, the details are beyond the scope of this book. Interested readers can find a more complete description in [Ellis 90].

Dispatch Tables

Because languages such as C++ or Object Pascal are statically typed, they can determine, at compile time, at least the parent class type of any object-oriented expression. Thus, a virtual method table needs to be only large enough to accommodate those methods actually implemented by a class. In a dynamically typed language, such as Objective-C, however, a virtual method table must include *all* messages understood by any class, and this table needs to be repeated for every class. If an application has 20 classes, for example, and they each on average implement 10 methods, then we would need 20 tables, each consisting of 200 entries. The size requirements quickly become exorbitant, and a better technique is called for.

An alternative technique is to associate with every class a table that, unlike the virtual method table, consists of selector–method pairs. This table is called a *dispatch table*. The selectors correspond to only those methods actually implemented in a class. Inherited methods are accessed through a pointer in this table, which points to the dispatch table associated with a superclass (Figure 19.5).

As in a system using virtual method tables, when dispatch tables are used every object carries with it an implicit (that is, not declared) pointer to the dispatch table associated with the class of the value it represents. This implicit pointer is known as the *isa* link. (The *isa* link should not be confused with the *is-a* relation between classes.)

A message expression in Objective-C, such as the following expression from the eight queens problem:

```
[neighbor checkrow: row column: column]
```

is translated by the Objective-C compiler[3] into:

```
objc_msgSend(neighbor,"checkrow:column:", row, column)
```

---

[3]The Objective-C system is actually a translator that produces conventional C code. In addition, the string form of the selector is not actually used; instead selectors are hashed into numeric values.

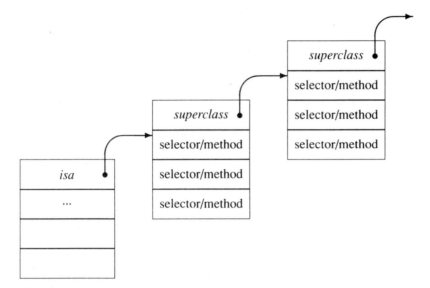

Figure 19.5 An object and its dispatch table.

The function objc_msgSend, called the *messaging function*, follows the *isa* link of the first argument to find the appropriate dispatch table. The messaging function then searches the dispatch table for an entry that matches the selector. If such an entry is found, the associated method is invoked. If no such method is found, the dispatch table of the superclass is searched. If the root class (class Object) is finally searched with no method having been found, then a run-time error is reported.

A Method Cache. Although, for dynamically typed languages, the dispatch-table method is more economical in space than is the virtual-method-table technique, the time overhead is considerably greater. Furthermore, this overhead is proportional to the depth of inheritance. Unless this penalty can be overcome, the latter point might lead developers to abandon the use of inheritance, trading the loss in power for the gain in efficiency.

Fortunately, we can largely circumvent this execution-time loss by means of a simple technique. We maintain a single system wide cache of methods that have been accessed recently. This cache is indexed by a hash value defined on the method selectors. Each entry in the cache consists of a pointer to a class (the dispatch table itself can serve this purpose), a selector value, and a pointer to a method (Figure 19.6).

When the messaging function is asked to find a method to match to a selector–class pair, it first searches the cache. If the entry in the cache at the hash-table location corresponds to the requested selector and class, then the associated method can be executed directly. If not, then the search process described

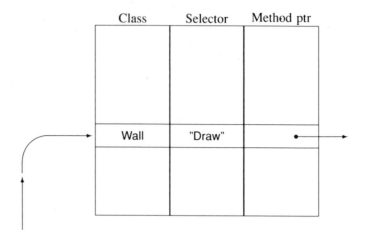

obj_msgSend(Wall, "Draw")

Figure 19.6 The messaging function checking the method cache.

earlier is performed. Following this search, immediately before executing the method, the cache is updated, overwriting whatever entry it contained previously at the hash location given by the message selector. Note that the value stored for the class entry in the cache is the class where the search began, not the class in which the method was eventually discovered.

By appropriate selection of hash functions and cache sizes, we can achieve cache hit ratios in the range of 90 to 95 percent, which reduces the overhead involved in a messaging expression to slightly over twice that of a conventional procedure call [Cox 86]. This figure compares favorably with the overhead incurred using the virtual-method-table technique.

19.2 INTERPRETERS

Interpreters are usually preferred over compilers if the amount of variation in a program is larger than can be accommodated easily in fixed code sequences. This variation can come from a number of sources; in a dynamically typed language, for example, we cannot predict at compile time the type of values that a variable can possess (although Objective-C is an example of a dynamically typed language that is nevertheless compiled). Another source of variation can occur if the user can redefine methods at run time.

A commonly used approach in interpreters is to translate the source program into a high-level "assembly language," often called a *bytecode* language (because typically each instruction can be encoded in a single byte). Figure 19.7 shows,

`0000` xxx	extended instruction with opcode xxx
`0001` xxx	push instance variable xxx on stack
`0010` xxx	push argument xxx on stack
`0011` xxx	push literal number xxx on stack
`0100` xxx	push class object number xxx on stack
`0101` xxx	push system constant xxx
`0110` xxx	pop into instance variable xxx
`0111` xxx	pop into temporary variable xxx
`1000` xxx	send message xxx
`1001` xxx	send message to super
`1010` xxx	send unary message xxx
`1011` xxx	send binary message xxx
`1100` xxx	send arithmetic message xxx
`1101` xxx	send ternary message xxx
`1110` xxx	unused
`1111` xxx	special instruction xxx

Figure 19.7 Bytecode values in the Little Smalltalk system.

for example, the bytecode instructions used in the Little Smalltalk system.[4]
The high-order four bits of the instruction are used to encode the opcode, and
the low order four bits are used to encode the operand number. If operand
numbers larger than 16 are needed, the extended instruction is used, and the
entire following byte contains the operand value. A few instructions, such as
"send message" and some of the special instructions, require additional bytes.

The heart of the interpreter is a loop that surrounds a large switch statement
(Figure 19.8). The loop reads each successive bytecode, and the switch statement
jumps to a code sequence that performs the appropriate action. We will avoid

---

[4]These are the bytecode instructions described in the book [Budd 87]. Later versions of the system
used a slightly different numbering, and the Smalltalk-80 system described in [Goldberg 83] uses
an entirely different instruction set.

```
while (timeslice-- > 0) {
  high = nextByte();  // get next bytecode
  low = high & 0x0F;  // strip off low nybble
  high >>= 4;         // shift left high nybble
  if (high == 0) {    // check extended form
    high = low;       // if so use low for opcode
    low = nextByte(); // get real operand
  }

  switch(high) {
    case PushInstance: ...
    ...
    case PushArgument: ...
    ...
  }
}
```

Figure 19.8   The main interpreter loop.

a discussion of the internal representation of a program (interested readers are referred to [Budd 87]), and will concentrate solely on the processing of message passing.

Just as objects in the compiled system presented in Section 19.1 all contained a pointer to a virtual table, objects in the Smalltalk system all contain a pointer to their class. The difference is that, as we saw in Chapter 18, the class is itself an object. Among the fields maintained in the class object is a collection containing all the methods corresponding to messages that instances of the class will understand (Figure 19.9). Another field points to the superclass for the class. (These fields were described earlier in Figure 18.3, page 264.)

When a message is to be sent, the interpreter must first locate the receiver for the message. By examining the class pointer for the receiver, it can find the object corresponding to the class of the receiver. It then searches the methods collection for a method that matches the name of the message being sent. If no such method is found, it follows the superclass chain, searching the classes in the superclass until either an appropriate method is found or the superclass chain is exhausted. In the latter case, the interpreter reports an error. This is exactly the same sequence of steps as that performed by the messaging function described in Section 19.1. As with the dispatch-table technique, a cache can be used to speed up the process of method search.

19.3   ADVANCED READING

For the reader interested in learning more about the implementation of object-oriented languages, the book by Cox [Cox 86] contains a detailed analysis of the time–space tradeoffs involved in various schemes. The implementation of multiple inheritance in C++ is sketched in [Ellis 90], which is based on an earlier

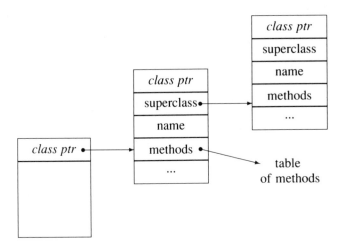

Figure 19.9   The internal structure of a class.

algorithm for Simula [Krogdahl 85]. The Smalltalk-80 interpreter is described in [Goldberg 83]. The collection of papers in [Krasner 83] contains several that describe techniques for improving the efficiency of the Smalltalk-80 system. A simple Smalltalk interpreter is detailed in [Budd 87]. Kamin [Kamin 90] presents a good general overview of the implementation issues involved in the implementation of nontraditional languages.

Exercises

1. Extend the dispatch-table technique to permit multiple inheritance.

2. The Objective-C compiler permits optional declarations for object variables. Explain how a compiler might make use of such declarations to speed processing of messages involving such values. Consider what needs to occur on assignment to a variable, and how messaging can be made more efficient.

3. Explain why methods that are not declared virtual in C++ can be invoked more efficiently than can virtual methods. How would you make measurements to determine whether the difference is significant?

4. Review the cache technique described in Section 19.1. Explain why the class stored in the cache is the class where the search for a method begins, and not the class where the method is eventually found. Explain how the cache lookup algorithm would need to be changed if the latter value were used. Do you think the new algorithm would be faster or slower? Explain your answer.

5. Sketch the outline of a Smalltalk interpreter based on the bytecodes shown in Figure 19.7.

20
Further Information

This book was intended to be not a tutorial or reference manual for any particular object-oriented language, but rather a discourse on the philosophy and ideas underlying object-oriented programming in general. The list of topics we have not discussed that are related to particular object-oriented languages, and even to object-oriented programming in general, is exceedingly large. In this chapter, we will simply mention some of these topics, and will provide pointers for interested readers to follow to find more complete information.

20.1   C++

The language C++ was designed as a successor to the C programming language, and not all the innovations added in C++ were related to object-oriented programming. In our discussions of C++, we have avoided mentioning those features incidental to the topic at hand. Among the many features not described in this book, or mentioned only briefly, are inline functions, function prototypes, the const and volatile modifiers, default and optional arguments on functions, the void keyword, stream based input and output, and linkage specifications.

The definitive reference manual for the language is the book written by the developer of C++, Bjarne Stroustrup [Stroustrup 86]. Unfortunately, as is common with programming languages, the language evolved once a large body of programmers started using the system, and thus the original book is somewhat outdated. A more up-to-date revision has been published [Ellis 90]. The latest language is called C++, Version 2.0 (after the AT&T version number). Hansen [Hansen 90] provides an extensive body of C++ code to examine in the form of heavily annotated solutions to the exercises in the Stroustrup book. The Hansen book makes a nice complement to the original.

For those people who are already familiar with the C programming language, a good introduction to C++ is the book by Pohl [Pohl 89].

There are dozens of tutorial books on C++. Among the more popular, beside the books already mentioned, are [Lippman 89], [Wiener 88] (companion book to [Pinson 88]), and [Dewhurst 89]. Others texts include [Chirlian 90], [Eckel 89] and [Weiskamp 90]. A series of graduated examples in C++ is presented in [Wiener 90].

The original C++ compiler is marketed and distributed by AT&T.

AT&T
Software Sales and Marketing
P.O. Box 25000
Greensboro, NC 27420 Telephone: 1-800-828-UNIX

The AT&T version is the language against which all other systems are measured. There are numerous commercial organizations that distribute either a port of the AT&T system to a particular platform or independently developed C++ systems.

An inexpensive but nevertheless high-quality implementation of C++ is the system distributed by the Free Software Foundation. This system is known as the GNU C++ compiler. You can obtain information on the GNU systems by writing directly to the Free Software Foundation:

Free Software Foundation
675 Massachusetts Ave.
Cambridge, MA 02139
Telephone: (617) 876-3296
E-mail: fsf@prep.ai.mit.edu

In the PC world, an inexpensive version of C++, called Turbo C++, is distributed by Borland International:

Borland International
1800 Green Hills Road
P.O. Box 660005
Scotts Valley, CA 95067

20.2 OBJECTIVE-C

The most readily accessible description of the principles of Objective-C is the book by the developer of the language, Brad Cox [Cox 86]. Unfortunately, as is the case with the analogous C++ text, the language has changed considerably since the publication of the original book. A small amount of slightly more up-to-date information is given in [Webster 89], which is a general introduction to the NeXT programming environment. Further information is available on-line in the NeXT system.

As was the case with C++, we have not discussed some of the more obscure features of the Objective-C language. In particular, the language permits the user direct access to the underlying messaging mechanisms, which can sometimes be useful for optimizing heavily used sections of code. The details are, however, too implementation-specific to be included in this book.

You can obtain further information on Objective-C and associated products by writing directly to Stepstone Corporation, the developers of the language:

Stepstone Corporation
75 Glen Road
Sandy Hook, CT 06482
Telephone: (203) 426-1875

20.3 SMALLTALK

The definitive description of Smalltalk-80, the standard Smalltalk system, is the book by Goldberg and Robson [Goldberg 83]. It is known colloquially as the "blue book" (because of the color on its cover), and is part of a series of books on Smalltalk-80. The blue book covers both the language and a description of the Smalltalk-80 implementation. Other books in the series include a book on the interactive programming environment [Goldberg 84], a book on the history of various aspects of the original Smalltalk implementation [Krasner 83], and a condensed version of the blue book dealing with only the language [Goldberg 89].

The book by Kaehler and Patterson [Kaehler 86] is a quick introduction to the concepts of Smalltalk-80, but does not go into any depth. Other books on Smalltalk-80 include [Pinson 88] (companion book to [Wiener 88]), and LaLonde and Pugh [LaLonde 90a], which is a two-volume set. The August 1981 issue of the popular journal *Byte* contained a series of articles on Smalltalk-80.

The original Smalltalk-80 system is distributed commercially by ParcPlace Systems, a spin off of Xerox Parc.

ParcPlace Systems
2400 Geng Road
Palo Alto, CA 94303
Telephone: (415) 859-1000

A similar system, called Smalltalk-V, is distributed by Digitalk, Inc.:

Digitalk, Inc.
5200 West Century Boulevard
Los Angeles, CA 90045

Telephone: (213) 645-1082

The Free Software Foundation (address given on Page 294) has recently announced the availability of GNU Smalltalk; presumably similar to the GNU C++ system.

Little Smalltalk is a nongraphical version of Smalltalk. The book *A Little Smalltalk* [Budd 87] describes not only the language, but also the implementation of the system. The Little Smalltalk system is distributed at low cost by the author:

Little Smalltalk Distribution
Department of Computer Science
Oregon State University
Corvallis, Oregon 97330

20.4   OBJECT PASCAL

Object Pascal was developed by Apple computer in consultation with the original designer of Pascal, Niklaus Wirth; it was partially based on an earlier Apple-developed extension of Pascal called Classical. The language is defined in a report from Apple [Tesler 85].

The QuickPascal system by Microsoft is an implementation of the Object Pascal system. The QuickPascal language is described in [Shammas 90].

A large application in Object Pascal is presented in [Schmucker 86], which also describes Classical and several other object-oriented languages.

Turbo Pascal

Turbo Pascal is an object-oriented version of Pascal developed by Borland International. The reference manual is [Turbo 88]. Other texts that describe Turbo Pascal include [O'Brian 89, Swan 89]. A drawback of all of these texts is that they first introduce programming in Pascal, and introduce the object-oriented extensions late in the discussion, seemingly more or less as an afterthought. Thus, the reader might be led to believe (incorrectly) that object-oriented extensions are simply an addition to programming in a conventional fashion, instead of a technique that requires a complete rethinking of the design process.

Despite the similarities in name and syntax, Turbo Pascal is very different from Object Pascal. Turbo Pascal borrows from C++ ideas such as constructors and a distinction between static and virtual methods.

Information concerning Turbo Pascal can be obtained from Borland, at the address given on Page 294.

20.5 OTHER LANGUAGES

The majority of the concepts we associate with object-oriented programming were first developed in the Simula [Birtwistle 79, Kirkerud 89] programming language. Unfortunately, in the United States Simula was viewed as simply an extension of ALGOL specifically oriented toward simulation, and relatively little attention was paid to the language.

The language Eiffel [Meyer 88a] is an object-oriented language designed specifically with modern software-engineering principles in mind. It includes features such as the ability to attach assertions, which are checked at run time, to classes and individual methods. It has been used in a large number of commercial software projects.

The Actor language [Actor 87], is a Pascal-based object-oriented language running chiefly on IBM PC systems. It should not be confused with the concept of actors [Agha 86], which is a way of structuring distributed computing.

There have been various object-oriented extensions proposed for Lisp [Moon 86, Bobrow 86, Schmucker 86, Kessler 88]. To provide a standard framework, researchers have proposed a new object system as part of the Common Lisp standard [Keene 89, Bobrow 88].

Object-oriented versions have been proposed or developed for a large number of programming languages. These include Forth [Pountain 87], Logo [Schmucker 86], and Assembler [Schmucker 86].

An excellent overview of the various aspects of object-oriented languages is given by Micallef [Micallef 88].

Because they cannot support inheritance, conventional languages cannot be considered truly object-oriented. Nevertheless, object-oriented design concepts have been applied in a number of languages, often with good effect. Coad and Yourdon [Coad 90] discuss object-oriented analysis in a manner that can be applied to non–object-oriented languages, such as Ada.

20.6 SELECTION OF AN OBJECT-ORIENTED LANGUAGE

Given the rich diversity of object-oriented languages, programmers are often confused about how to select a programming language for a particular project. Here are points to consider: decision:

- *Familiarity.* If many programmers are already familiar with a given language, then it is reasonable to exploit that familiarity by continuing to use the language. But it is important not to place too much weight on familiarity; particularly not on familiarity with non–object-oriented languages. Knowledge of Pascal does not automatically translate into knowledge of Object Pascal, and a good C programmer does not necessarily make a good C++ programmer. Indeed, too great a familiarity can blind a programmer to the fundamental shifts in design necessary to program in an object-oriented manner.

- *Platforms.* Not all object-oriented languages run on all hardware platforms. Object Pascal is associated largely with the Macintosh/PC world, whereas C++ runs mostly on Unix workstations. A commitment to a particular language must be tied to a commitment to the hardware platform on which the final application is to run.

- *Importance of programming time relative to execution time.* On the one hand, we have languages, such as C++, that are designed with efficiency of execution foremost in mind. On the other hand, there are languages such as Smalltalk, where the emphasis is placed on ease of program development, often at the expense of execution time. Languages such as Object Pascal and Objective-C fall somewhere in between.

- *Ubiquity.* A popular language, such as C++, will attract a much more diverse collection of tutorials, training guides, tools, and reading material than will a less widely known language.

- *Access to existing code.* Access is useful not only for pedagogy (often, the best way to learn how to program in a new style is to study existing code), but also for reusability. If a large fraction of an existing application can be constructed out of readily available libraries in a particular language, then the development time of a new application can be considerably shortened.

- *Programming environment.* The availability of editors, debuggers, and other software tools simplifies the creation of new applications.

- *Delivery issues.* In interpreted languages, the programming environment is often bundled together with the running program. Although the development of an application in Smalltalk may be faster than in C++, the final product cannot be delivered to the end user without the entire Smalltalk run-time system being included. Languages such as C++ or Object Pascal, on the other hand, generate a conventional binary executable file.

20.7   FURTHER TOPICS

There is a large number of topics related to object-oriented programming that we have not addressed in this book. The reasons for these omissions are varied. In some cases, the topics are still somewhat advanced, appearing only in the research literature or in experimental languages. In other cases, the topics are only marginally related to the objectives of this book. Nevertheless, a few of these ideas deserve at least a comment and a pointer to where to obtain further information.

Programming Environments

The term programming environment refers to the entire support system that is provided to the programmer to assist in the development of new software applications. In practice, the environment in which a program is developed may have an even larger effect on the programming process than does the language in which the programmer writes an application. The interest in the Smalltalk project at Xerox Parc, for example, was probably due as much to the novel innovations in the programming environment as to the language itself.

In general, a programming environment provides the following facilities:

- An organized repository of code. This must necessarily include the code itself; it may also include information such as creator and creation times. It need not be any thing more complicated than a simple file system.

- A system to permit the programmer easy access to existing code, and to facilitate sharing of code among programmers and projects. The object-oriented design philosophy encourages the reuse of existing code. So that this process is facilitated, it must be possible to scan libraries of code rapidly. This scanning process is often called *browsing*.

- A mechanism to permit updates or modifications of code in the repository. This includes editors, as well as facilities for multiprogrammer cooperation, such as version control systems.

- Tools to document not only the code itself (using mechanisms such as comments), but also higher-level libraries or collections of objects.

- Facilities for expediting the programming process itself, such as run-time debuggers.

Probably the best-known object-oriented programming environment is the Smalltalk-80 system described in [Goldberg 84]. Other common environments are dictated not so much by the programming language but by the underlying operating system. C++ is usually associated with the Unix operating system [Kernighan 84], Object Pascal with the Macintosh [Schmucker 86], the Objective-C with the NeXT [Webster 89].

Generic Dispatching

As we saw in Chapter 19, from the point of view of the implementation, a receiver in an object-oriented message-sending expression is simply the first argument. Thus, message sending can be viewed as a form of overloading in which resolution is based on the type of the first argument. The question then naturally arises why the first argument should be treated differently from subsequent arguments. Proponents of generic dispatch languages argue that there is no valid reason. In a generic dispatch language, such as CLOS [Keene 89], message dispatching can be performed based on the type of any argument, or of any combinations of arguments. A feature called *identity specializers* even permits methods to be defined that are invoked only if an argument is a certain constant value. Although such features are powerful, they greatly complicate the algorithm used to match a method to a message selector [Snyder 87, Bobrow 88].

Generic dispatching is most commonly associated with Lisp-based languages; the technique has also been proposed for use in Pascal-like languages [Grogono 89].

Persistence

A *persistent* object is one that can maintain its value across multiple program executions, either simultaneously or sequentially over time. In contrast to persistent values, objects that are created and destroyed with each execution of a program are called *ephemeral*. As with garbage collection (a concept to which persistence is closely related), persistence can be managed either automatically by the system or explicitly by the user.

None of the object-oriented languages we have described in this book provide persistence as an automatic feature. However, libraries are available for some of them.

Object Databases

It has proved useful to view a collection of persistent values as representing a generalized form of database. There is a rich literature on object-oriented databases. The collections of papers in [Atkinson 88, Zdonik 90] are good representative samples.

20.8 RESEARCH REFERENCES

Object-oriented programming continues to be a rapidly expanding area of research. The technical literature is extensive. Good introductions to the major areas of work are the books by Shriver and Wegner [Shriver 87] and Kim and Lochovsky [Kim 89].

The major conferences on object-oriented programming are the *OOPSLA* conference (Conference on Object-Oriented Programming Systems, Languages and Applications) in the United States and the ECOOP conference (European Conference on Object-Oriented Programming) in Europe. Proceedings of the OOPSLA conference are published routinely as special issues of the journal *Sigplan Notices* [Meyrowitz 89]; the proceedings of ECOOP are published as books by Springer-Verlag [Bézivin 87, Gjessing 88]. The Unix users group USENIX sponsors an annual workshop devoted exclusively to C++ [Usenix 87].

The *Journal of Object-Oriented Programming* is devoted to object-oriented topics; several smaller journals deal with C++ exclusively.

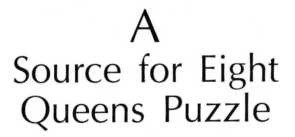

A
Source for Eight Queens Puzzle

This appendix gives in full the programs for the eight queens puzzle discussed in Chapter 5.

A.1 EIGHT QUEENS IN OBJECT PASCAL

```
program queens;
  type
    Queen = object
      row : integer;
      column : integer;
      neighbor : Queen;
      procedure initial (col : integer; ngh : Queen);
      function canAttack (r, c : integer) : boolean;
      function first : boolean;
      function testOrAdvance : boolean;
      function next: : boolean;
      procedure print;
    end;
  var
    neighbor, lastqueen : Queen;
    i : integer;

    (* initialize the newly created queen object *)
  procedure Queen.initial(col : integer; ngh : Queen);
  begin
    column := col;
    neighbor := ngh;
```

```
end;


  (* can queen or neighbors attack position? *)
function Queen.canAttack(r, c : integer) : boolean;
var
  cd : integer;
begin
  if row = r then
    canAttack := true
  else
    begin
      cd := c - column;
      if (row + cd = r) or (row - cd = r) then
        canAttack := true
      else if neighbor = nil then
        canAttack := false
      else
        canAttack := neighbor.canAttack(r, c)
    end
end;


  (* generate first acceptable solution *)
function Queen.first : boolean;
begin
  row := 1;
  if neighbor = nil then
    first := true
  else if not neighbor.first then
    first := false
  else
    first := self.testOrAdvance
end;


  (* test and possibly advance solution *)
function Queen.testOrAdvance : boolean;
begin
  if neighbor = nil then
    testOrAdvance := true
  else if neighbor.canAttack(row, column) then
    testOrAdvance := self.next
  else
    testOrAdvance := true
end;


  (* generate next acceptable solution *)
```

```
   function Queen.next : boolean;
   begin
     if row = 8 then
       if neighbor = nil then
         next := false
       else if not neighbor.next then
         next := false
       else
         begin
           row := 1;
           next := self.testOrAdvance;
         end
     else
       begin
         row := row + 1;
         next := self.testOrAdvance;
       end
   end;

     (* print out solution *)
   procedure Queen.print;
   begin
     if neighbor <> nil then
       neighbor.print;
     writeln(' row ', row, ' column ', column);
   end;

begin     (* main program *)
   neighbor := nil;
   for i := 1 to 8 do
     begin
       new(lastQueen);
       lastQueen.initial(i, neighbor);
       neighbor := lastQueen;
     end;
   if lastQueen.first then
     lastQueen.print;
end.
```

A.2   EIGHT QUEENS IN C++

```
class Queen {
  int row;
  int column;
```

```
    Queen *neighbor;
    int canAttack(int r, int c);
    int testOrAdvance();
public:
    Queen(int c, Queen * ngh);
    int first();
    int next();
    void print();
};

    // construct a new queen, setting neighbor and column
    //    number
Queen::Queen(int c, Queen * ngh)
{ column = c; neighbor = ngh; }

    // check to see if queen or neighbor can attack
    // position
Queen::canAttack(int r, int c)
{  int cd;
   if (row == r) return 1;
   cd = c - column;
   if ((row + cd == r) || (row - cd == r)) return 1;
   if (neighbor) return neighbor->canAttack(r, c);
   return 0;
}

    // compute first legal position for queen and neighbor
int Queen::first()
{    row = 1;
    if (neighbor && neighbor->first())
      return testOrAdvance();
    return 1;
}

    // test or advance a position
int Queen::testOrAdvance()
{  if (neighbor && neighbor->canAttack(row, column))
      return next();
   return 1;
}

    // compute another legal position for queen and
    // neighbor
int Queen::next()
{  if (row == 8) {
```

```
      if (!(neighbor && neighbor->next()))
        return 0;
      row = 0;
      }
    row = row + 1;
    return testOrAdvance();
  }


    // print solution
  void Queen::print()
  {   if (neighbor) neighbor->print();
      printf("column %d row %d\n", column, row);
  }


  main()    // main program
  {   Queen *lastQueen = 0;

      for (int i = 1; i <= 8; i++)
        lastQueen = new Queen(i, lastQueen);
      if (lastQueen->first()) lastQueen->print();
  }
```

A.3 EIGHT QUEENS IN OBJECTIVE-C

Note that for both the classes Queen and NullQueen implementation sections
are presented without prior interface definitions. This will produce a warning
from the compiler, but no error.

```
    # import <objc/Object.h>

    @implementation NullQueen : Object
    {
    }
    - (int) first {return 1;}
    - (int) next {return 0;}
    - (int) checkrow: (int) r column: (int) c { return 0; }
    - (int) print {};
    @end

    @implementation Queen : Object
    {
      int row;
      int column;
      id neighbor;
    }
```

```
   /* initialize the column and neighbor values */
-  (void) initialColumn: (int) c neighbor: ngh
{  column = c; neighbor = ngh;  }

   /* check to see if queen or neighbors can attack a */
   /* given position */
-  (int) checkrow: (int) r column: (int) c
{  int cd;
   if (row == r) return 1;
   cd = c - column;
   if ((row + cd == r) || (row - cd == r)) return 1;
   return [ neighbor checkrow: r column: c];
}

   /* test a given position, advancing if not
      acceptable */
-  (int) testOrAdvance
{  if ([neighbor checkrow: row column: column])
     return [ self next ];
   return 1;
}

   /* compute first legal position for queen and
      neighbors */
-  (int) first
{  row = 1;
   if ([ neighbor first ])
     return [ self testOrAdvance ];
   return 0;
}

   /* compute next legal position for queen and
      neighbors */
-  (int) next
{  if (row == 8) {
     if (! [ neighbor next ]) return 0;
     row = 0;
     }
   row = row + 1;
   return [ self testOrAdvance ];
}

   /* print out solution */
-  (int) print
```

```
{   [ neighbor print ];
    printf("row %d column %d\n", row, column);
}
@end

    /* main program */
main() {
id lastQueen, nghbor;
int i;

nghbor = [ NullQueen new ];
for (i = 1; i <= 8; i++) {
    lastQueen = [ Queen new ];
    [lastQueen initialColumn: i neighbor: nghbor];
    nghbor = lastQueen;
    }
if ([lastQueen first]) [lastQueen print];
}
```

A.4 EIGHT QUEENS IN SMALLTALK

The class NullQueen in the Smalltalk solution has no instance variables. It uses
the following methods.

first
" a null queen can always produce first solution "
↑ true

next
" a null queen cannot produce a subsequent solution "
↑ false

checkRow: row **column:** column
" a null queen cannot attack anything "
↑ false

result
" produce list to hold solution "
↑ List new

The class Queen has three instance variables, corresponding to the values
of the row, column, and neighbor. It defines the following methods.

setColumn: aNumber **neighbor:** aQueen
" initialize column and neighbor values for new queen "
column ← aNumber.
neighbor ← aQueen

checkRow: testRow **column:** testColumn | columnDifference |
" check to see if this queen, or any neighbor "
" can attack the position given in the argument "
columnDifference ← testColumn - column.
(((row = testRow) or:
[row + columnDifference = testRow]) or:
[row - columnDifference = testRow])
ifTrue: [↑ true].
↑ neighbor checkRow: testRow column: testColumn

first
" generate the first acceptable solution "
neighbor first.
row ← 1.
↑ self testPosition

next
" generate the next acceptable solution "
↑ (self advance) and: [self testPosition]

advance
" advance current queen "
(row = 8)
ifTrue: [(neighbor next) ifFalse: [↑ false].
row ← 0].
row ← row + 1.
↑ true

testPosition
" test and possibly advance current queen "
[neighbor checkRow: row column: column]
whileTrue: [(self advance) ifFalse: [↑ false]].
↑ true

result
" produce a list containing the current solution "
↑ neighbor result addLast: row

The solution can be found by invoking the following method

```
queen   | lastQueen |
" produce a list containing solution to queen puzzle "
lastQueen ← NullQueen new.
(1 to: 8) do: [:i | lastQueen ← Queen new;
setColumn: i neighbor: lastQueen ].
lastQueen first.
↑ lastQueen result
```

B
Source for Solitaire Game

The solitaire game described in Chapter 10 is built on top of the InterViews windowing-interface construction system [Linton 89]. Thus, the following program must be linked with the InterViews library before an executable program can be produced.

B.1 FILE SOLITAIRE.CC

```
//
//   solitaire game using Interviews interface
//
//   written by tim budd, oregon state university, 1990
//

# include <InterViews/world.h>
# include <InterViews/sensor.h>
# include <InterViews/button.h>
# include <InterViews/box.h>
# include <InterViews/canvas.h>
# include <InterViews/painter.h>
# include <InterViews/shape.h>

# include "game.h"

# define BoardWidth 600
# define BoardHeight 450

GameWindow *game;

extern "C" {
```

```
    void exit();
    }


    // The Quit button at the bottom of the screen halts game
    class QuitButton : public PushButton
    {
    public:
      QuitButton() : PushButton("quit", new ButtonState(false),
        true) {;}
      void virtual Press() { exit(0); }
    };


    // The Start button at the bottom of the screen starts
    //   game class StartButton : public PushButton
    {
    public:
      StartButton() : PushButton("start", new ButtonState(false),
        true) {;}
      void virtual Press() { game->newGame(); }
    };


    Canvas *  drawField;   // the drawing area for game
    Painter *  painter;    // the object used to draw the cards
    DealPile *  newDeck;     // the original unshuffled deck


    //
    //   the main program
    //     create a new game window
    //   map it onto the screen with two buttons at bottom
    //   start it up
    //

    int main (int argc, char ** argv) {

      World *world = new World("solitaire", argc, argv);

      game = new GameWindow;

      world->InsertApplication( new VBox(game,
        new HBox(new QuitButton, new StartButton)));

      drawField = game->GetCanvas();

      world->Run();
    }
```

```
//
//    initialize the game window
//
GameWindow::GameWindow() {
  int i, j, hight;

  // create a new shape for our drawing area
  shape = new Shape;
  shape->Rect(BoardWidth, BoardHeight);
  shape->Rigid(hfil, hfil, vfil, vfil);

  // create a new sensor so that we can catch mouse down
  //    events
  input = new Sensor;
  input->Catch(DownEvent);

  // create a new painter for drawing
  painter = new Painter;

  // now some game specific initialization
  // create the original (unshuffled) deck
  newDeck = new DealPile();
  for (i = 0; i < 4; i++)
    for (j = 1; j <= 13; j++)
      newDeck->addCard(new CardLink(i, j));

  // create suit piles
  hight = BoardHeight - round(1.5*CardView::CardHeight);
  // create the deck and discard piles
  allPiles[0] = deck = new DeckPile(500, hight);
  allPiles[1] = discard = new DiscardPile(400, hight);
  // create suit piles
  for (i = 0; i < 4; i++)
    allPiles[i+2] = suitPiles[i] =
      new SuitPile(30 + (round(1.4*CardView::CardWidth) * i),
        hight);


  // create tableau
  hight = BoardHeight - round(2.7*CardView::CardHeight);
  for (i = 0; i < 7; i++)
    allPiles[i+6] = table[i] =
      new TablePile(i, 10
        + (round(1.2*CardView::CardWidth) * i), hight);
```

```
}

//
//  start up a new game
//
void GameWindow::newGame()
{   int i;

    // initialize all the piles
    for (i = 0; i < 13; i++)
      allPiles[i]->initialize();

    // then redraw the game window
    Draw();
}

//
//    redraw the window
//
void GameWindow::Redraw(Coord a, Coord b, Coord c,
Coord d)
{   int i;

    // first clear the entire playing area
    clearArea(0,0, BoardWidth, BoardHeight);

    // then display the piles
    for (i = 0; i < 13; i++)
      allPiles[i]->display();
}

//
//  handle a mouse down event in the game window
//
void GameWindow::Handle (Event& e)
{   int i;

    // we are only interested in mouse down events
    if (e.eventType != DownEvent) return;

    for (i = 0; i < 13; i++)
      if (allPiles[i]->contains(e.x, e.y)) {
        allPiles[i]->select(e.x, e.y);
        return;
```

```
        }
    return;
}

//
//   see if any of the suit piles can add a specific card
//
int   GameWindow::suitCanAdd(Card *aCard)
{   int i;

    for (i = 0; i < 4; i++)
        if (suitPiles[i]->canTake(aCard)) return 1;
    return 0;
}

//
//   see if any of the table piles can add a specific card
//
int   GameWindow::tableCanAdd(Card *aCard)
{   int i;

    for (i = 0; i < 7; i++)
        if (table[i]->canTake(aCard)) return 1;
    return 0;
}

//
//    return which of the suit piles can add a card
//
CardPile *GameWindow::suitAddPile(Card *aCard)
{   int i;

    for (i = 0; i < 4; i++)
        if (suitPiles[i]->canTake(aCard))
            return suitPiles[i];
    // hopefully this won't happen
    return newDeck;
}

//
//    return which of the table piles can add a card
//
CardPile *GameWindow::tableAddPile(Card *aCard)
{   int i;
```

```
  for (i = 0; i < 7; i++)
    if (table[i]->canTake(aCard))
      return table[i];
  // hopefully this won't happen
  return newDeck;
}


//
//  clear out a given area in the game window
//
void GameWindow::clearArea(int a, int b, int c, int d)
{ Color *fg, *bg;

  // first get the foreground and background colors
  fg = painter->GetFgColor();
  bg = painter->GetBgColor();
  // then reverse them
  painter->SetColors(bg, fg);
  // then draw a filled rectangle
  painter->FillRect(drawField, a, b, c, d);
  // then restore the colors
  painter->SetColors(fg, bg);
}
```

B.2   FILE GAME.H

```
// interface description of game window for
// solitaire game
//
//  written by tim budd, oregon state university, 1990
//

# ifndef SeenGameh
# define SeenGameh

# include <InterViews/event.h>
# include <InterViews/scene.h>

# include "pile.h"

class GameWindow : public MonoScene
{
public:
```

```
  CardPile *discard;      // the discard pile
  CardPile *deck;      // the unplayed card deck

  GameWindow();

  void    newGame();      // start a new game
  void    clearArea (int, int, int, int);
  int     suitCanAdd(Card*);
  CardPile *  suitAddPile(Card*);
  int     tableCanAdd(Card*);
  CardPile *  tableAddPile(Card*);

protected:
  CardPile *  allPiles[13];   // all piles
  CardPile *  suitPiles[4];   // the pile of suits
  CardPile *  table[7];     // the playing table

  void virtual Handle (Event&);
  void virtual Redraw(Coord,Coord,Coord,Coord);
};
# endif
```

B.3   FILE CARD.H

```
//
//   card.h - definition file for card behavior
//      cards have a suit, a rank, and a color
//
//   written by tim budd, oregon state university, 1990
//

# ifndef Cardh
# define Cardh

//
//   --------------------------- class Card
//
class Card
{
  public:
    // constructor
    Card(int, int);
```

```
int     color ();
int     rank ();
int     suit ();

private:
int s;      // suit value
int r;      // rank value
};

inline Card::Card(int sv, int cv) { s = sv; r = cv; }

inline int Card::rank () { return r; }

inline int Card::suit () { return s; }

inline int Card::color() { return suit() % 2; }

# endif
```

B.4   FILE CARDVIEW.H

```
//
//   cardview.h - definition for viewing a card
//
//     provides protocol for displaying a card on an
//     output device
//
//   written by tim budd, oregon state university, 1990
//

# ifndef CardViewh
# define CardViewh

# include "card.h"

//
// --------------------------- class Card
//
class CardView
{
  public:
    // constructor
  CardView(Card *);
  CardView(int s, int c);
```

```
   // constants
const int CardWidth = 68;
const int CardHeight = 75;

Card *  card();
void    draw ();
void    erase ();
int     faceUp ();
void    flip ();
int     includes (int, int);
int     x ();
int     y ();
void    moveTo (int, int);

private:
Card * theCard;    // the card value
int up;         // true if face up
int locx;       // x location of card
int locy;       // y location of card
};

inline Card* CardView::card() { return theCard; }

inline int CardView::faceUp() { return up; }

inline void CardView::flip() { up = ! up; }

inline int  CardView::x() { return locx; }

inline int  CardView::y() { return locy; }

inline void CardView::moveTo(int sx, int sy)
  { locx = sx; locy = sy; }

# endif
```

B.5   FILE CARDVIEW.CC

```
//
//  card.c - implementation of card behavior
//
//  written by tim budd, oregon state university, 1990
//
```

```cpp
# include "cardview.h"
# include <InterViews/canvas.h>
# include <InterViews/painter.h>

// the actual drawing is done using interview tools:
extern Canvas * drawField;
extern Painter * painter;

//
//  --------------------------    class CardView
//

static char *suits[ ] = {"Heart", "Club", "Diamond",
  "Spade" };

static char *ranks[ ] = {"blank", "Ace", "2", "3", "4",
  "5", "6", "7", "8", "9", "10", "Jack", "Queen",
    "King" };

//const int CardView::CardWidth = 68;
//const int CardView::CardHeight = 75;

//        constructors
CardView::CardView(Card * c)
{
  theCard = c;
  up = 0;
  locx = locy = 0;
}

CardView::CardView(int s, int c)
{
  theCard = new Card(s, c);
  up = 0;
  locx = locy = 0;
}

//        draw
void CardView::draw()
{
  // erase the card and redraw it
  erase();
  painter->Rect(drawField,  x(), y(), x()+CardWidth,
    y()+CardHeight);
```

```
    if (up) {   // draw the card face up
      painter->MoveTo(x()+12, y()+round(CardHeight*0.80));
      painter->Text(drawField, suits[theCard->suit()]);
      painter->MoveTo(x()+15, y()+round(CardHeight*0.60));
      painter->Text(drawField, ranks[theCard->rank()]);
      }
    else {   int n;   // draw the card face down
      n = x()+round(CardWidth*0.3);
      painter->Line(drawField, n, y()+5, n,
        y()+CardHeight-10);
      n = x()+round(CardWidth*0.7);
      painter->Line(drawField, n, y()+5, n,
        y()+CardHeight-10);
      n = y()+round(CardHeight*0.3);
      painter->Line(drawField, x()+5, n,
        x()+CardWidth-10, n);
      n = y()+round(CardHeight*0.7);
      painter->Line(drawField, x()+5, n,
        x()+CardWidth-10, n);
      }
}


//          erase
void CardView::erase()
{ Color *fg, *bg;

  // first get the foreground and background colors
  fg = painter->GetFgColor();
  bg = painter->GetBgColor();
  // then reverse them
  painter->SetColors(bg, fg);
  // then draw a filled rectangle
  painter->FillRect(drawField, x(), y(), x()+CardWidth,
    y()+CardHeight);
  // then restore the colors
  painter->SetColors(fg, bg);
}


//          includes
int CardView::includes(int a, int b)
{
  return (a >= x()) && (a <= x() + CardHeight) &&
      (b >= y()) && (b <= y() + CardWidth);
}
```

B.6   FILE PILE.H

```
//
//  pile.h - interface for class Pile, representing a
//      pile of cards
//    uses instances of class Card
//
//  written by tim budd, oregon state university, 1990
//

# ifndef Pileh
# define Pileh

# include "cardview.h"

//
// ------------------------- class CardLink
//
class CardLink : public CardView
{
  public:
  CardLink(int s, int c);
  CardLink(Card *c);
  CardLink *  next ();
  void      setLink (CardLink * aCard);

  private:
  CardLink *  link;
};

inline CardLink::CardLink(int s, int c) : CardView(s, c)
  { ; }

inline CardLink::CardLink(Card * c) : CardView(c) { ; }

inline CardLink * CardLink::next() { return link; }

inline void CardLink::setLink (CardLink * aCard)
  { link = aCard; }

//
// ------------------------- class CardPile
//
class CardPile
{
```

```
public:
  CardPile();
  CardPile(int, int);

  void virtual    addCard (CardLink *);
  int  virtual    canTake(Card *);
  int       contains (int, int);
  void virtual    display();
  void virtual    initialize();
  CardLink *  removeCard ();
  void virtual    select(int, int);

private:
  int  x;     // x location of pile
  int  y;     // y location of pile

protected:
  CardLink *top;   // first card in pile
};

# define nilLink (CardLink *) 0

inline CardPile::CardPile(int a, int b)
  { x = a; y = b; top = nilLink; }

//
// -------------------------- class DealPile
//
class DealPile : public CardPile
{
public:
  DealPile();

  void       shuffleTo (CardPile *);
};

inline DealPile::DealPile() : CardPile(0, 0) { ; }

//
// -------------------------- class SuitPile
//
//
// SuitPile - the pile of suit cards
//      at the top of the board
```

```
class SuitPile : public CardPile
{
public:
  int  virtual   canTake (Card *);
};


//
// --------------------------- class TablePile
//
//
class TablePile : public CardPile
{
 public:
  TablePile(int c, int x, int y) : CardPile(x, y)
    { column = c; }

  void virtual   addCard (CardLink *);
  int  virtual   canTake (Card *);
  void      copyBuild (CardLink *, CardPile *);
  void virtual   display ();
  void virtual   select (int, int);
  void virtual   initialize ();

private:
  int  column;  // our column number
};



//
// --------------------------- class DeckPile
//
//


class DeckPile : public CardPile
{
public:
  void virtual   addCard (CardLink *);
  void virtual   initialize ();
  void virtual   select (int, int);
};


//
// --------------------------- class DiscardPile
//
//
```

```
class DiscardPile : public CardPile
{
public:
  void virtual    addCard (CardLink *);
  void virtual    select (int, int);
};

# endif
```

B.7   FILE PILE.CC

```
//
//   pile.c - implementation for class CardPile
//
//
//   written by tim budd, oregon state university, 1990
//

# include "game.h"

extern GameWindow *   game;
extern DealPile *   newDeck;

//
//   --------------------------  class CardPile
//

void CardPile::addCard(CardLink *aCard)
{
  if (aCard != nilLink) {
    aCard->setLink(top);
    top = aCard;
    top->moveTo(x, y);
    }
}

int CardPile::canTake(Card *aCard)
{
  return 0;
}

int CardPile::contains(int a, int b)
{
```

```
    for (CardLink *p = top; p != nilLink; p = p->next())
      if (p->includes(a, b))
        return 1;
    return 0;
}

void CardPile::display()
{
  if (top == nilLink)
      game->clearArea(x, y, x+CardView::CardWidth,
        y+CardView::CardHeight);
  else
    top->draw();
}

void CardPile::initialize()
{
  top = nilLink;
}

CardLink * CardPile::removeCard()
{  CardLink *p;

  if (top == nilLink)
    return nilLink;
  p = top;
  top = top->next();
  return p;
}

void CardPile::select(int x, int y)
{ /* do nothing */ ; }

//
//  ----------------------------  class DealPile
//

extern "C" { int rand(); }

void DealPile::shuffleTo(CardPile *aPile)
{  CardLink *p, *q;
  int max, limit, i;

  // first see how many cards we have
  for (max = 0, p = top; p != nilLink; p = p->next()) {
```

```
    max++;
    if (p->faceUp()) p->flip();
    }

  // then pull them out, randomly, one at a time
  for (; max > 0; max--) {
    limit = ((rand() >> 3) % max) + 1;
    for (i = 1, p = top; i <= limit; ) {
      while (p->faceUp()) p = p->next();
      i += 1;
      if (i <= limit) p = p->next();
      }
    q = new CardLink(p->card());
    aPile->addCard(q);
    p->flip();
    }
}

//
// --------------------------- class DeckPile
//

void DeckPile::initialize()
{
  CardPile::initialize();
  newDeck->shuffleTo(this);
}

void DeckPile::addCard(CardLink *c)
{
  if (c->faceUp())
    c->flip();
  CardPile::addCard(c);
}

void DeckPile::select(int x, int y)   // turn over a new
                                      // card
{  CardLink *c;

  if (top == nilLink)
    ;
  else {
    c = removeCard();
    if (c != nilLink)
      (game->discard)->addCard(c);
```

```
      }
   display();
   (game->discard)->display();
}

//
//  -------------------------  class DiscardPile
//

void DiscardPile::addCard(CardLink *c)
{
   if (!(c->faceUp()))
      c->flip();
   CardPile::addCard(c);
}

void DiscardPile::select(int x, int y)   // play the
                                         //   current face card
{  CardPile *aPile;

   if (top == nilLink) return;
   // see if we can move it to a suit pile
   if (game->suitCanAdd(top->card())) {
      aPile = game->suitAddPile(top->card());
      aPile->addCard(removeCard());
      display();
      aPile->display();
      return;
      }
   // else see if we can move to a table pile
   if (game->tableCanAdd(top->card())) {
      aPile = game->tableAddPile(top->card());
      aPile->addCard(removeCard());
      display();
      aPile->display();
      return;
      }
   // else do nothing
}

//
//  -------------------------  class SuitPile
//

int  SuitPile::canTake(Card *aCard)
```

```
{
  if (top == nilLink) {   // we're empty, can take an ace
    if (aCard->rank() == 1) return 1;
    return 0;
    }
  if ((top->card())->suit() != aCard->suit())
    return 0;
  if (((top->card())->rank() + 1) == aCard->rank())
    return 1;
  return 0;
}

//
//  --------------------------  class TablePile
//

void TablePile::initialize()
{   int i;

  // put the right number of cards on the table
  CardPile::initialize();
  for (i = 0; i <= column; i++)
    addCard((game->deck)->removeCard());
  // flip the last one
  if (top != nilLink) {
    top->flip();
    }
}

void TablePile::addCard(CardLink *aCard)
{   int tx, ty;

  if (top == nilLink)
    CardPile::addCard(aCard);
  else {
    tx = top->x();
    ty = top->y();
    // figure out where to place the card
    if (top->faceUp() && top->next() != nilLink &&
      (top->next())->faceUp())
      ; // do nothing, place on top of top card
    else
      // else move it down a bit
      ty -= round(CardView::CardHeight * 0.5);
    CardPile::addCard(aCard);
```

```
  top->moveTo(tx, ty);
  }
}

int TablePile::canTake(Card *aCard)
{
  if (top == nilLink) {  // can take kings on an
                         //    empty pile
    if (aCard->rank() == 13) return 1;
    return 0;
    }
  // see if colors are different
  if ((top->card())->color() == aCard->color()) return 0;
  // see if numbers are legal
  if (((top->card())->rank() - 1) == aCard->rank())
    return 1;
  return 0;
}

void TablePile::copyBuild(CardLink *c, CardPile *aPile)
{  CardLink *d;

  top->erase();
  d = removeCard();
  display();
  if (c != d) copyBuild(c, aPile);
  aPile->addCard(d);
  aPile->display();
}

static void stackDisplay(CardLink *p)
{
  if (p->next())
    stackDisplay(p->next());
  p->erase();
  p->draw();
}

void TablePile::display()
{  Card *p;

  // zero or one cards, can't do any better
  if (top == nilLink)
    CardPile::display();
  // otherwise half display all the covered cards
```

```
    else {
      stackDisplay(top);
      }
  }

  void TablePile::select(int x, int y)
  {  CardLink *c;
     int i;

     // no cards, do nothing
     if (top == nilLink) return;

     // if top card is not flipped, flip it now
     if (! top->faceUp()) {
       top->erase();
       top->flip();
       top->draw();
       return;
       }
     // if it was to top card, see if we can move it
     if (top->includes(x, y)) {
       // see if we can move it to a suit pile
       if (game->suitCanAdd(top->card())) {
         copyBuild(top, game->suitAddPile(top->card()));
         return;
         }
       // else see if we can move to a table pile
       // but only if it is not part of pile
       if ((top->next() == nilLink)
               || ! (((top->next())->faceUp()))))
         if (game->tableCanAdd(top->card())) {
           copyBuild(top, game->tableAddPile(top->card()));
           return;
           }
       }
     // else see if we can move a pile
     for (c = top->next(); c != nilLink; c = c->next())
       if (c->faceUp() && c->includes(x, y)) {
         if (game->tableCanAdd(c->card())) {
           copyBuild(c, game->tableAddPile(c->card()));
           }
         return;
         }
     // else do nothing
  }
```

C

Source for Billiards Game

This appendix lists the complete source code for the billiards simulation described in Chapter 16.

C.1 FILE SIMPLEWINDOW.P

The file "simplewindow.p" provides tools to simplify the development of graphical user interfaces. It is similar to, although simpler than, several other widely available systems, such as the MacApp collection [Wilson 90].

```
{ simple window interface for Object Pascal }
{ written by Tim Budd, Oregon State University }
{ April 1990 }

unit SimpleWindow;

interface

  type
    SimpleMenu = object
        { data fields }
      theMenuID: Integer;
      theMenuPtr: MenuHandle;
      link: SimpleMenu;
        { creation methods }
      procedure readFromResource (id: integer);
      procedure createNewMenu (title: Str255);
      procedure createAppleMenu (aboutTitle: Str255);
        { adding elements to menu }
      procedure addItem (title: Str255);
      procedure addSeparator;
```

```
                    { action to take when selected }
                    { must be overridden by user }
                procedure selectItem (itemNumber: integer);
            end;

      SimpleWindow = object
                { data fields }
            theWindowPtr: windowPtr;
            name: STR255;
            windowRect: Rect;
            winType: integer;
            done: boolean;
            event: eventRecord;
                { creation methods }
            procedure setAttributes;
            procedure establish;
                { event handling }
            procedure eventLoop;
            procedure eventLoopTask;
            procedure endEventLoop;
                { window events - seldom overridden }
            procedure activate;
            procedure deactivate;
            procedure menu (which: LongInt);
            procedure menuChoice (theMenu, theItem: integer);
            procedure buttonDownEvent;
            procedure keyEvent;
            procedure handleDrag;
            procedure handleGrow;
            procedure doGoAway;
                { window events - often overridden }
            procedure buttonDown (x, y: integer);
            procedure keyPressed (c: char);
            procedure update;
            end;
      var
        nextMenuID: Integer;
        globalMenuList: SimpleMenu;

      procedure setNextMenuID (id: integer);
      procedure globalInitializations;

  implementation

      { the necessary Macintosh initializations }
```

```
procedure globalInitializations;
begin
  initGraf(@ThePort);
  InitFonts;
  InitWindows;
  FlushEvents(everyEvent, 0);
  InitMenus;
  DrawMenuBar;
  TEInit;
  InitDialogs(nil);
  initCursor;
  nextMenuID := 512;
  globalMenuList := nil;
end;

{ set the attributes on the simple window }
procedure SimpleWindow.setAttributes;
begin
  name := 'unknown window';
  SetRect(windowRect, 50, 70, 350, 270);
  winType := DocumentProc;
  done := false;
end;

{ open (establish) a simple window }
procedure SimpleWindow.establish;
  var
    tempPort: Grafptr;
begin
  GetPort(tempPort);
  theWindowPtr := NewWindow(nil, windowRect, name,
    TRUE, winType, WindowPtr(-1), TRUE, LongInt(0));
  SelectWindow(theWindowPtr);
  ShowWindow(theWindowPtr);
end;

{ start up a main event loop }
procedure SimpleWindow.eventLoop;
begin
  while not done do
    self.eventLoopTask;
end;

procedure SimpleWindow.eventLoopTask;
  var
```

```
      ignore: boolean;
begin
  systemTask;
  ignore := GetNextEvent(everyEvent, event);

  case event.what of

    mouseDown:
      self.buttonDownEvent;

    keyDown:
      self.keyEvent;

    activateEvt:
      if BitAnd(event.modifiers, activeFlag) <> 0 then
        self.activate
      else
        self.deactivate;

    updateEvt:
      self.update;

    otherwise
        ;
  end;
end;


procedure SimpleWindow.endEventLoop;
begin
  done := true
end;


procedure SimpleWindow.buttonDownEvent;
  var
    localPoint: Point;
    wp: WindowPtr;
begin
  case FindWindow(event.where, wp) of

    inSysWindow:
      SystemClick(event, wp);

    inMenuBar:
      self.menu(menuSelect(event.where));
```

```
    inGrow:
      self.handleGrow;

    inDrag:
      self.handleDrag;

    inContent:
      if wp <> FrontWindow then
        SelectWindow(wp)
      else
        begin
          localPoint := event.where;
          GlobalToLocal(localPoint);
          self.buttonDown(localPoint.h, localPoint.v);
        end;

    inGoAway:
      self.doGoAway;

  end;
end;

procedure SimpleWindow.keyEvent;
  var
    chCode: integer;
    ch: char;
begin
  chCode := BitAnd(event.message, CharCodeMask);
  ch := chr(chCode);
  if BitAnd(event.modifiers, CmdKey) <> 0 then
    begin
      if event.what <> AutoKey then
        self.menu(MenuKey(ch))
    end
  else
    self.keyPressed(ch);
end;

{ handle a conventional key press - overridden in
    subclasses }
procedure SimpleWindow.keyPressed (c: char);
begin
end;

{ handle a window activation }
```

```
procedure SimpleWindow.activate;
begin
  SetPort(self.theWindowPtr);
end;

procedure SimpleWindow.deactivate;
begin
  { subclasses may do something, we don't }
end;

procedure SimpleWindow.menu (which: LongInt);
  var
    theMenu, theItem: integer;
begin
  if which <> 0 then
    self.menuChoice(HiWord(which), LoWord(which));
end;

procedure SimpleWindow.handleDrag;
begin
  dragWindow(theWindowPtr, event.where,
    ScreenBits.bounds);
end;

procedure SimpleWindow.handleGrow;
begin
  { assumption is that windows can't grow  }
  { can be overridden in subclasses }
end;

{ handle a menu selection }
procedure SimpleWindow.menuChoice (theMenu,
    theItem: Integer);
  var
    menuPtr: SimpleMenu;
begin
  menuPtr := globalMenuList;
  while menuPtr <> nil do
    if menuPtr.theMenuID = theMenu then
      begin
        menuPtr.selectItem(theItem);
        menuPtr := nil
      end
    else
      menuPtr := menuPTr.link;
```

```
end;

{ handle a window update - usually modified in
    subclasses }
procedure SimpleWindow.update;
begin
  SetPort(self.theWindowPtr);
  ClipRect(self.theWindowPtr^.portRect);
end;

{ handle a button down event - usually overridden in
    subclasses}
procedure SimpleWindow.buttonDown (x, y: integer);
begin
end;

{ handle button press in go away box }
procedure SimpleWindow.doGoAway;
begin
end;

{ insert a menu into the menu bar }
procedure insertAndDraw (menu: SimpleMenu);
begin
  InsertMenu(menu.theMenuPtr, 0);
  DrawMenuBar;
  menu.link := globalMenuList;
  globalMenuList := menu;
end;

{ read a menu description from resource file }
procedure SimpleMenu.readFromResource (id: integer);
begin
  theMenuPtr := GetMenu(id);
  theMenuID := id;
  insertAndDraw(self);
end;

{ create a new menu }
procedure SimpleMenu.createNewMenu (title: Str255);
begin
  theMenuID := nextMenuID;
  nextMenuID := nextMenuID + 1;
  theMenuPtr := NewMenu(theMenuID, title);
  InsertAndDraw(self);
```

```
    end;

    { create the special Apple menu item }
    procedure SimpleMenu.createAppleMenu
        (aboutTitle: Str255);
      var
        appleTitle: Str255;
    begin
      appleTitle := '@';
      appleTitle[1] := CHR(AppleMark);
      self.createNewMenu(appleTitle);
      self.addItem(aboutTitle);
      self.addSeparator;
      AddResMenu(theMenuPtr, 'DRVR');
    end;

    { add an item to a menu }
    procedure SimpleMenu.addItem (title: Str255);
    begin
      AppendMenu(theMenuPtr, title);
    end;

    { add a separator bar to a menu }
    procedure SimpleMenu.addSeparator;
    begin
      self.addItem('(-----------------');
    end;

    procedure SimpleMenu.selectItem (itemNumber: integer);
      var
        accName: Str255;
        accNumber: Integer;
    begin
    { this is just to handle the Apple menu }
    { should be overridden in all other subclasses }
      if itemNumber > 1 then
        begin
          GetItem(self.theMenuPtr, itemNumber, accName);
          accNumber := OpenDeskAcc(accName);
        end;
    end;
  end.
```

C.2   FILE GRAPH.P

```
{ graphical simulation class }
{ written by Tim Budd, Oregon State University }
{ April 1990 }

unit graphicUniverse;

interface

  type

    GraphicalObject = object
        link: GraphicalObject;
        region: Rect;
        procedure moveTo (x, y: integer);
        function intersectsWith
          (anObject: GraphicalObject): boolean;
        procedure erase;
          { the following overridden in subclasses }
        procedure update;
        procedure draw;
        procedure hitBy (anObject: GraphicalObject);
      end;

    ObjectUniverse = object
        moveableObjects: GraphicalObject;
        fixedObjects: GraphicalObject;
        continueUpdate: boolean;
        procedure initialize;
        procedure installFixedObject
          (newObj: GraphicalObject);
        procedure installMovableObject
          (newObj: GraphicalObject);
        procedure draw;
        procedure updateMoveableObjects;
        procedure continueSimulation;
        function hitObject
          (anObject: GraphicalObject):GraphicalObject;
      end;

implementation

  procedure GraphicalObject.moveTo (x, y: integer);
  begin
```

```
    OffsetRect(region, region.top, region.left);
    OffsetRect(region, x, y);
  end;


procedure GraphicalObject.update;
begin
  { implemented in subclass }
end;


procedure GraphicalObject.erase;
begin
  EraseRect(region);
end;


procedure GraphicalObject.draw;
begin
  { implemented in subclass }
end;


function GraphicalObject.intersectsWith
      (anObject: GraphicalObject): boolean;
  var
    theIntersection: Rect;
begin
  intersectsWith := SectRect(region, anObject.region,
    theIntersection);
end;


procedure GraphicalObject.hitBy
  (anObject: GraphicalObject);
begin
  { behavior provided by subclass }
end;


procedure ObjectUniverse.initialize;
begin
  fixedObjects := nil;
  moveableObjects := nil;
end;


procedure ObjectUniverse.installFixedObject
    (newObj: GraphicalObject);
begin
  newObj.link := fixedObjects;
  fixedObjects := newObj;
```

```
end;

procedure ObjectUniverse.installMovableObject;
begin
  newObj.link := moveableObjects;
  moveableObjects := newObj;
end;

procedure ObjectUniverse.updateMoveableObjects;
  var
    currentObject: GraphicalObject;
begin
  repeat
    continueUpdate := false;
    currentObject := moveableObjects;
    while currentObject <> nil do
      begin
        currentObject.update;
        currentObject := currentObject.link;
      end;
  until not continueUpdate
end;

procedure ObjectUniverse.continueSimulation;
begin
  continueUpdate := true
end;

procedure ObjectUniverse.draw;
  var
    currentObject: GraphicalObject;
begin
  currentObject := fixedObjects;
  while currentObject <> nil do
    begin
      currentObject.draw;
      currentObject := currentObject.link;
    end;
  currentObject := moveableObjects;
  while currentObject <> nil do
    begin
      currentObject.draw;
      currentObject := currentObject.link;
    end;
end;
```

```
function ObjectUniverse.hitObject
        (anObject: GraphicalObject): GraphicalObject;
    var
      currentObject: GraphicalObject;
      hit: GraphicalObject;
begin
  currentObject := fixedObjects;
  hit := nil;
  while (hit = nil) and (currentObject <> nil) do
    begin
      if (anObject <> currentObject) then
        if (anObject.intersectsWith(currentObject)) then
          hit := currentObject;
      currentObject := currentObject.link;
    end;
  currentObject := moveableObjects;
  while (hit = nil) and (currentObject <> nil) do
    begin
      if (anObject <> currentObject) then
        if (anObject.intersectsWith(currentObject)) then
          hit := currentObject;
      currentObject := currentObject.link;
    end;
  hitObject := hit;
  end;
end.
```

C.3   FILE COMPONENTS.P

```
{ components for billiard simulation }
{ written by Tim Budd, Oregon State University }
{ April 1990 }

unit billiardComponents;
interface
  uses
    graphicUniverse;

  type

    wall = object(GraphicalObject)
        convertFactor: real;
        procedure setBounds (left, top, right,
```

```
            bottom: integer; cf: real);
        procedure draw; override;
        procedure hitBy (anObject: GraphicalObject);
            override;
      end;

  hole = object (GraphicalObject)
      procedure setCenter (x, y: integer);
      procedure draw; override;
      procedure hitBy (anObject: GraphicalObject);
          override;
      end;

  ball = object (hole)
      direction: real;
      energy: real;
      procedure draw; override;
      procedure update; override;
      procedure hitBy (anObject: GraphicalObject);
          override;
      function x: real;
      function y: real;
      end;

var
  theUniverse: ObjectUniverse;
  cueBall: ball;
  saveRack: integer;

function hitAngle (dx, dy: real): real;

implementation

  function hitAngle (dx, dy: real): real;
    const
      PI = 3.14159;
    var
      na: real;
    begin
      if (abs(dx) < 0.05) then
        na := PI / 2
      else
        na := arctan(abs(dy / dx));
      if (dx < 0) then
        na := PI - na;
```

```
    if (dy < 0) then
      na := -na;
    hitAngle := na;
  end;


procedure wall.setBounds (left, top, right,
    bottom: integer; cf: real);
begin
  convertFactor := cf;
  SetRect(region, left, top, right, bottom);
end;


procedure wall.draw;
begin
  PaintRect(region);
end;


procedure wall.hitBy (anObject: GraphicalObject);
  var
    theBall: ball;
begin
  theBall := ball(anObject);
  theBall.direction := convertFactor - theBall.direction;
  theUniverse.continueSimulation;
  draw;
end;


procedure hole.setCenter (x, y: integer);
begin
  SetRect(region, x - 5, y - 5, x + 5, y + 5);
end;


procedure hole.draw;
begin
  PaintOval(region);
end;


procedure hole.hitBy (anObject: GraphicalObject);
  var
    theBall: ball;
begin
  theBall := ball(anObject);
  if (theBall = cueBall) then
    theBall.setCenter(50, 100)
  else
```

```
    begin
      saveRack := saveRack + 1;
      theBall.setCenter(10 + saveRack * 15, 250);
    end;
  theBall.energy := 0.0;
  anObject.draw;
end;

function ball.x: real;
begin
  x := (region.left + region.right) / 2;
end;

function ball.y: real;
begin
  y := (region.top + region.bottom) / 2;
end;


procedure ball.draw;
begin
  if (self = cueBall) then
    FrameOval(region)
  else
    PaintOval(region);
end;

procedure ball.update;
  var
    hit: GraphicalObject;
    dx, dy: integer;
    i, xdir, ydir, ymove: integer;
begin
  if (energy > 0.5) then
    begin
      erase;
      energy := energy - 0.05;
      if energy > 0.5 then
        theUniverse.continueSimulation;
      dx := trunc(5.0 * cos(direction));
      dy := trunc(5.0 * sin(direction));
      offsetRect(region, dx, dy);
      hit := theUniverse.hitObject(self);
      if hit <> nil then
        begin
```

```
            hit.hitBy(self);
            theUniverse.draw;
         end
      else
         draw;
   end;
end;


procedure ball.hitBy (anObject: GraphicalObject);
  var
    aBall: ball;
    da: real;
begin
  aBall := ball(anObject);
  energy := aBall.energy / 2;
  aBall.energy := energy;
  direction := hitAngle(self.x - aBall.x,
        self.y - aBall.y);
  da := aBall.direction - direction;
  aBall.direction := aBall.direction + da;
  theUniverse.continueSimulation;
  end;
end.
```

C.4   FILE BILLIARD.P

```
{ Billiards Program Simulation - main program }
{ written by Tim Budd, Oregon State University }
{ April 1990 }

program billiards;

  uses
    SimpleWindow, graphicUniverse, billiardComponents;
  type
      { the menu containing the quit command }
    BilliardMenu = object(SimpleMenu)
        procedure initialize (title: STR255);
        procedure selectItem (itemNumber: Integer);
            override;
      end;

      { the main simulation window }
    BilliardSimulation = object(SimpleWindow)
```

```
         procedure initialize;
         procedure buttonDown (x, y: integer); override;
         procedure update; override;
         procedure keyPressed (c: char); override;
         procedure createWalls;
         procedure createHoles;
         procedure rackBalls;
      end;
var
   theGame: BilliardSimulation;

{ create a new menu }
procedure BilliardMenu.initialize (title: Str255);
begin
   self.createNewMenu(title);
   self.addItem('quit');
end;

{ when the user selects quit, we quit }
procedure BilliardMenu.selectItem (itemNumber: integer);
begin
   theGame.endEventLoop;
end;

{ initialize the billiard window }
procedure BilliardSimulation.initialize;
   var
      appleMenu: SimpleMenu;
      newMenu: BilliardMenu;
begin
   setAttributes;
   name := 'billiard Simulation';
   setRect(windowRect, 20, 50, 400, 350);

   new(theUniverse);
   theUniverse.initialize;

   createWalls;
   createHoles;
   rackBalls;

   new(appleMenu);
   appleMenu.createAppleMenu('about
           BilliardSimulation...');
```

```
  new(newMenu);
  newMenu.initialize('billiards');

  establish;
end;


{ when the button goes down, hit the cue ball }
procedure BilliardSimulation.buttonDown (x, y: integer);
begin
  cueBall.energy := 20.0;
  cueBall.direction := hitAngle(cueBall.x - x,
      cueBall.y - y);
  theUniverse.updateMoveableObjects;
end;


{ to update the simulation, draw everything }
procedure BilliardSimulation.update;
begin
  inherited update;
  theUniverse.draw;
end;


procedure BilliardSimulation.createWalls;
  var
    newWall: wall;
begin
  new(newWall);
  newWall.setBounds(10, 10, 300, 15, 0.0);
  theUniverse.installFixedObject(newWall);
  new(newWall);
  newWall.setBounds(10, 200, 300, 205, 0.0);
  theUniverse.installFixedObject(newWall);
  new(newWall);
  newWall.setBounds(10, 10, 15, 200, 3.114159);
  theUniverse.installFixedObject(newWall);
  new(newWall);
  newWall.setBounds(300, 10, 305, 205, 3.114159);
  theUniverse.installFixedObject(newWall);
end;


procedure BilliardSimulation.createHoles;
  var
    newHole: hole;
begin
  new(newHole);
```

```
      newHole.setCenter(15, 15);
      theUniverse.installFixedObject(newHole);
      new(newHole);
      newHole.setCenter(15, 200);
      theUniverse.installFixedObject(newHole);
      new(newHole);
      newHole.setCenter(300, 15);
      theUniverse.installFixedObject(newHole);
      new(newHole);
      newHole.setCenter(300, 200);
      theUniverse.installFixedObject(newHole);
    end;

    procedure BilliardSimulation.rackBalls;
      var
        i, j: integer;
        newBall: ball;
    begin
      saveRack := 0;
      new(cueBall);
      cueBall.setCenter(50, 96);
      cueBall.direction := 0.0;
      theUniverse.installMovableObject(cueBall);

      for i := 1 to 5 do
        for j := 1 to i do
          begin
            new(newBall);
            newBall.setCenter(190 + i * 8,
                    100 + 16 * j - 8 * i);
            theUniverse.installMovableObject(newBall);
          end;
    end;

    { quit on any key press }
    procedure BilliardSimulation.keyPressed (c: char);
    begin
      endEventLoop;
    end;

{ ********** main program ********* }
begin
  globalInitializations;

  new(theGame);
```

```
    theGame.initialize;
    theGame.eventLoop;
end.
```

D
Source for
Container Classes

This appendix gives the complete source code for the container classes described in Chapter 17.

D.1   FILE COLLECT.H

```
# ifndef collecth
# define collecth
//
//  C++ Container Class Definitions
//  Written by Tim Budd
//     Oregon State University
//     June, 1990
//

//
//---------------------------------------- Element
//  the basic elements of a linked list
//

typedef int Boolean;

class Element
{
   friend class List;

public:
   Element();
```

```
    virtual Boolean    operator == (Element& x) ;
    virtual Boolean    operator != (Element& x) ;
    virtual unsigned  hash() ;

private:
  Element *  lnk;
  Element *  link ();
  void     setLink (Element* n);
  void     insert (Element& n);
  void     removeNext ();
};

inline void Element::setLink(Element* n)
{  lnk = n; }

inline Element::Element()
{  setLink(0); }

inline Element* Element::link()
{  return lnk; }

//
//------------------------------------------- List
//

class List : private Element  {
public:
    // addition
  void     addFirst (Element& x);
  void     addLast (Element& x);
    // removal
  void     removeEqual (Element& x);
  void     removeFirst ();
  void     removeLast ();
    // testing
  Boolean    includes (Element& x);
  Boolean    isEmpty ();
  int     size ();
    // access
  Element *  first ();
  Element *  last ();
  Element *  next();
  void     reset ();
  Boolean    operator++();
```

```
    Element *  operator()();

protected:
  void     addAfterCurrent(Element& y);

private:
  Element *  current;
};

inline void List::reset()
{  current = 0;  }

inline Element* List::operator()()
{  return current;  }

inline void List::addFirst(Element& x)
{  Element::insert(x);  }

inline Element* List::first()
{  return Element::link();  }

inline int List::isEmpty()
{  return first() == 0;  }

inline void List::addAfterCurrent(Element& y)
{   current->insert(y); }

inline void List::removeFirst()
{  List::removeNext();  }

//
//---------------------------------------- Set
//

class Set : private List {
public:
  void     add (Element& x);
  void     remove (Element& x);
    // alter accessibility on the following
  List::includes;
  List::size;
  List::reset;
  //List::operator ++;
  Boolean operator ++() { return List::operator++(); }
  //List::operator ();
```

```
    Element * operator()() { return List::operator()(); }
};

inline void Set::remove(Element& x)
{  List::removeEqual(x);  }

//
//----------------------------------- OrderedElement
//

class OrderedElement : public Element {
public:
  Boolean virtual      operator <  (OrderedElement& x) ;
  Boolean virtual      operator <= (OrderedElement& x) ;
  Boolean virtual      operator >  (OrderedElement& x) ;
  Boolean virtual      operator >= (OrderedElement& x) ;
};

//
//----------------------------------------- Ordered
//

class Ordered : private List {
public:
  void         add (OrderedElement& x);
  OrderedElement *  max();
  OrderedElement *  min();
  void         remove (OrderedElement& x);
  OrderedElement *  operator()();
  OrderedElement *  next();

  List::includes;
  List::size;
  List::reset;
  //List::operator++;
  Boolean operator++() { return List::operator++(); }
};

inline void Ordered::remove(OrderedElement& x)
{  List::removeEqual(x);  }

inline OrderedElement *  Ordered::min()
{  return (OrderedElement *) List::first();  }

inline OrderedElement *  Ordered::max()
```

```
{  return (OrderedElement *) List::last(); }

inline OrderedElement * Ordered::operator()()
{  return (OrderedElement *) List::operator()(); }

inline OrderedElement * Ordered::next()
{  return (OrderedElement *) List::next(); }

//
//---------------------------------------- Table
//

class AssociationList;    // forward declaration

class Table
{
public:
  Table (int sz = 17);    // constructor - size of table

  Boolean    includesKey (Element& x);
  List&      keys ();
  void       removeKey (Element& x);
  int        size ();
  List&      values ();
  Element*&   operator [] (Element& x);

protected:
  const int tablesize;      // size of the table
  AssociationList *elements;  // table values

};
# endif
```

D.2 FILE COLLECT.CC

```
//
//  C++ Container Class Implementation File
//  Written by Tim Budd
//     June, 1990
//

# include "collect.h"

//
```

```
//   virtual methods and non-inline methods from class
//     Element
//

Boolean Element::operator == (Element& x)
{  return this == &x; }

Boolean Element::operator != (Element& x)
{  return ! ( *this == x); }

unsigned Element::hash()
{  return 0; }

void Element::insert (Element& n)
{
  // insert new element, updating links
  n.setLink(link());
  setLink(&n);
}

void Element::removeNext ()
{
  // remove next element, if there is one
  if (link())
    setLink(link()->link());
}


//
//   virtual methods and non-inline methods from class
//     List
//

void List::addLast(Element& x)
{
  if (isEmpty())
    addFirst(x);
  else
    last()->insert(x);
}

Boolean List::includes(Element& x)
{
  reset();
  while ((*this)++)
    if (*current == x)
```

```
      return 1;
  return 0;
}

Element * List::last()
{
  // empty list - just return nothing
  if (isEmpty())
    return (Element *) 0;

  // else iterate until we find end of list
  reset();
  while ((*this)++) {
    if (! next())
      return (*this)();
    }
  return (Element *) 0;
}

void List::removeLast()
{  Element* p;

  // empty list, do nothing
  if (isEmpty()) return;

  // if only one element, remove it
  p = first();
  if (! (p->link()))
    Element::setLink(0);

  // need to find next to last element
  reset();
  while ((*this)++) {
    if (!(next()->link()))
      (*this)()->removeNext();
    }
}

void List::removeEqual(Element& x)
{

  // if first element, remove it
  if (*first() == x)
    removeFirst();
```

```
    // loop over elements, checking next one
    reset();
    while ((*this)++)
      if (next() && *next() == x) {
        (*this)()->removeNext();
        return;
        }
}

int List::size()
{  int i = 0;

   reset();
   while ((*this)++) i++;
   return i;
}

Boolean List::operator++()
{
   if (current)
     current = current->link();
   else
     current = Element::link();
   return current != 0;
}

Element* List::next()
{  if (current)
     return current->link();
   else
     return 0;
}

//
//  virtual methods and non-inline methods from class Set
//

void Set::add(Element& x)
{  if (! includes(x))
     List::addFirst(x);
}

//
//  virtual methods and non-inline methods from class
//     OrderedElement
```

```
//

Boolean OrderedElement::operator < (OrderedElement& x)
{   return x > *this; }

Boolean OrderedElement::operator <= (OrderedElement& x)
{   return (*this < x) || (*this == x); }

Boolean OrderedElement::operator > (OrderedElement& x)
{   return x < *this; }

Boolean OrderedElement::operator >= (OrderedElement& x)
{   return x <= *this; }

//
//  virtual methods and non-inline methods from
//     class Ordered
//

void Ordered::add(OrderedElement& x)
{   OrderedElement *p;

  p = (OrderedElement *) List::first();
  // base cases - empty list or first element
  if ((!p) || (x < *p)) {
    List::addFirst(x);
    return;
    }

  // looping case, loop until we find right location
  reset();
  while ((*this)++)
    if (next() && (x < *next())) {
      List::addAfterCurrent(x);
      return;
      }
  List::addLast(x);
}

//
//--------------------------------------- Association
//

class Association : public Element
{
```

```
  friend class Table;

public:
  Association (Element&);  // constructor - arg is key

  Boolean virtual   operator == (Element&) ;

private:
  const Element&  associationKey;
  Element*  associationValue;
  Element&  key() ;
  Element*&  value();
};

inline Element&  Association::key()
{   return associationKey; }

inline Element*& Association::value()
{   return associationValue; }

inline Association::Association(Element& x) :
        associationKey(x)
{   associationValue = (Element *) 0; }

//
//------------------------------------- AssociationList
//

class AssociationList : public List
{
public:
  void      add(Association& x);
  Association *  operator()();
};

inline void AssociationList::add(Association& x)
{  List::addFirst(x); }

inline Association * AssociationList::operator()()
{  return (Association *) List::operator()(); }

//
//
// virtual methods and non-inline methods from class
//    Association
```

```
//

Boolean Association::operator == (Element& x)
{
  return key() == x;
}

//
//  virtual methods and non-inline methods from class
//     Table
//

Table::Table (int sz) : tablesize(sz)
{   elements = new AssociationList[tablesize]; }

Element*& Table::operator [] (Element& x)
{   AssociationList& list =
         elements[x.hash() % tablesize];

  // see if already there
  list.reset();
  while (list++)
    if (*list() == x)
      return list()->value();

  // not there, make new association
  Association *p = new Association(x);
   list.add(*p);
  return p->value();
}

int Table::size()
{   int i; int sz = 0;
    for (i = 0; i < tablesize; i++)
    sz += elements[i].size();
  return sz;
}

List& Table::keys()
{   List& theList = *new List;
  int i;

  for (i = 0; i < tablesize; i++) {
    AssociationList& p = elements[i];
    p.reset();
```

```
    while (p++)
      theList.addFirst(p()->key());
    }
  return theList;
}


List& Table::values()
{   List& theList = *new List;
    int i;

    for (i = 0; i < tablesize; i++) {
      AssociationList& p = elements[i];
      p.reset();
      while (p++)
        theList.addFirst(*(p()->value()));
      }
    return theList;
}


Boolean Table::includesKey (Element& x)
{   return elements[x.hash() % tablesize].includes(x); }

void Table::removeKey(Element& x)
{   elements[x.hash() % tablesize].removeEqual(x); }
```

D.3   FILE CTEST.CC

Although it is not part of the container classes themselves, the following file
shows how the container classes can be subclassed to hide details of the use of
the class Element.

```
//
//  routines to test the C++ container classes
//
# include <stdio.h>
# include "collect.h"

//
//  IntElement - integer elements
//     elements which maintain integer values
//
class IntElement : public OrderedElement {
public:
  const int value;
  IntElement (int i);
```

```
  unsigned virtual hash();

  Boolean virtual operator== (Element&);
  Boolean virtual operator< (OrderedElement&);

  int &  intReference();
  void display();
};

inline IntElement::IntElement (int i) : OrderedElement(),
  value(i)
{ ; }

unsigned IntElement::hash()
{ return (unsigned) value; }

int &  IntElement::intReference()
{ return value; }

void IntElement::display()
{ printf(" %d ", value); }

// define equality and relations in terms of underlying
//     integers
Boolean IntElement::operator == (Element& x)
{  return value == ((IntElement &) x).value; }

Boolean IntElement::operator < (OrderedElement& x)
{  return value < ((IntElement &) x).value; }


//
//  Now define collections which manipulate integer
//     elements specifically
//
class IntList : public List {
public:
  IntElement *    first ();
  IntElement *    last ();
  void    add (int);
  void    addFirst (int);
  void    addLast (int);
  void    remove (int);
  IntElement *  operator()();
```

```
};

IntElement * IntList::operator()()
{  return (IntElement *) List::operator()(); }

IntElement * IntList::first()
{ return (IntElement *) List::first(); }

IntElement * IntList::last()
{ return (IntElement *) List::last(); }

void IntList::add(int i)
{ List::addFirst(* new IntElement(i)); }

void IntList::addFirst(int i)
{ List::addFirst(* new IntElement(i)); }

void IntList::addLast(int i)
{ List::addLast(* new IntElement(i)); }

void IntList::remove(int i)
{ IntElement p(i);
  List::removeEqual(p); }

void print(IntList& x)
{
  x.reset();
  while (x++)
    x()->display();
  printf("\n");
}

class IntSet : public Set {
public:
  void     add (int);
  void     remove (int);
  IntSet&    operator += (int);
  IntElement *  operator()();
};

void    IntSet::add(int i)
{ Set::add(* new IntElement(i)); }

void    IntSet::remove(int i)
{  IntElement p(i);
```

```
      Set::remove(p);  }

  IntSet&     IntSet::operator += (int x)
  { add(x); return *this; }

  IntElement * IntSet::operator()()
  {   return (IntElement *) List::operator()();  }

  void print(IntSet& x)
  {
    x.reset();
    while (x++)
      x()->display();
    printf("\n");
  }

  class IntOrdered : public Ordered {
  public:
    void  add (int);
    void  remove (int);
    IntElement *  operator()();
  };

  void  IntOrdered::add(int i)
  { Ordered::add(* new IntElement(i));  }

  void  IntOrdered::remove(int i)
  { IntElement p(i);
    Ordered::remove(p);  }

  IntElement * IntOrdered::operator()()
  {   return (IntElement *) List::operator()();  }

  void print(IntOrdered& x)
  {
    x.reset();
    while (x++)
      x()->display();
    printf("\n");
  }

  class IntTable : public Table {
  public:
    IntList&  keys();
    IntList&  values();
```

```
  Boolean     includesKey (int);
  void      removeKey (int);
  int&      operator [] (int);
};


IntList& IntTable::keys()
{ return (IntList&) Table::keys(); }


IntList& IntTable::values()
{ return (IntList&) Table::values(); }


Boolean IntTable::includesKey(int i)
{ return Table::includesKey(* new IntElement(i));}


void IntTable::removeKey(int i)
{ IntElement p(i);
  Table::removeKey(p);}


int& IntTable::operator [] (int i)
{   Element*& x = Table::operator[](* new IntElement(i));
  // if not there, make new element
  if (!x) x = new IntElement(0);
  return ((IntElement *) x)->intReference();
}



main() {
  IntList A;

  printf("List tests\n");
  // first add new elements
  A.addFirst(5);
  A.add(23);
  A.addFirst(4);
  A.addLast(6);
  print(A);
  printf("size is %d\n", A.size());

  // display the first and last elements
  printf("first last ");
  A.first()->display();
  A.last()->display();
  printf("\n");

  // try removing a few
```

```
printf("remove element ");
A.remove(23);
print(A);
printf("remove first ");
A.removeFirst();
print(A);
printf("remove last ");
A.removeLast();
print(A);

printf("Set test\n");
IntSet S;

// add a few elements to the set
S.add(12);
(S += 14) += 23;
S.add(12);
print(S);
// remove the element that was added twice
S.remove(12);
print(S);
printf("size is %d\n", S.size());

printf("Ordered Test\n");
IntOrdered B;

// put one value into test
B.add(12);
// display it
print(B);

B.add(15);
print(B);
B.add(10);
B.add(13);
B.add(14);
B.add(17);
print(B);
printf("size is %d\n", B.size());

IntTable T;
int i;

for (i = 7; i < 200; i += 7)
  T[i] = -i;
```

```
        printf("keys ");
        IntList &k = T.keys();
        print(k);

        printf("values ");
        IntList &v = T.values();
        print(v);

        printf("size %d\n", T.size());

        printf("includes tests %d %d %d\n", T.includesKey(14),
            T.includesKey(-14), T.includesKey(15));

        T.removeKey(14);

        printf("size %d\n", T.size());

        printf("includes tests %d %d %d\n", T.includesKey(14),
            T.includesKey(-14), T.includesKey(15));
}
```

E
Glossary

Object-oriented programming techniques introduce many new ideas and terms that may not be familiar to the novice, even if he or she has had extensive experience with other programming languages. Even more problematic, among the various object-oriented languages, several different terms often are used to denote the same idea. Such terms are listed as synonyms in the following glossary. Also indicated are situations where a term is given a particular meaning in a language that is not shared with other languages.

abstract superclass Syn. *deferred class*. A class that is not used to make direct instances, but rather is used only as a base from which other classes inherit. In C++, the term is often reserved for classes that contain at least one *pure virtual method*.

accessor method A method designed to provide access to the internal data maintained by instances of a class. Such functions are necessary in languages such as Smalltalk where access is not permitted, and their use generally is considered good programming style even when direct access to the data is available.

ad hoc polymorphism Syn. *overloading*. A procedure or method identifier that denotes more than one procedure.

allocated class Syn. *dynamic class*. See *static class*.

ancestor class Syn. *base class, superclass*. (Object Pascal) A type from which an object type inherits. The type named in an object type definition statement is called the *immediate ancestor*.

ancestor type See *ancestor class*.

argument signature (C++) In internal encoding of a list of argument types; the argument signature is used to disambiguate overloaded function invocations, with that function body being selected that matches most closely the signature of the function call. See *parametric overloading*.

automatic storage management See *garbage collection*. A policy in which the underlying run-time system is responsible for the detection and reclamation of memory values no longer accessible, and hence of no further use to the computation. Among the object-oriented languages discussed in this book, only Smalltalk provides automatic storage management.

automatic variable A variable that is allocated space automatically when a procedure is entered. Contrast to *dynamic variables*, which must have space allocated by the user.

base class Syn. *ancestor type, superclass*. (C++) A class from which another class is derived.

binding The process by which a name or an expression is associated with an attribute, such as a variable and the type of value the variable can hold.

binding time The time at which a binding takes place. *Early* or *static binding* generally refers to binding performed at compile time, whereas *late* or *dynamic binding* refers to binding performed at run time. Dynamically bound languages, such as Smalltalk and Objective-C, do not bind a variable and the type of value the variable can hold at compile time. Message passing is a form of procedure calling with late binding.

browser A software tool that simplifies the examination of code associated with a software system. It is useful for exploratory programming. (Smalltalk) A software tool used to examine the classes already defined as part of the Smalltalk class hierarchy.

child class Syn. *subclass, derived class*. (C++) A class that is defined as an extension of another class, which is called the *parent class*.

class Syn. *object type*. An abstract description of the data and behavior of a collection of similar objects. The representatives of the collection are called *instances* of the class.

class description protocol The complete definition of all properties, features, and methods that are descriptive of any object that is an instance of a class.

class object Syn. *factory object*. (Smalltalk) The single special object, and instance of class Class, that is associated with each class. New instances of the class are created by the message new being sent to this object.

class method (C++) A method declared with the keyword static. Class methods are not permitted to access instance variables; they can access only class variables. Class methods can be invoked independent of instances using explicit name qualification.

class variable A variable shared by all instances of a class. (C++) A data member declared as static. (Smalltalk) A variable declared as a class variable in the class-construction message.

cohesion The degree to which components of a single software system (such as members of a single class) are tied together. Contrast with *coupling*.

collection classes See *container classes*.

constructor (C++) A method having the same name as the class in which it is defined. A constructor is invoked to initialize new instances of the class. Constructors can be overloaded. (Turbo Pascal) A special method, defined using the reserved word constructor, that initializes an object containing virtual methods. Calling a virtual method for an object without first calling that object's constructor generates a run-time error.

container classes Classes used as data structures that can contain a number of elements. Examples include lists, sets, and tables. Chapter 17 develops a number of container classes in C++.

coupling The degree to which separate software components are tied together. Contrast with *cohesion*.

data member (C++) See *instance variable*.

deferred class See *abstract superclass*.

deferred method A method that defines an interface (that is, argument and result types), but no implementation. Implementation is provided by subclasses that override the deferred method, preserving the interface. See *pure virtual method*.

delegation An alternative to class-based organization. Using delegation, objects can defer the implementation of behavior to other objects, called *delegates*. This technique permits sharing of behavior without the necessity to introduce classes or inheritance.

derived class Syn. *descendant type, subclass, child class*. (C++) A class that is defined as an extension or a subclass of another class, which is called the *base* class.

descendant type Syn. *subclass, child class*. See *derived class*.

destructor (C++) A method that is invoked immediately before memory is released for an object. The destructor can perform any actions required for the management of the object. The name of the destructor is formed by a tilde being prepended to the name of the class.

dispatch table (Objective-C) A table of method selectors and associated methods. Created when a class is compiled, the dispatch table is searched as part of the message-passing operation.

domain (Object Pascal) When used to refer to variables of object types, the set of object types that represent legal values for the variable. The domain consists of the declared type, and all of that latter's descendants (subtypes).

dynamic class See *static class*.

dynamic variable A variable for which space must be allocated explicitly by the user. Contrast to *automatic* variables, which have space allocated for them automatically when a procedure is entered.

dynamically typed language A language in which programmers do not declare any specific type in variable declarations.

early binding See *binding time*.

exported name An identifier (variable, type name, function, or method) available for use outside of the context in which it is defined. (Objective-C) A variable, type, function or method that is global or is defined in an interface (*.h) file. (Object Pascal) A variable, type, function, or method defined within the interface section of a unit.

factory method (Objective-C) A method recognized only by the class object for a class. Contrast to *instance methods*, which are recognized by instances of the class.

factory object Syn. *class object*. (Objective-C) The unique object, associated with each class, used to create new instances of the class. Each factory object is an instance of class Class. New instances of the class are created by the message new being sent to this object.

friend function (C++) A function that is permitted access to the otherwise private or protected features of a class. Friend functions must be explicitly declared as such by the class that is protecting the features to which the friend is being given access. Friend classes and friend methods also can be defined.

function member (C++) See *method*.

garbage collection The component of a system for performing automatic storage management that is specifically concerned with the detection and recovery of memory storage areas that are no longer accessible and thus are candidates for collection and reuse.

generic method Syn. *virtual method*.

has-a **relation** See *is-a relation*. The relation that asserts that instances of a class possess fields of a given type.

immutable variables A variable the value of which is assigned once, and cannot be reassigned. See *single-assignment variable*.

information hiding The principle that users of a software component (such as a class) need to know only the essential details of how to initialize and access the component, and do not need to know the details of the implementation. By reducing the degree of interconnectedness between separate elements of a software system, the principle of information hiding helps in the development of reliable software.

inheritance The property of objects by which instances of a class can have access to data and method definitions contained in a previously defined class, without those definitions being restated. See *superclass*.

inheritance graph An abstract structure that illustrates the inheritance relationships within a collection of classes.

inherited (Object Pascal) A keyword used to activate the execution of an over-ridden procedure. (See Section 9.3.)

initialize (Objective-C, Smalltalk) A special message sent to the class object before the class receives instances of any other message. Can be redefined as a factory method to set up the appropriate run-time environment before instances of a class are used.

inline function A function that is expanded internally by the compiler as code at the point of call, thus avoiding the overhead of a subroutine call and return sequence. Since the code for an inline function can be duplicated many times, the feature is used mainly for functions that generate very little code, such as accessor methods.

instance Syn. *object.* (C++) A variable of a class type. (Object Pascal) A variable of an object type. (Smalltalk) A specific example of the general structure defined by a class.

instance variable The data associated with each instance of a class. Every instance maintains a distinct set of instance variables.

instance method Syn. *method.* (Objective-C) A method recognized by in-stances of a class. See *factory method.*

is-a **relation** See *has-a relation.* The relation that asserts that instances of a sub-class must be more specialized forms of the superclass. Thus, instances of a subclass can be used where quantities of the superclass type are required.

isa link (Objective-C) An implicit pointer, contained in every object, that points to the dispatch table for the object. Since objects are characterized only by their behavior, this pointer in effect encodes the class of the object.

late binding See *binding time.*

Member (Object Pascal) A system-provided Boolean function that can be used to determine whether the value (dynamic type) of a variable is a member of a specific object type. An example illustrating the use of this function is given in Section 4.3.

member (C++) A general term for the attributes associated with instances of a class. Instance variables are called *data members* in C++; methods are called *procedure* or *function* members.

message passing See *method lookup.* The process of locating and executing a method in response to a message.

message selector Syn. *method designator, method selector, selector.* The tex-tual string that identifies a message in a message-passing expression. During the process of message passing, this string is used to find a matching method as part of the method-lookup process.

message expression (Objective-C) A Smalltalk-like message-passing expres-sion enclosed in a pair of square braces, [...]. The braces are used to differentiate message-passing code from normal C code.

metaclass (Smalltalk) The class of a class object. For each class, there is an associated metaclass. The class object is typically the only instance of this metaclass. Metaclasses permit the specialization of class behavior. Without them, all classes would need to behave in the same way.

method A procedure or function associated with a class (or object type) and invoked in a message-passing style.

method declaration The part of a class declaration specific to an individual method.

method designator Syn. *message selector*. A method name identifier used as a procedure or function name in a message-passing expression. The method designator is used to search for the appropriate method during the process of message sending. In general, you cannot determine from the program text which method a method designator will activate during execution.

method lookup The process of locating a method matching a particular message, generally performed as part of the message-passing operation. Usually, the run-time system finds the method by examining the class hierarchy for the receiver of the message, searching from bottom to top until a method is found with the same name as the message.

method selector See *message selector*.

multiple inheritance The feature that allows a subclass to inherit from more than one immediate superclass. Multiple inheritance is not supported by all object-oriented languages.

object See *instance*. (Object Pascal) A keyword used to indicate the definition of an object type.

object field designator (Object Pascal) A (perhaps qualified) identifier that denotes a field within an object.

object hierarchy Syn. *class hierarchy*. (Object Pascal) A group of object types all related through inheritance.

object type Syn. *class*. (Object Pascal) A data structure, similar to a Pascal record type definition, that can contain fields (methods) of procedures and functions, as well as data fields.

overload Used to describe an identifier that denotes more than one object. Procedures, functions, methods, and operators can all be overloaded. A virtual method, or a method that is overridden, can be said to also be overloaded. See *parametric overloading*.

override The action that occurs when a method in a subclass with the same name as a method in a superclass takes precedence over the method in the superclass. Normally, during the process of binding a method to a message (see *message passing*), the overriding method will be the method selected. (Object Pascal) A keyword used to indicate that a method is to override the similarly named method in an ancestor type.

paradigm An illustrative model or example, which by extension provides a way of organizing information. The object-oriented paradigm emphasizes organization based on behaviors and responsibilities.

parameterized classes Classes in which some types are left unbound at the time of class definition. These bindings are filled in, resulting in qualified classes, before instances of the class are created.

parametric overloading Overloading of function names in which two or more procedure bodies are known by the same name in a given context, and are disambiguated by the type and number of parameters supplied with the procedure call. (Overloading of functions, methods, and operators can also occur.)

parent class Syn. *superclass, ancestor class.* An immediate superclass of a class.

Parnas' Principles Principles that describe the proper use of modules.

persistent object An object that continues to exist outside of the execution time of programs that manipulate the object.

polymorphic See *pure polymorphism, ad hoc polymorphism.* Literally "many shapes". A feature of a variable that can take on values of several different types, or of a function is a function that has at least one polymorphic argument. The term is also used for a function name that denotes several different functions.

primitive (Smalltalk) See *primitive operation.*

primitive operation (Smalltalk) An operation that cannot be performed in the programming language, and thus must be accomplished with the aid of the underlying run-time system.

private inheritance (C++) Inheritance used for the purposes of implementation, which does not preserve the *is-a* relation. The inheriting class is permitted access to the features of the parent class, but instances of the child class cannot be assigned to variables declared as the parent class.

procedure call The transfer of control from the current point in execution to the code associated with a procedure. Procedure calling differs from *message passing* in that the section of code to be transferred to is decided at compile time (or link time), rather than at run time.

protocol See *class description protocol.*

prototype (C++) A function declaration that includes the types of the arguments.

pure polymorphism See *ad hoc polymorphism.* A feature of a single function that can be executed using arguments of a variety of types.

pure virtual method (C++) A virtual method without a body, created by the value 0 being assigned to the function in the class definition. Pure virtual methods provide specification for subclasses. See *deferred method.*

qualified name (C++) A name of a method that indicates explicitly the class in which the method is located. In C++, the class name and method name are separated by two colons (class::method); in Object Pascal, a period is used. Since the class of the method is named explicitly, a call on a qualified name can be performed using procedure calling in place of message passing.

rapid prototyping See *exploratory programming*. A style of software development in which less emphasis is placed on creation of a complete formal specification than on rapid construction of a prototype pilot system, with the understanding that users will experiment with the initial system and suggest modifications or changes, probably leading to a complete redevelopment of a subsequent system.

receiver The object to which a message is sent. In Smalltalk and Objective-C, the receiver is indicated as the object to the left of the message selector. In C++ and Object Pascal, the receiver is the object to the left of the field qualifier (period). Within a method, the current receiver is indicated in various ways: In C++, the variable this is a *pointer* to the current receiver, in Objective-C, Object Pascal, and Smalltalk the pseudo-variable self contains the current receiver.

reference variable (C++) A variable declared using the address-of (&) modifier. The variable points to another value, and is an alias for this value. Changes to the reference variable will be reflected in changes in the object to which the reference has been assigned.

responsibility-driven design A design technique that emphasizes the identification and division of responsibilities within a collection of independent agents.

scope When applied to a variable identifier, the (textual) portion of a program in which references to the identifier denote the particular variable.

selector See *message selector*.

self See *this*. (Objective-C, Object Pascal, Smalltalk) When used inside a method, **self** refers to the receiver for the message that caused the method to be invoked.

single-assignment variable A variable the value of which is assigned once, and cannot be redefined. (C++) Single-assignment variables can occur in C++ using either the const modifier or through the definition of a reference variable (in the latter case, the reference is single assignment; the variable to which the reference points, on the other hand, can be modified repeatedly). A single-assignment variable can also be created by assigning a data member in a constructor and then not permitting any other method to modify the value.

slicing (C++) The process by which an argument of a derived type is passed to an argument declared as a base type. In effect, the fields and methods of the derived type are sliced off from the base fields. This is described in Chapter 11.

specification class An abstract superclass used only to define an interface. The actual implementation of the interface is left to subclasses.

static (C++) A declaration modifier that, when applied to global variables and functions, means that the variables are not accessible outside of the file in which they are declared; when applied to local variables, means that they continue to exist even after the procedure in which they are declared has exited; and, when applied to class declaration fields, indicates that the fields are shared by all instances of the class. (Object Pascal) A variable that is allocated space automatically when a procedure is entered. Contrast to dynamic variables, which must have space allocated by the user. Because of the confusion with the term in C++, we have used the synonym *automatic variable* for static variables.

static method A method that can be called using early binding. The method body can be determined uniquely at compile time, and thus no message passing is required to process a message to a static method.

static class In statically typed object-oriented languages, such as C++ and Object Pascal, the declared class of a variable. It is legal, however, for the value of the variable to be an instance of either the static class or any class derived from the static class. The class of the value for the variable is known as the *dynamic class*.

statically typed object (Objective-C) A variable that is declared using a class name, as opposed to simply being declared using the type id. Statically typing an object permits certain errors to be detected at compile time, rather than at run time, and permits certain optimizations.

statically typed language A language in which the type of every variable must be declared at compile time.

strongly typed language A language in which the type of every expression can be determined at compile time.

subclass Syn. *descendant type, derived class*. (Smalltalk) A class that inherits from another class.

subclass client A class that makes use of the facilities of a superclass to implement its own functionality.

subclass coupling The connection formed between a parent and child class. Subclass coupling is a very weak form of coupling, since instances of the subclass can be treated as though they were simply instances of the superclass. See *coupling* and *cohesion*.

super (Objective-C, Smalltalk) When used inside a method, a synonym for *self*. However, when used as the receiver for a message, the search for an appropriate method will begin with the *superclass* of the class in which the current method is defined.

superclass Syn. *ancestor type, base class.* (Smalltalk) A class from which another class inherits attributes.

symbol (Smalltalk) A value that is characterized only by its unique value. Similar to an enumerated value in C or Pascal, with the exception that symbols can print themselves textually at run time.

this See *self.* (C++) When used inside a method, **this** is a pointer to the receiver for the message that caused the method to be invoked. Note that the pointer must be dereferenced to obtain the value of the receiver; for example, to send further messages to the receiver.

user client A class that makes use of the facilities provided by another distinct object. See *subclass client.*

virtual method (C++) A method that must be called using late binding. The method body to be invoked cannot be determined at compile time, and thus a run-time search must be performed to determine which of several methods should be invoked in response to a message. See *pure virtual method.*

virtual-method pointer (C++) A pointer, maintained by every object that uses virtual methods, that points to the virtual-method table associated with the type of the value currently contained in the variable.

virtual-method table (C++) A table of pointers to methods. A virtual method table is constructed for each class, and all instances of the class point to this table.

void (C++) A type name used to indicate a function returning no value — that is, a procedure.

yo-yo problem Repeated movements up and down the class hierarchy may be required when the execution of a particular method invocation is traced.

Bibliography

[Abelson 81]   Harold Abelson and Andrea diSessa, *Turtle Geometry: The Computer as a Medium for Exploring Mathematics*, MIT Press, Cambridge, MA, 1981.

[Actor 87]   *Actor Language Manual*, The Whitewater Group, Inc., Evanston, IL, 1987.

[Agha 86]   Gul Agha, "An Overview of Actor Languages," *Sigplan Notices*, 21(10): 58–67, 1986.

[Aho 85]   Alfred V. Aho, Ravi Sethi, and Jeffrey D. Ullman, *Compilers: Principles, Techniques, and Tools*, Addison-Wesley, Reading, MA, 1985.

[Appel 87]   Andrew W. Appel, "Garbage Collection can be Faster than Stack Allocation," *Information Processing Letters*, 25(4): 275–279, 1987.

[Atkinson 88]   Malcolm P. Atkinson, Peter Buneman, and Ronald Morrison (Eds), *Data Types and Persistence*, Springer-Verlag, New York, 1988.

[Beck 89]   Kent Beck and Ward Cunningham, "A Laboratory for Teaching Object-Oriented Thinking," *Proceedings of the 1989 OOPSLA — Conference on Object-Oriented Programming Systems, Languages and Applications*; reprinted in *Sigplan Notices*, 24(10): 1–6, 1989.

[Berztiss 90]   Alfs Berztiss, *Programming with Generators*, Ellis Horwood, New York, 1990.

[Bézivin 87]   Jean Bézivin, Jean-Marie Hullot, Pierre Cointe, and Henry Lieberman (Eds), *ECOOP '87 European Conference on Object-Oriented Programming*, Springer-Verlag, New York, 1987.

[Birtwistle 79]   Graham M. Birtwistle, Ole-Johan Dahl, Bjørn Myhrhaug, and Kristen Nygaard, *Simula Begin*, Studentlitteratur, Lund, Sweden, 1979.

[Bobrow 86]   Daniel G. Bobrow, Kenneth Kahn, Gregor Kiczales, Larry Masinter, Mark Stefik, and Frank Zdybel, "Common-Loops: Merging Lisp and Object-Oriented Programming,"

Proceedings of the 1986 OOPSLA — Conference on Object-Oriented Programming Systems, Languages and Applications; reprinted in *Sigplan Notices*, 21(11): 17–29, 1986.

[Bobrow 88]   Daniel G. Bobrow, Linda G. DeMichiel, Richard P. Gabriel, Sonya E. Keene, Gregor Kiczales, and David A. Moon, "Common Lisp Object System Specification X3J13 Document 88-002R," *Sigplan Notices*, 23, 1988.

[Brooks 75]   Frederick P. Brooks, Jr., *The Mythical Man-Month; Essays on Software Engineering*, Addison-Wesley, Reading, MA, 1975.

[Budd 87]   Timothy A. Budd, *A Little Smalltalk*, Addison-Wesley, Reading, MA, 1987.

[Budd 91]   Timothy A. Budd, *"Generalized Arithmetic in C++,"* *Journal of Object-Oriented Programming*, 3(6): 11–23, February 1991.

[Cardelli 85]   Luca Cardelli and Peter Wegner, "On Understanding Types, Data Abstraction, and Polymorphism," *Computing Surveys*, 17(4): 471–523, 1985.

[Carroll 60]   Lewis Carroll, *The Annotated Alice: Alice's Adventures in Wonderland & Through The Looking Glass*, with Notes by Martin Gardner, Bramhall House, New York, 1960.

[Chirlian 90]   Paul M. Chirlian, *Programming in C++*, Merrill, Columbus, OH, 1990.

[Coad 90]   Peter Coad and Edward Yourdon, *Object-Oriented Analysis*, Yourdon Press, Englewood Cliffs, NJ, 1990.

[Cohen 81]   Jacques Cohen, "Garbage Collection of Linked Data Structures," *ACM Computing Surveys*, 13(3): 341–367, 1981.

[Cox 86]   Brad J. Cox, *Object Oriented Programming: An Evolutionary Approach*, Addison-Wesley, Reading, MA, 1986.

[Cox 90]   Brad J. Cox, "Planning the Software Industrial Revolution," *IEEE Software*, 7(6): 25–35, November 1990.

[Danforth 88]   Scott Danforth and Chris Tomlinson, "Type Theories and Object-Oriented Programming," *ACM Computing Surveys*, 20(1): 29–72, 1988.

[Dewhurst 89]   Stephen C. Dewhurst and Kathy T. Stark, *Programming in C++*, Prentice-Hall, Englewood Cliffs, NJ, 1989.

[Dijkstra 76]   Edsger W. Dijkstra, *A Discipline of Programming*, Prentice-Hall, Englewood Cliffs, NJ, 1976.

[Eckel 89]   Bruce Eckel, *Using C++*, McGraw-Hill, New York, 1989.

[Ellis 90]   Margaret A. Ellis and Bjarne Stroustrup, *The Annotated C++ Reference Manual*, Addison-Wesley, Reading, MA, 1990.

[Fairley 85]   Richard Fairley, *Software Engineering Concepts*, McGraw-Hill, New York, 1985.

[Fischer 88]   Charles N. Fischer and Richard J. LeBlanc, Jr., *Crafting A Compiler*, Benjamin Cummings, Menlo Park, CA, 1988.

[Ghezzi 82]   Carlo Ghezzi and Mehdi Jazayeri, *Programming Language Concepts*, John Wiley and Sons, New York, 1982.

[Gillett 82]   Will D. Gillett and Seymour V. Pollack, *An Introduction to Engineered Software*, Holt, Rinehart & Winston, New York, 1982.

[Gjessing 88]   Stein Gjessing and Kristen Nygaard (Eds), *ECOOP '88 European Conference on Object-Oriented Programming*, Springer-Verlag, New York, 1988.

[Goldberg 83]   Adele Goldberg and David Robson, *Smalltalk-80: The Language and Its Implementation*, Addison-Wesley, Reading, MA, 1983.

[Goldberg 84]   Adele Goldberg, *Smalltalk-80: The Interactive Programming Environment*, Addison-Wesley, Reading, MA, 1983.

[Goldberg 89]   Adele Goldberg and David Robson, *Smalltalk-80: The Language*, Addison-Wesley, Reading, MA, 1989.

[Gorlen 90]   Keith Gorlen, Sandy Orlow, and Perry Plexico, *Data Abstraction and Object-Oriented Programming in C++*, John Wiley and Sons, New York, 1990.

[Gries 81]   David Gries, *The Science of Programming*, Springer-Verlag, New York, 1981.

[Griswold 83]   Ralph E. Griswold and Madge T. Griswold, *The Icon Programming Language*, Prentice-Hall, Englewood Cliffs, NJ, 1983.

[Grogono 89]   Peter Grogono and Anne Bennett, "Polymorphism and Type Checking in Object-Oriented Languages," *Sigplan Notices*, 24(11): 109–115, 1989.

[Hailpern 86]   Brent Hailpern, "Multiparadigm Languages and Environments," *IEEE Software*, 3(1):6–9, 1986.

[Halbert 87]   Daniel C. Halbert and Patrick D. O'Brien, "Using Types and Inheritance in Object-Oriented Programming," *IEEE Software*, 4(5): 71–79, 1987.

[Hansen 90]   Tony L. Hansen, *The C++ Answer Book*, Addison-Wesley, Reading, MA, 1990.

[Hanson 78]   David R. Hanson and Ralph E. Griswold, "The SL5 Pro-
                   cedure Mechanism," *Communications of the ACM*, 21(5):
                   392–400, 1978.

[Hanson 81]   David R. Hanson, "Is Block Structure Necessary?" *Software
                   Practice & Experience*, 1(8): 853–866, 1981.

[Hebel 90]   Kurt J. Hebel and Ralph E. Johnson, "Arithmetic and Double
                   Dispatching in Smalltalk-80," *Journal of Object-Oriented
                   Programming*, 2(6): 40–44, 1990.

[Horowitz 84]   Ellis Horowitz, *Fundamentals of Programming Languages*,
                   Computer Science Press, Rockville, MD, 1984.

[Ingalls 81]   Daniel H. H. Ingalls, "Design Principles Behind Smalltalk,"
                   Byte, 6(8):286–298, 1981.

[Ingalls 86]   Daniel H. H. Ingalls, "A Simple Technique for Handling
                   Multiple Polymorphism," *Proceedings of the 1986 OOP-
                   SLA — Conference on Object-Oriented Programming Sys-
                   tems, Languages and Applications*; reprinted in *Sigplan No-
                   tices*, 21(11): 347–349, 1986.

[Kaehler 86]   Ted Kaehler and Dave Patterson, *A Taste of Smalltalk*, W.W.
                   Norton & Company, New York, 1986.

[Kamin 90]   Samuel N. Kamin, *Programming Languages: An Inter-
                   preter-Based Approach*, Addison-Wesley, Reading, MA,
                   1990.

[Kay 77]   Alan Kay, "Microelectronics and the Personal Computer,"
                   Scientific American, 237(3): 230–244, 1977.

[Keller 90]   Daniel Keller, "A Guide to Natural Naming," *Sigplan No-
                   tices*, 25(5): 95–102, May 1990.

[Kernighan 84]   Brian W. Kernighan and Rob Pike, *The UNIX Programming
                   Environment*, Prentice-Hall, Englewood Cliffs, NJ, 1984.

[Kessler 88]   Robert R. Kessler, *LISP, Objects, and Symbolic Program-
                   ming*, Scott, Foresman and Company, Glenview, IL, 1988.

[Keene 89]   Sonya E. Keene, *Object-Oriented Programming in Common
                   Lisp*, Addison-Wesley, Reading, MA, 1989.

[Kim 89]   Won Kim and Frederick H. Lochovsky (Eds), *Object-
                   Oriented Concepts, Databases, and Applications*, Addison-
                   Wesley, Reading, MA, 1989.

[Kirkerud 89]   Bjørn Kirkerud, *Object-Oriented Programming with Simula*,
                   Addison-Wesley, Reading, MA, 1989.

[Knolle 89]   Nancy T. Knolle, "Why Object-Oriented User Interface
                   Toolkits Are Better," *Journal of Object-Oriented Program-
                   ming*, 2(4): 63–67, 1989.

[Koenig 89a]   Andrew Koenig, "References in C++," *Journal of Object-Oriented Programming*, 1(6), 1989.

[Koenig 89b]   Andrew Koenig, "Objects, Values, and Assignment," *Journal of Object-Oriented Programming*, 2(2): 37–38, 1989.

[Koenig 89c]   Andrew Koenig, "What Are Friends For?" *Journal of Object-Oriented Programming*, 2(4): 53–54, 1989.

[Krasner 83]   Glenn Krasner, *Smalltalk-80: Bits of History, Words of Advice*, Addison-Wesley, Reading, MA, 1983.

[Kristensen 87]   Bent Bruun Kristensen, Ole Lehrmann Madsen, Birger Møller-Pedersen, and Kristen Nygaard "The BETA Programming Language," in Bruce Shriver and Peter Wegner (Eds) *Research Directions in Object-Oriented Programming*, MIT Press, Cambridge, MA, 1987.

[Krogdahl 85]   Stein Krogdahl, "Multiple Inheritance in Simula-Like Languages," *BIT*, 25:318–326, 1985.

[Kuhn 70]   Thomas S. Kuhn, *The Structure of Scientific Revolutions*, 2nd ed., University of Chicago Press, Chicago, IL, 1970.

[LaLonde 90a]   Wilf LaLonde and John Pugh, "Integrating New Varieties of Numbers into the Class Library: Quaternions and Complex Numbers," *Journal of Object-Oriented Programming*, 2(5): 64–68, 1990.

[LaLonde 90a]   Wilf LaLonde and John Pugh, *Inside Smalltalk*, Prentice-Hall, Englewood Cliffs, NJ, 1990.

[Lieberherr 89a]   Karl J. Lieberherr and Ian M. Holland, "Assuring Good Style for Object-Oriented Programs," *IEEE Software*, 6(5): 38–48, 1989.

[Lieberherr 89b]   Karl J. Lieberherr and Arthur J. Riel, "Contributions to Teaching Object-Oriented Design and Programming," *Proceedings of the 1989 OOPSLA — Conference on Object-Oriented Programming Systems, Languages and Applications*; reprinted in *Sigplan Notices*, 24(10): 11–22, October 1989.

[Lieberman 86]   Henry Lieberman, "Using Prototypical Objects to Implement Shared Behavior in Object-Oriented Systems," *Proceedings of the 1986 OOPSLA — Conference on Object-Oriented Programming Systems, Languages and Applications*; reprinted in *Sigplan Notices*, 21(11): 214–223, 1986.

[Linton 89]   Mark A. Linton, John M. Vlissides, and Paul R. Calder, "Composing User Interfaces with InterViews," *Computer*, 22(2): 8–22, 1989.

[Lippman 89]   Stanley B. Lippman, *C+ Primer*, Addison-Wesley, Reading, MA, 1989.

[Logan 86]   Robert K. Logan, *The Alphabet Effect*, St. Martin's Press, New York, 1986.

[MacLennan 87]   Bruce J. MacLennan, *Principles of Programming Languages*, Holt, Rinehart & Winston, New York, 1987.

[Marcotty 87]   Michael Marcotty and Henry Ledgard, *The World of Programming Languages*, Springer-Verlag, New York, 1987.

[Meyer 88a]   Bertrand Meyer, *Object-oriented Software Construction*, Prentice-Hall International, London, 1988.

[Meyer 88b]   Bertrand Meyer, "Harnessing Multiple Inheritance," *Journal of Object-Oriented Programming Languages*, 1(4): 48–51, 1988.

[Meyrowitz 89]   Normal Meyrowitz (Ed), Object-Oriented Programming: Systems, Languages and Applications, *Sigplan Notices* 24(10), October 1989.

[Micallef 88]   Josephine Micallef, "Encapsulation, Resuability and Extensibility in Object-Oriented Programming Languages," *Journal of Object-Oriented Programming Languages*, 1(1): 12–35, 1988.

[Milner 90]   Robin Milner, Mads Tofte and Robert Harper, *The Definition of Standard ML*, MIT Press, Cambridge, MA, 1990.

[Moon 86]   David A. Moon, "Object-Oriented Programming with Flavors," *Proceedings of the 1986 OOPSLA — Conference on Object-Oriented Programming Systems, Languages and Applications*; reprinted in *Sigplan Notices*, 21(11): 1–8, 1989.

[Morehead 49]   Albert H. Morehead and Geoffrey Mott-Smith, *The Complete Book of Solitaire and Patience Games*, Grosset & Dunlap, New York, 1949.

[O'Brian 89]   Stephen K. O'Brian, *Turbo Pascal 5.5: The Complete Reference*, McGraw-Hill, New York, 1989.

[Parnas 72]   David L. Parnas, "On the Criteria to Be Used in Decomposing Systems into Modules," *Communications of the ACM*, 15(12):1059–1062, 1972.

[Pemberton 87]   Steven Pemberton, "An Alternative Simple Language and Environment for PCs," *IEEE Software*, 4(1): 56–64, 1987.

[Perry 90]   Dewayne E. Perry and Gail E. Kaiser, "Adequate Testing and Object-Oriented Programming," *Journal of Object-Oriented Programming*, 2(5): 13–19, 1990.

[Pinson 88]   Lewis J. Pinson and Richard S. Wiener, *An Introduction to Object-Oriented Programming and Smalltalk*, Addison-Wesley, Reading, MA, 1988.

[Pohl 89]   Ira Pohl, *C++ for C Programmers*, Addison-Wesley, Reading, MA, 1989.

[Pountain 87]   Dick Pountain, *Object-Oriented Forth*, Academic Press, New York, 1987.

[Rosenberg 71]   Jay F. Rosenberg and Charles Travis (Eds), *Readings in the Philosophy of Language*, Prentice-Hall, Englewood Cliffs, NJ, 1971.

[Sakkinen 88]   Markku Sakkinen, "Comments on 'the Law of Demeter' and C++," *Sigplan Notices*, 23(12): 38–44, 1988.

[Scheifler 88]   Robert W. Scheifler, James Gettys, and Ron Newman, *X Window System*, Digital Press, Bedford, MA, 1988.

[Schmucker 86]   Kent J. Schmucker, *Object-Oriented Programming for the Macintosh*, Hayden, Hasbrouck Heights, NJ, 1986.

[Simonian 89]   Richard Simonian and Michael Crone, "True Object-Oriented Programming in Ada," *Signal*, 61–67, 1989.

[Stefik 86]   Mark Stefik and Daniel G. Bobrow, "Object-Oriented Programming: Themes and Variations," *AI Magazine*, 6(4): 40–62, 1986.

[Sethi 89]   Ravi Sethi, *Programming Languages: Concepts and Constructs*, Addison-Wesley, Reading, MA, 1989.

[Shammas 90]   Namir Shammas, *Object-Oriented Programming with Quick-Pascal*, John Wiley and Sons, New York, 1990.

[Snyder 86]   Alan Snyder, "Encapsulation and Inheritance in Object-Oriented Programming Languages," *Proceedings of the 1986 OOPSLA — Conference on Object-Oriented Programming Systems, Languages and Applications*; reprinted in *Sigplan Notices*, 21(11): 38–45, 1986.

[Snyder 87]   Alan Snyder, "Inheritance and the Development of Encapsulated Software Components," in Bruce Shriver and Peter Wegners (Eds) *Research Directions in Object-Oriented Programming*, MIT Press, Cambridge, MA, 1987.

[Shriver 87]   Bruce Shriver and Peter Wegner, *Research Directions in Object-Oriented Programming*, MIT Press, Cambridge, MA, 1987.

[Stein 87]   Lynn Andrea Stein, "Delegation Is Inheritance," *Proceedings of the 1987 OOPSLA—Conference on Object-Oriented Programming Systems, Languages and Applications*; reprinted in *Sigplan Notices*, 22(12): 138–146, 1987.

[Stevens 81]   W. Stevens, G. Myers and L. Constantine, "Structured De-
                    sign," *IBM Systems Journal*, 13(2), 1974; Reprinted in
                    Edward Yourdon (Ed) *Classics in Software Engineering*,
                    Prentice-Hall, Englewood Cliffs, NJ, 1979.

[Stroustrup 86]   Bjarne Stroustrup, *The C++ Programming Language*,
                    Addison-Wesley, Reading, MA, 1986.

[Stroustrup 87a]   Bjarne Stroustrup, "Possible Directions for C++," *Proceed-
                    ings of the 1987 USENIX C++ Workshop*, Santa Fe, NM,
                    1987.

[Stroustrup 87b]   Bjarne Stroustrup, "Multiple Inheritance for C++," *Pro-
                    ceedings of the European Unix Users Group Conference*,
                    Helsinki, Finland, May 1987.

[Stroustrup 88]   Bjarne Stroustrup, "What is 'Object-Oriented Program-
                    ming?' " *IEEE Software*, 5(3): 10–20, May 1988.

[Swan 89]   Tom Swan, *Mastering Turbo Pascal 5.5*, Hayden, Indianapo-
                    lis, Indiana, 1989.

[Taenzer 89]   David Taenzer, Murthy Ganti, and Sunil Podar, "Object-
                    Oriented Software Reuse: The Yoyo Problem," *Journal of
                    Object-Oriented Programming*, 2(3): 30–35, 1989.

[Tello 89]   Ernest R. Tello, *Object-Oriented Programming for Artificial
                    Intelligence*, Addison-Wesley, Reading, MA, 1989.

[Tesler 85]   Larry Tesler, "Object Pascal Report," Apple Computer,
                    Santa Clara, CA, 1985.

[Tomlinson 90]   Chris Tomlinson, Mark Scheevel and Won Kim, "Shar-
                    ing and Organization Protocols in Object-Oriented Sys-
                    tems," *Journal of Object-Oriented Programming*, 2(4): 25–
                    36, 1989.

[Turbo 88]   *Turbo Pascal 5.5 Object-Oriented Programming Guide*, Bor-
                    land International, Scotts Valley, CA., 1988.

[Ungar 87]   David Ungar and Randall B. Smith, "Self: The Power of
                    Simplicity," *Proceedings of the 1987 OOPSLA — Confer-
                    ence on Object-Oriented Programming Systems, Languages
                    and Applications*; reprinted in *Sigplan Notices*, 22(12): 227–
                    242, 1987.

[Unger 87]   J. Marshall Unger, *The Fifth Generation Fallacy*, Oxford
                    University Press, New York, 1987.

[Usenix 87]   *Proceedings of the C++ Workshop*, USENIX Association,
                    Berkeley, CA, 1987.

[Webster 89]   Bruce F. Webster, *The NeXT Book*, Addison-Wesley, Read-
                    ing, MA, 1989.

[Wegner 86]   Peter Wegner, "Classification in Object-Oriented Systems," *Sigplan Notices*, 21(10):173–182, October 1986.

[Weiskamp 90]   Keith Weiskamp and Bryan Flamig, *The Complete C++ Primer*, Academic Press, New York, 1990.

[Wiener 88]   Richard S. Wiener and Lewis J. Pinson, *An Introduction to Object-Oriented Programming and C++*, Addison-Wesley, Reading, MA, 1988.

[Wiener 89]   Richard S. Wiener and Lewis J. Pinson, "A Practical Example of Multiple Inheritance in C++," *Sigplan Notices*, 24(9): 112–115, 1989.

[Wiener 90]   Richard S. Wiener and Lewis J. Pinson, *The C++ Workbook*, Addison-Wesley, Reading, MA, 1990.

[Wikström 87]   Åke Wikström, *Functional Programming Using Standard ML*, Prentice-Hall International, London, 1987.

[Wilson 90]   David A. Wilson, Larry S. Rosenstein and Dan Shafer, *Programming With MacApp*, Addison-Wesley, Reading, MA, 1990.

[Wirfs-Brock 89a] Allen Wirfs-Brock and Brian Wilkerson, "Variables Limit Reusability," *Journal of Object-Oriented Programming*, 2(1): 34–40, May 1990.

[Wirfs-Brock 89b] Rebecca Wirfs-Brock and Brian Wilkerson, "Object-Oriented Design: A Responsibility-Driven Approach," *Proceedings of the 1989 OOPSLA — Conference on Object-Oriented Programming Systems, Languages and Applications*; reprinted in *Sigplan Notices*, 24(10): 71–76, October 1989.

[Wirfs-Brock 90]   Rebecca Wirfs-Brock, Brian Wilkerson and Lauren Wiener, *Designing Object-Oriented Software*, Prentice-Hall, Englewood Cliffs, NJ, 1990.

[Whorf 56]   Benjamin Lee Whorf, *Language Thought & Reality*, MIT Press, Cambridge, MA, 1956.

[Wulf 72]   William A. Wulf, "A Case Against the GOTO," *Proceedings of the twenty-fifth National ACM Conference*, 1972; Reprinted in Edward Yourdon (Ed) *Classics in Software Engineering*, Prentice-Hall, Englewood Cliffs, NJ, 1979.

[Wulf 73]   William A. Wulf and Mary Shaw, "Global Variable Considered Harmful," *Sigplan Notices*, 8(2): 28–43, 1973.

[Yonezawa 87]   Akinori Yonezawa and Mario Tokoro, *Object-Oriented Concurrent Programming*, MIT Press, Cambridge, MA, 1987.

[Zdonik 90]   Stanley B. Zdonik and David Maier, *Readings in Object-Oriented Database Systems*, Morgan Kaufmann Publishers, 1990.

I N D E X

abstract data types, as an abstraction
   mechanism, 13
abstract superclass:
   definition, 7
   definition, 371
abstraction mechanisms, 11
access and visibility:
   C++, 226
   Object Pascal, 226
   Objective-C, 231
   Smalltalk, 225
accessor method, definition, 371
activation record, 282
active value, 221
ad. hoc polymorphism, 187
   definition, 371
Ada, 13, 191
addition, of methods, 122
Aho, Alfred, 282
allocated class, definition, 371
ambiguity, multiple inheritance, 173
ancestor class, definition, 371
ancestor type, definition, 371
ANSI standard C, 54
anthropomorphic aspects of object-oriented
      programming, 9
Appel, Andrew, 152
argument signature, 191
   definition, 371
arithmetic, smalltalk, 113
assertions, 123, 262
assignment:
   C++, 158
   copy semantics, 157
   effect of OOP on, 151
   Object Pascal, 159
   Objective-C, 161
   pointer semantics, 156
   Smalltalk, 160

automatic storage management, definition,
   372
automatic variable, 62
   definition, 372

base class, definition, 372
Beck, Kent, 25
Berztiss, Alfs, 75, 76
Beta, programming language, 129
binding:
   definition, 372
   method, 106
   type, 103
binding time, 4, 103
   definition, 372
blocks, Smalltalk, 48
blue book, 113
Bobrow, D., 221
Brooks, Frederick P., 10
browser, 267
   definition, 372
   Smalltalk, 45
Budd, Elizabeth H., 4, 169, 189
Budd, Elsie, 3
bytecode instructions, 288

C++:
   access and visibility, 226
   assignment, 158
   class definition, 52
   class variables, 270
   constant members, 230
   constructors, 66
   constructors, overridden, 125
   creation, 65
   data member initialization, 231
   default initializers, 67
   deferred method, 195
   design philosophy, 111, 125
   destructor, 67